ॐ द्यौः शान्तिरन्तरिक्षꣳ शान्तिः पृथिवी शान्तिरापः शान्तिरोषधयः शान्तिः। वनस्पतयः शान्तिर्विश्वे देवाः शान्तिर्ब्रह्म शान्तिः सर्वꣳ शान्तिः शान्तिरेव शान्तिः सा मा शान्तिरेधि॥ ॐ शान्तिः शान्तिः शान्तिः॥

Culture and Development
No. 6

General Editor
Kapila Vatsyayan

Culture of Peace

Experience and Experiment

UNESCO Chair in the field of Cultural Development

Indira Gandhi National Centre for the Arts

Culture of Peace

Experience and Experiment

Edited by
Baidyanath Saraswati

Indira Gandhi National Centre for the Arts
New Delhi

D.K. Printworld (P) Ltd.
New Delhi

Cataloging in Publication Data — DK

The Culture of Peace: experience and experiment/edited by
Baidyanath Saraswati.
(Culture and development; no.6).
Includes bibliographical references.

1. Culture and peace — Congresses. 2. Peace — Social aspects — Congresses. 3. Peace — Religious aspects — Congresses. I. Saraswati, Baidyanath, 1932 - II. Series: Culture and development; no. 6.

ISBN 81-246-0124-0

First published in India, 1999

Publishers
Indira Gandhi National Centre for the Arts
Central Vista Mess, Janapath, New Delhi - 110001

D.K. Printworld (P) Ltd.
Regd. office: *'Sri Kunj'*, F-52, Bali Nagar, New Delhi - 110015

Printed in India.

Foreword

Kapila Vatsyayan

PERHAPS one of man's earliest awareness was the need for a harmonious peaceful life with all living beings. In India the Vedic seers evoked 'peace' (*santi*) in many hymns. They inchanted the verses, invoking peace on earth, with the vegetative, the animal and the human world. Over the millenniums, the more strife man creates, the more he (she) calls out for peace.

Modern civilisation lives in the paradox of ever increasing capacity of man to comprehend the universe ascend to spaces unknown and the imminent threat of total annihilation.

The late Mrs. Indira Gandhi had eloquently summed it up:

> Development, independence, disarmament and peace are closely inter-related. Can there be peace alongside nuclear weapons? Without peace, all our dreams of development turn to ashes. No peace today, no life tomorrow.

The interface of development and peace, and of course disarmament has been the subject of many international conferences and global debates. The Indira Gandhi National Centre for the Arts (IGNCA) cannot address the question of nuclear weapons and non-proliferation, but it is concerned with the cultural fabric of societies, life-styles and their interface with development models which create disharmony and ruptures at the human level. On the occasion of Mrs. Indira Gandhi's martyrdom anniversary, the Centre considered it appropriate to hold an international conference on the Culture of Peace, as a tribute to her. The volume is dedicated to her memory.

The conference was also in continuation of other initiatives taken by the Centre to study the interface of culture with other domains of life. Three conferences and seminars and workshops addressed a variety of issues, such as identity, indigenous knowledge system, the interface of culture and ecology, culture and education. As early as 1989 an international workshop on Cross-cultural Lifestyle Studies with Multimedia Computerizable Documentation was organised under the aegis of UNESCO. The proceedings of the Workshop have been published in two volumes. The deliberations on general concepts, theories and methods were followed by a series of pilot studies of various cohesive communities in different parts of India. In 1993, the UNESCO responded again to this concern of the IGNCA and facilitated another international seminar which went a little further in exploring the Interface of Cultural Identity and Development. The proceedings of this seminar constituted the First Volume of the IGNCA's *Culture and Development Series*. The Second Volume, *Integration of Endogenous Cultural Dimension into Development*, aimed at suggesting positive strategies for intergrating all that could be understood by the term 'indigenous cultural knowledge'. The Third Volume, *the Cultural Dimension of Education*, addressed itself to a cross-cultural comparison and assessment of problems involved in the modern system of education. The Fourth Volume, *the Cultural Dimension of Ecology*, devoted itself to critical issued pertaining to the natural environment. The Fifth Volume, *Lifestyle and Ecology*, emerged as an outcome of some pilot studies on the inter-relationship of nature, social structure, world view, cosmology, daily routine, lifecycle, annual calendar, knowledge, skills and traditional technologies. Closely linked with the fluid dynamics of a culture is the issue of peace. The Sixth Volume presents the proceedings of the Asian conference on the Culture of Peace, held in 1996.

I must hasten to acknowledge that in organising this conference we have received moral support and encouragement from H.E. Dr. Felix Marti Ambel, Director of the UNESCO de Catalunya, Barcelona, who has pioneered a series of dialogues on 'The Contribution by Religions to the Culture of Peace'. Professor B.N. Saraswati is associated with this dialogue since its beginning in 1993. Dr. Marti could not attend our conference, but I am indeed very gald that he has contributed to this volume a very valuable prologue which brings to light the importance of making such dialogue a fundamental practice and a living part of all traditions. The fact that six participants of the Barcelona dialogue took part in the IGNCA conference clearly shows that we have moved a step further towards realising this goal.

Although in a certain sense this conference was a renewal of the Barcelona dialogue, its framework was different in so far as it did not aim at evaluating the role of the religion in building a culture of peace. It was planned with intention of sharing the experience of beauty and peace and working toward the moral basis of experiments in peace as reflected in the wisdom tradition of Asian peoples and cultures.

The distinctive nature of the culture of peace in the present volume is treated at several different levels by eminent peace researchers, educators and actors in peace, Gandhian scholars, religious leaders, spiritual luminaries, philosophers, poets painters, artists, choreographers, musicologists, archaeologists, anthropologists, indologists, doctors, and other professionals coming from different cultural traditions and background. The presence of this impressive group of participants, who came from Bangladesh, China, India, Iran, Japan, Russia, Sri Lanka, Thailand, the USA and Vietnam, was the proof and the confirmation that this world driven with war and violence is in need of a new culture of peace.

While addressing themselves to various themes of the conference, the participants came out with several formulations; Peace is not absence of war, rather it is a state of integration with Nature. Peace is the condition of mind. The vision of peace is countered by materialism and consumerism. Art is the best means of spreading peace. Meditation helps the art of peaceful living. The awareness of peace starts from childhood and motherhood. Peace is a basic requirement of every living being. Peace is scarce these days, it has been threatened by internal forces and external powers. Peace is a state of being, culture is an expression, and religion is the source for both state and expression. Major religions of the world such as Hinduism, Buddhism, Christianity and Islam have contributed to the culture of peace. The method and the message of Mahatma Gandhi have given a healing touch to the ailing humanity today.

It is my sincere hope that through diverse voices of the participants there will be a renewal of the sense of urgency to adopt plural paths for the single goal of establishing a culture of peace in this our strife-torn world of our own making.

Prologue

Félix Martí Ambel

Reading some of the contributions from the seminar organised in 1996 by my friend Baidyanath Saraswati on the Culture of Peace that are gathered in this book I feel called to reflect once again on cultural diversity and on the possibility of a common Culture of Peace on our responsibilities as crafters of peace.

I think one of the most important cultural events of recent decades has been the discovery of the regional nature of all cultures, including the culture of science and technology which the dominant powers in the world today have tried to impose on all the continents as though it were a superior culture to others. Today, knowledgeable people, East and West, North and South, are agreed on the local, partial, limited nature of all cultures. None of them can be considered globally superior to the others. For centuries the cultures of the colonisers were imposed on people everywhere, in the conviction that their values were objectively superior to those characterising the people they colonised, their religions and their way of life. The nineteenth and twentieth centuries have seen large-scale attacks by the culture of science and technology against the so-called inferior cultures.

We are coming to the end of the twentieth century (if we measure time by Christian standards) with the certainty that no one culture has a monopoly on knowledge, values or the art of living. For this reason I feel we are beginning an interesting cultural period which will be characterised by a long, patient struggle to understand cultures different to our own. This is a time for intercultural dialogue, for discovering the spiritual, conceptual and experiential originality of other cultures and for respect for the untranslatable or intransferable nature of many poems, concepts or experiences in each specific culture. In this respect, we realise that each language is a universe full of enigmas, mysteries and wonders that can be revealed through sensitivity and respect.

Some of the articles in this book interest me precisely because they bring me closer to symbolic universes and forms of knowledge that are still a long way from my own intellectual tradition. I would like many academics in the Western tradition to reap the benefits of this valuable material. When people in Western universities or research centres speak of the culture of peace or simply of peace they tend to look at political, social or — especially — economic issues, and they lack the conceptual instruments necessary to extend their reflection to anthropological, aesthetic, cosmic or spiritual issues. I am delighted at this book's contribution to extending the debate on the culture of peace and I think that from now on, luckily, we shall no longer be able to speak of the culture of peace without taking into account its multi-dimensional nature and the original approach taken by the book's authors. I am convinced that without this type of contribution the search for the culture of peace could become a repetition of the experience of cultural colonialism.

The second reflection arising from reading the contributions to the seminar in New Delhi in 1996 is whether, over and above respect for cultural pluralism, it will possible to agree on a universal Culture of Peace. In the atmosphere at the seminars in Barcelona in 1993 and 1994 and in New Delhi in 1996 we have cause for optimism.

The religious and ideological patterns of our various human communities are different. Extreme injustices exist that make violence understandable. Economic models of development are unsustainable and prevent our establishing a harmonious relationship with nature. Human history, until today, has always included war as an expression of conflict. In this respect we can ask ourselves if it is possible to find a common ground of ideas and actions which we can share and whether we can begin a new culture of peace. I think the essential orientation of the great religious and cultural traditions is similar. Using different myths and languages they speak out in favour of a desirable cosmic order which dignifies human life and makes more harmonious co-existence possible. The different relations they establish between the cosmos, human beings and the divinity always inspire ways of life and responsibilities that keep chaos and violence at bay. I think a leaning towards peace is common to all traditions, although each one picks out certain aspects of peace. To work together for peace, we need not be inspired in the same mythological and symbolic universe or have exactly the same priorities. It is enough if we recognise our common intentions and are willing to discuss the conditions of peace.

The issue of dialogue appears as a fundamental practice which must be made a living part of all traditions. There cannot be dialogue when traditions attempt to be the sole bearers of knowledge or salvation. I think this pretension arises out of the ignorance caused by the isolation or political manipulation of religious and cultural traditions. Those cultures that are not afraid, because they are convinced of their values in any context, are open cultures. So are those traditions which manage to keep clear of political interests. I believe that in a context of ever easier communications and ever stronger interdependences, only open cultures prepared to dialogue will have a future. It could seem that shutting themselves away in ideological and political citadels is a guarantee for the future, but precisely the opposite is true. Cultures, like living species, have a future when, in dialogue with their surroundings, they evolve and adapt. Our traditions, faithful to their sources of inspiration, must generate dialogue, reasonable explanations and proposals for life that oppose chaos, pain, ignorance, alienation and injustice. Our traditions must be well disposed, that is able to stand back wisely from even the appearance of excessive mythicism in their own tradition. Religious fanaticism is not well disposed and is a superficial form of religious life. The depths of religion are mystical, free, luminous, joyful and open.

We are beginning to locate the common ground of the Culture of Peace. Some contributions by the Hindu tradition draw attention to cosmic harmony; some contributions by the Buddhist tradition insist on non-violence; some contributions by the Judaeo-Christian tradition call for recognition of human dignity; some contributions by the Islamic tradition remind us of the need for justice; some contributions by non-religious humanism value rationality and ethical qualities. But each of these contributions connects with the others and this is why no tradition can consider as alien the Universal Declaration of Human Rights or Agenda 21 from Rio de Janeiro or aspirations for human development for all peoples.

My third reflection refers to the responsibilities we need to exercise. We must see to it that the value placed on active non-violence becomes generalised. Until now non-violence has been limited to the circles of relatively marginal groups. Policies in most states and international political relations include the resort to war as something quite normal. There are some international decisions in favour of disarmament, but they are still hesitant and insufficient. We must see to it that war gradually ceases to be a normal way of resolving conflicts. We must fight against the historical inertia that colonises our imagination and prevents our thinking of a future without wars. We must make it possible for politicians to have alternative instruments to war. We need to develop more and better mechanisms for solving conflicts. We must multiply the courts of appeal and of law to which demands for the application of justice can be directed. We must create tribunals and mediating authorities for the different types of conflict. We must, above all, create the certainty that any conflict can be solved without the need for violence. At the same time, state and international laws must make life impossible for the mafias of violence. Disarmament and democratic conflict-solving must become priorities on the national and international political agenda.

All these changes will be possible on condition that the great spiritual and cultural traditions are clearly oriented towards the culture of peace. Our traditions have the power to shape the hearts of human beings: the desires, the secret dreams, the most mysterious energies, love and hate, generosity. If our traditions make clear their position in favour of the culture of peace, this will set up a powerful trend that will make it all possible. We need a broad-based agreement to bring together behind a single aim spiritual leaders, artists, thinkers, journalists, educators and scientists. I think UNESCO is the right platform to facilitate the necessary agreement. I hope that in the coming years we shall be able to multiply initiatives in favour of the culture of peace on every continent. The seminars in Barcelona and New Delhi are significant contributions in the right direction. I believe one of their great virtues is that they have created a universal network of friendship between religious and cultural leaders working for peace in different contexts, but in the same spirit. After these three seminars, I am sure our work will continue with renewed enthusiasm.

Contents

PART - II
EXAMINING THE EMPERICAL REALITY OF BEAUTY AND PEACE

PART - III
WORKING TOWARDS THE RESTORATION OF PEACE

PART - IV
FORMING THE NETWORK OF ACTORS IN PEACE

Introduction
Diffusing Glory With Peace

Baidyanath Saraswati

WE have moved from the age of monlogue to the age of dialogue. We live in the Global Village. But what if the Global Village were to become the arena of violence and war? The climate of modern world is wholly hostile. What we see without believing that we see it is a dehumanized fragmented world: the human family is broken by exploitative social order; the village is destroyed by technocentric development; the city is corrupted by conspicuous consumerism; injustice is caused by man-made laws; discrimination is made by claims of equity; oppression is committed by those demanding rights-without-duties; violence is done by self-appointed guardians of humanity; and faith is feebled by lust. In such a state of human degeneration, can we diffuse Glory with Peace? Can we identify ourselves with peace? Can peace be ever brought through totalitarian dictatorships — republics disseminating fear? Can there be a world without wars? Can the disorderly world be brought back to order? Is the clash of civilizations inevitable? Is the human race doomed to extinction? Or is there a way out?

There are today a large number of national and international organizations concerned with peace. The United Nations is the main political forum for worldpeace. Peace-making and peace-keeping are its core functions. The UNESCO, which is an organization of states within the United Nations, had held meetings in Barcelona in 1993, 1994 on "Contributions by Religions to the Culture of Peace". Peace is still a dream. Violence is unleashed all over, particularly in Asia, Africa and Eastern Europe. The dialogue on peace must continue. The practical way to live peacefully must be found.

Indira Gandhi National Centre for the Arts has tried to take the Barcelona dialogue further. A five-day conference on Asian perspective in the culture of peace was organized in New Delhi on 25th November 1996 when people of India were celebrating 527th birth anniversary of Guru Nanak, great mystic and votary of world peace. More than 29 distinguished scholars and missionaries of peace from Bangladesh, China, India, Iran, Japan, Russia, Sri Lanka, Thailand, United States and Vietnam gathered on this occasion to discuss major aspects of peace. Happily, six members of the Barcelona dialogue took part in this Asian conference. Dr. Felix Marti, the leader of the Barcelona group, could not attend the meeting but has graciously filled up his absence by writing a thoughtful prologue.

Asians are the people to whom the Veda, the *Bible*, the *Koran* and the *Zend Avesta* were revealed. Asia is the place where all major religions of the world were born and where great prophets have left an unimpeachable testimony of peace through prayer. India is the land where Buddha spoke of silence and lead the liberation from anguish and suffering. Buddhism spread all over Asia without shedding a drop of blood. In our own times, Gandhi, the Mahatma, made experiments with truth and non-violence. He was the first in human history to extend the principle of non-violence from individual to social and political planes. He refused to admit that truth and non-violence are meant only for saints. Also he did not hesitate saying: "I would risk violence a thousand times than the emasculation of the whole race". India achieved Independence by non-violence and self-suffering. The Spirit of Asia is not a caged bird; it soars in the sky and evokes sweet sounds of life that enlighten the race of men.

This volume consists of papers presented at the Asian conference on Peace. Each paper is richly illustrated and brilliantly conceived. While some of these papers are conceptually more ambitious, others address practical issues. But all of these focus on the culture of peace.

I. Sharing the Experience of Beauty and Peace

To situate the place of experience (sensual, intellectual and spiritual) in the culture of peace, it is absolutely necessary to know how musicians, painters, poets, dancers, actors, and creative geniuses are naturally oriented towards peace. And also, how do they foster the act of faith and goodness? The Sanskrit word for peace is *shanti*. The dormant state of body and mind — as in sleep or in death — is called 'lying in peace' or 'becoming peaceful'. What it suggests is a sublime ontology of peace. At the highest level of thought peace is 'self-reflexive consciousness' as well as 'self-reflective intelligence'. This double concurrent awareness can possibly be kept active. Natural experience has a hold upon man. Movement in time and space is man's existential necessity. There is a call for him also to move beyond time and space. Both of these constitute the truth of human living. Metaphysical experience of peace is true; it is higher than natural experience. But one cannot say that natural experience is false or deceptive or misleading. The holy yearning for peace is realized at the experiential level. Not all human creativities but only special works of special people, we call 'artists', can illuminate the mind of man. The man who works for the glory of God, displays in his work the sovereign Beauty. Beauty is perfection, and perfection is peace. The artist who works in love for God is sensitive to human suffering. Many cultures talk about suffering as good, suffering as virtue, suffering to bear the grace of God. At the end of the Mahabharata war, Kunti, the mother of the Pandavas, asked Lord Krishna to suffer all her life so that she may progress in her spritual journey — devotion to God. The acceptance of suffering as spiritual power is of highest prudence.

The Japanese culture views suffering precisely in the sense of ultimate good. The case of Hikare, a mentally handicapped musician, reveals that art is very much spiritual; being healed through expressing despair, the dark night of the soul being transformed through healing and sharing the joy of recovery with others. Sufferings such as being handicapped, being sick, and being victims of violence are lives of the family and of society. Cosmos and humanity are healing families. Hikari and Oe's family and prayers of the surviving victims of Hiroshima and Nagasaki are witnesses of healing families. The mystery of art reveals this reality. The perspective and experience of the culture of peace cannot be conceived of without a healing family (Minoru Kasai).

The Chinese civilization has conceived of peace as the law and the logic of the universe. Confucius talked about peace a goal from the view point of a philosopher. Chinese poets have highlighted the eternal dilemma of war and peace. One Chinese empress composed a song of peace seeking blessings of the sacred. Many poets have voiced against warlike policies, and have painted pictures of tragedies of war. Passive resistence to war and longing for the sentient-world reflect clearly in several poems. There is an unmistakable touch of Buddhist philosophy in Chinese poems. Poets visualize natural peace and beauty as the fundamental rhythm of the universe, and they play 'the music of tranquillity' (Tan Chung).

Peace and friendship are important topics within Chinese Buddhist art. Artists create a type of Buddha image in which benevolence is nestled within the beauty of its solemnity. He deals with its awesomeness and its kindness or benevolence, which are completely different and even mutually cancelling elements, but still melds them together, so that the Buddha has an external image of gravity and an inner store of kindness. (Jim Weinuo)

From Russia the voice of Nicholas Roerich sounds — 'realization of beauty will save the world'. The inner discipline of Russian artists is expressed in the art of icon painting. Before starting a painting, the artist practices prayer and silence and maintains mental and emotional purity, which help him to achieve resonance like a musical instrument. It is the duty and responsibility of the artist to stress on the expression of inner beauty and spiritual power (Natalia Kravtchenko and Vladimir Zaitsev)

Human individual is by nature an artist, a creator. Creative activities are those disciplines in which senses quite intuitively seek harmony, proportion and wholeness of any experience. The uses of media and tools, such as clay, cotton, wool, leather, wood, stone, brushes, potter's wheel, saws, impose upon this discipline by their very nature. Moreover, it draws us closer to nature, which alone is the supreme example of harmony, sympathy and union. These are the same laws on which the human community depends for its own unity and integrity. The crucial point here is that unless we as individuals feel ourselves parts of the whole we cannot experience the whole, which is the ultimate aim of humanity. And without that personal experience we cannot be happy and feel fulfilled. Art assists the individual in creating the desired unity with the universe (Devi Prasad).

Theatrical art demonstrates the value of peace. European theatre, for instance, projects the futility of war, and heroism as an argument for peace. But peace in this theatrical tradition is argued for as a value, not portrayed as a presence. The dramatic action hardly ever shows an experience of peace. Greek drama was devoted to the portrayal of the conflict between the human and the divine. Peace here was known as an epiphany. Theatrical activity in ancient India created an experience of peace through emotional purification and elation, which led to the deeper aesthetic experience called *rasa*, a profoundly peace-giving experience. Theatre, as the oldest art of communication, is best suited to highlight consonances between cultures and promotes the common scale of peace. (Bharat Gupt)

II. Examining the Empirical Reality of Beauty and Peace

Experience can neither be measured nor can it be expressed fully. It can be gained only in the crossing of temporal reality. Why? The uncritical mind is satisfied with what is given; and what is given is taken as real. The critical mind is not satisfied with what is given; it goes deeper into what is observable. The spiritual mind is not limited by empiricity; it has an inward power of feelings. Feelings differ from emotions. Modern man has a critical mind. He lacks inwardness and gives himself to emotions. Violence becomes a part of his emotionality. His mind thinks horizonatally, hence his contact with the reality is limited. He who thinks vertically moves into the celestial, the universal, the divine. Kabir, a medieval saint-poet, has described three kinds of being:

He who treads within limits is man.
He who treads without limits is saint.
He who treads within and without limits,
his mind is immeasurable.

Modern man, who treads within limits, is incapable of experiencing peace. He draws consequences from his limited perception and projected emotion. He has no sense of beauty, hence no peace. He does not relate himself with the whole; gets confused with emotions and becomes fragmented and degraded, hence no peace. He does not seek uplift, does not move towards inner radiance, hence peace remains for him an illusion. This implies that the reality of peace can be understood only in terms of relativity, and not in its absoluteness. At the highest level of "understanding", beauty and peace are symbolically adequate, that is, in conformity with reality, hence absolute. At another level, beauty and peace are "things" which infact appear other than what they are, hence relative. The principle of relativity operates in minds of modern men moving away from God.

We find that there are good things in the modern world: there are electric light and the flash system, two admittedly very important acquirements. But these are only good means, now unwittingly made out as ends. Means are not ends. The all-important end is the flavour man gives to his life, or to put it better, the consumption of beauty. This end is quite unrelated to the accumulation of skills of civilization. Meditation or *yoga*, or whatever, to men already cast in this form, becomes no more than a technology, a magical means of control over others. But there is no inner tranquility. A growing will to power, yes, but a rapid loss of the sense of beauty — and therefore no peace. (Keshav Malik)

At this degenerate state of the contemporary culture, violence has become endemic. The present-day individual is fast losing ethical sense of personal responsibility. The modernity in the success of its technology and the capitalistic modes of human relationship have brought into the open (perhaps the primordial) loneliness — insecurity — fear syndrome, and liberated the avarice in man, whose satisfaction he sees as the only way to deal with his pitiable condition. This 'liberation' is the main cause of his fragmentation. To achieve integration within, therefore, the individual must turn to himself in a holistic perspective upon life. Only then that sense of responsibility can reborn in him and can transform the 'given' into a culture of peace. (M.M. Agrawal)

In our times, internally, inwardly, man is contradicting himself, e.g., the problem of ends and means, where his left hand does not know what his right one does. It is a state of schizophrenic existence, where the head and the heart are no longer resonating with each other. This split behaviour is not confined to the East or the West, since, evolutionarily speaking, the human brain itself is in disorder. Given this situation, what chance is there for peace? What is peace in any case, who knows it and for whom is it? Is it not true that all we see is turmoil, crisis and conflict? Can a mind-brain in this condition know peace? Is it not just chasing a mirage? (S.C. Malik)

There is a possibility to change from our present status of 'mental' beings to a status of beings poised in the Spirit. A transition to be made from the state of extreme fragmentation in which we live today to a future possbility of re-creating life on the basis of a concrete experience of 'wholeness'. From 'within' to 'without' is the innate movement of the spiritual consciousness, till, in its own unfolding, it reaches a point where the 'without' ceases to be, for all are contained in one whole. We feel that a very concrete help can come to us from the experience and work of Sri Aurobindo and Swami Vivekananda. (Mira Aster Patel)

III. Working Towards the Restoration of Peace

Truth is not limited by empiricity. It is not an object of physical experimentation, as the natural sciences do. Truth is God; God is Truth. Hence the experiment with Truth (the nature of being) means following the way proper to religion (faith in and about God). Great men like Buddha, Confucius, and Gandhi made internal experimentation with Truth. They found that the world is ill, and that there are ways to make a beautiful world to live in. They not only preached but also realized the Truth by which peace is supported. They did not follow the method of the moderns who want to build a culture of peace while destroying culture (by militant atheism, consumerism, individualism). They taught tolerance, the sacred art of living (goodness in action), grounded in peace (by fighting against violence, materialism, technocracy), and spoke the language of traditional symbolism. The compassion of Buddha, the intelligence of Cofucious, and the truthfulness of Gandhi were directed towards building a normal human society. They tried to pull down barriers between man and God, man and man, and man and other beings, so as to bring divine peace for all. They were universal redeemers of man. Teachings and healings of Jesus Christ and the Prophet Muhammad were also an integral manifestation of peace. The repeated appearance of such restorers of peace signifies sanctification of history: the reminder that peace is under sovereignty of Time.

Confronted with an almost similar situation of conflict and crisis, as of today, about twenty-six centuries ago, Gautam, the Buddha, made a supreme effort, unparalleled in the annals of human history, in the quest for a solution to the all-pervading phenomenon of misery. In that process he re-discovered the ancient technique of *vipassana*, the most sublime and noblest heritage of India. Anyone can practise it to purify one's mind. It involves no blind faith nor conversion from one organized religion to another organized religion. With it, the individual mind begins to experience peace and harmony. This paves the way for peace within and amongst families, societies and nations. (S.N. Goenka)

Apart from meditation (*vipassana*), Buddhist teachings of loving kindness, forgiveness, and non-anger are ways of peace. The peace of mind or internal peace is the source of external peace of the world. Besides moral cultivation, peace can be attained through all religious arts, e.g., paintings, sculptures, images, and so on. In Thailand, Buddha-images are intentionally made to inspire peace in all who have seen them. In Buddhist culture of peace, people are encouraged to 'diffuse loving kindness' to humans and animals as often as they can. Proper educational system should be established to promote humaneness and moral wisdom. The right education will endow students with noble hearts and make them complete human beings. (Pataraporn Sirikanchana)

In Vietnam, since early times, peace has been largely conceived of as peace in one's mind, peace towards one's fellows, and peace with nature. These aspects of peace are greatly influenced by Buddhism. If Buddhism provided Vietnamese people with a good-natured heart, Confucianism provided them with *wisdom* translated into the sense of order, discipline and responsibility. Two major contributions of Confucianism to traditional Vietnamese societies are materialization and institutionalization of benevolence as advocated by Buddhism into regulations and laws; and defining of the responsibility and duty of each individual towards himself and the community in which he is living. (Cao Xuan Pho)

Sri Lankan Buddhists follow a fourfold moral path: loving kindness, compassion, sympathetic joy and equanimity. These moral qualities are practised at all stages of life: as students, as family members and fellow members of the community at large. They convey to the world at large the message of universal peace and universal benevolence. (Sirima Goonesinghe)

Iranian Suffism offers the traveller with the spiritual path a three fold state of peace: *Islam* (submission, abandonment, to the Divine Will), *Iman* (the Divine Peace that enters believer's heart) and *Ishan* (the Sanctifying Virtue by which sovereignty of evils come to an end). Peace at the stage of *Islam* pertains to the corporeal and social aspects of human beings, whereas at the stage of *Iman*, it pertains to the heart and the microcosm, and, finally, at the stage of *Islam*, peace pertains to the Spirit and the macrocosm. The way to Universal Peace is from microcosm to macrocosm, and not *vice versa*. In Sacred Scriptures, the Awaited Universal Peace-Makers who will eventually come and establish Universal Peace throughout the world are referred to by different names but possess same characteristics. Universal Peace is a station in which the spiritual traveller lives amongst people only bodily, but is not with people heartly, actually, the face of his heart has been turned from the world of materiality to the world of spirituality. Having one's hands busy with work, while having one's heart with the Beloved. That is the only way to Universal Peace. (Mohammad Reza Rikhtehgaran)

Contributions of Indian Sufis to society lie in their sincere and dedicated struggle to find a unity for heterogeneous elements that make up its totality. They appreciated the multi-racial, multi-religious and multi-lingual pattern of Indian society. Sufis identified the service of God with the service of man. They not only preached it but practised it and helped in pulling down barriers between various religious groups. Chaitanya, Kabir, Guru Nanak, Namadev, Pipa, Sen and others familiarized themselves with the cosmopolitan ideas of the Sufi cult and broadcast them in their respective religions. (K.A. Nizami)

The Vedas never pray for peace of man alone, as we in our blind narcissism dare to do. When the Vedas pray for peace they pray, first, for the peace of the heaven, of the sky, of the earth, of all those who live on earth and of all those which grow on it and then for the peace of man. Even the peace of gods and of *Brahman*, the Absolute, has precedence in this prayer over the peace of man. They make this prayer because the self of man is not merely a human self; it is self of all. Unless and until his self becomes expansive enough to become all and small enough to become each he cannot know what peace is. For those who live alienated from themselves, their own native beings, can only be creatures of fear and of violence, not creatures of peace and bliss. It was for this reason that the Upanishadic seers found the creative centre of a peaceful civilization in the forest and not in the village or the town. For man could, they believed, live in genuine peace only if he loved all those he beheld from the sky to the earth, from the birds of the air to the beast of the jungle. (Som Raj Gupta)

Gandhi made an experiment with Truth, to which he called the other side of the coin, non-violence. His personal experiment with Truth had become an extension programme when it was accepted both as an end and a means for attaining independence for India. Earlier preachers of *bhakti* in medieval India went a step ahead of non-violence by preaching love for all living beings. Love is dynamic, non-violence is passive. The mythology of ancient India throws light on cultivation of peace in a climate of self-disciplined freedom. Visvamitra wanted to usher in universal peace by controlling intelligence with physical force. He failed, and so tried to acquire intellectual power. Vasishtha wanted to keep the world under control by intellectual power but failed. Valmiki appealed to the heart of the mankind to adjure violence and appreciate the beauty of mutual love. His message was received well by warriors, intellectuals and commoners alike. (Biswanarayan Shastri)

Peace, as Gandhi envisaged it, is far more than the absence of war and violence. It is a state of positive and constructive world-view and world-order, where individuals, groups and nations eschew to dominate or exploit one another and live in cooperation and mutual aid. This means that peace needs a new life-style and a new culture. However, such a philosophy of civilization of peace does not work in a vacuum. Therefore, Gandhi enunciates both an epistemology of peace and non-violence and he also formulates a sociology of peace. Gandhi had a vision of self-sufficient and self-managed village republics serving as grassroots of democracy as an alternative to a centralized party system and parliamentary democracy. Gandhi advocated, 'think globaly and act locally'. (Ramjee Singh)

Gandhi, with his advocacy of the development of self-sufficient village communities, trusteeship, disapproval of desires beyond the minimum manual labour, the community based basic education, was aiming at developing a social order where nobody could be an exploiter or exploited and which would ensure equitable distribution of wealth and justice. He wrote in his little classic *Hind Swaraj*: "We notice that the mind is a restless bird, the more it gets the more it wants, and still remains unsatisfied. The more we indulge our passions the more unbriddled they become. Our ancestors, therefore, set a limit to our indulgence. They saw that happiness was largely a mental condition. A man is not necessarily happy because he is rich, or unhappy because he is poor". (N. Radhakrishnan)

IV. Forming the Network of Actors in Peace

Knowing, willing and doing are three moments of the soul of man. We know that happiness can not be achieved unless everything is grounded in peace. But unless we have the will to promote a culture of peace, through the spiritual vision of shared human responsibility, we can make no beginning. To act is to pray. Prayer is the discipline by means of which the holiness (wholeness) is achieved. The holy man is the complete man. Peace can be achieved only by the holy man. To bring peace in the world, we have to form a network of holy men, the actors in peace, contemplating sovereign goodness and bringing peace and pleasure within every man. What is to be done is to counter false ideologies of materiality with spirituality which is still within every man's reach; to build a culture of peace brick by brick, act by act, and community by community; to maintain the balance between this-worldy and the other-worldly needs actualized by moral education; and to make people realize that the Kingdom of Heaven is within them.

Here is a case study of the Sarvodaya Shramadana Movement in Sri Lanka which began in mid-1950s. Mahatma Gandhi's vision of Village Republics or Lord Buddha's teachings on Right Livelihood Society provided the movement with a lot of insights into this stage of experiment. This experiment, including the economic and political aspects, is already going on in over 2,500 advanced villages out of 10,000 villages where the movement is active. These villages are going through what is described as social, economic and political empowerment. The very fact that this people's movement, working towards non-violent transformation of man and society has survived amidst many obstacles, shows that change based on moral principles is still possible. Turn to the spring of spirituality which is still within our reach, it depollutes and cleans the stream of morality that flows from it, and on either side of the stream it builds a culture of peace, sustainability and joy of living. (A.T. Ariyaratne)

Gandhiji gave a blue-print for the culture of peace to be built brick by brick, act by act, community by community. "In this structure composed of innumerable villages, there will be ever-widening, never-ascending circles. Life will not be a pyramid with the apex sustained by the bottom. But it will be an oceanic circle whose centre will be the individual, always ready to perish for the village, the village ready to perish for the circle of villages, till at last the whole becomes one life composed of individuals never aggressive in their arrogance but ever humble, sharing the majesty of the oceanic circle of which they are integral parts." (M. Aram)

Following the Unesco programme of working towards a culture of peace, people in different countries, including Bangladesh, took active part in prevention and solution of conflicts in campaigns of peace education, mobilization of public opinion and building of a mass movement promoting peace. (Ali Aksad)

The movement of bishops of Asia concerning the theology underlying inter-religious dialogue has led to a study on the theology of harmony. The movement 'Basic Education for All' was initiated in 1990 at the International Catholic Education Office in Brussels. Special features of the movement are that children of the formal school system, acting as agents or levers of change, carry to family units of slums in their neighbourhood a basic education package programme that includes, besides literacy, developmental components, basic skills, values and attitudes. This is the first step in education for peace. (Angelo Fernandes)

The starting point for the application of Bahai principles to educational reform is the understanding that continuing reform and evolution of education is essential to the life of the mind and spirit. Two of the specific Bahai principles of education that will influence the emergence of world peace are that education must become a virtuous process and that we must learn to celebrate errors as part of essential processes and products will then foster the type of environment necessary to promote independent investigation of truth to facilitate interdependency of the process, content, and objectives of education. (Dwight W. Allen)

From Bahai writings we can discern following requirements on the part of the present-day society for the establishment of a new World Order and permanent peace on earth: unity of nations, unity in the political realm, unity of thought, unity of freedom, unity of religion and adoption by majority of humankind of a world religion, unity of races and unity of languages. (A.K. Merchant)

The approach to peace must be universal, not merely institutional, but with the backing of all. All citizens, communities and groups must participate actively, honestly and dutifully in a concerted effort to do away with war in all its forms. Of the groups who must be involved, we can identify the younger generation, the youth, students and their teachers. Add to them the sensitive community of mothers, and businessmen, brahmans, maulvis, priests and rabbis who impart true education by precept and by example. (M. Ishaq Jamkhanawala)

Man is the actor. He acts in war and in peace. What matters is his role in the cosmic play. He plays a specific role in the course of living. His destiny lies in the role that he chooses for himself. Depending on the self-reflexivity with which he is gifted, he relates himself either to Truth or to untruth. He is, thus, the marker of his destiny. He has an innate tendency to organize his self. Moving from one body to another he is re-made and re-organized again and again. In truth, he is without a centre. His roots are upward. The traditional model of human organization is diametrically opposed to the pattern of the modern global village, organizing itself in fear and tension. (Baidyanath Saraswati)

* * *

It is fairly evident that authors of these essays have made us possible to think of culture as an organisation of peace. The truth of proportion of war and peace is critical in the understanding of culture. Human behaviour is complex. Culture is by necessity selective. No culture is made up of more than a fraction of the total range of human behaviour. A culture that capitalizes a considerable proportion of peace is the culture of peace. The influence of spirituality on early culture made peace possible. The influence of materiality on modern culture is a threat to the culture of peace. In a world plenty of knowledge and skill, the cow of peace is limping. Who will offer the wisdom, the compassion and the healing faith that strengthen it?. . . The world's people, not the Asians alone.

Part - I

Sharing the Experience of Beauty and Peace

1

The Cosmos and Humanity as a Healing Family

Minoru Kasai

A recent publication *A Healing Family* by Kenzaburo and Yukari Oe is a quiet best seller in Japan. Kenzaburo Oe is a Nobel Prize winner in literature and Yukari is his wife. *A Healing Family* is a collection of essays on their life with Hikari, mentally handicapped because of brain damage, by Oe with Yukari's paintings of Hikari.

One of the basic tones of the book is the utter pain, agony and groaning of Hikari, their first child born. Oe's despair is reflected in his novel *A Personal Matter*. He himself gives the essence of the story.

> *A Personal Matter* is the story of a young man whose first child is born with a cranial deformity. The work describes what might be called a rite of passage, as the young father struggles to accept the infant as a member of his family.[1]

The young father reflects Oe's despair to a great extent. He hoped the baby would die. Considering all factors, he thought it would be the best solution. He was so much for the idea of his baby's death that he couldn't wait for it to happen and tried to find a doctor to help the baby die because of the misery to be expected. He was also tempted to run away from the baby, after divorcing his wife, to Africa with his former girl friend. He was utterly egocentric, shaken to the bottom of his heart. However, he finally overcame his confusion, pain, temptation and irresponsibility. Oe states briefly the young father's final position.

> In the end the young man experiences a kind of epiphany, realizing that abandoning the child to die was tantamount to destroying himself.[2]

The actual turning point for Oe to live with and for his baby came from his meeting and dialogue with Dr Fumio Shigeto, the head of the hospital for the victims of the Hiroshima atomic bomb. Dr Shigeto himself was a victim of the atomic bomb. He was wounded by Pika Don, the murderous light of the bomb on 6 August 1945. But as a medical doctor, he worked day and night without returning to his home for the first two weeks. Since then he has been a living witness to the reality of the Hiroshima disaster: Heaven burnt red and bodies melted.

Dr Shigeto told Oe about a young doctor working with him soon after the disaster. He was overwhelmed by the futility of medical works for the dying victims. He wanted to consult Dr Shigeto. But he could not wait for the occasion of thinking together with Dr Shigeto. He committed suicide, hanging himself with the rope tied to the support of the ceiling. Dr Shigeto regretted that he could not spare his time for that young doctor because of the crying need of the victims. He wanted to tell the young doctor before his final decision, 'Yes, helpless and powerless, but the patients are waiting for us. Let's just get on with it.'

Oe's response to the meeting with Dr Shigeto is reflected in the young father's decision:

> He sheds his romanticism, parts with the girl friend who is bound for Africa, and accepts the child, deciding in favour of a life-saving operation. His decision is for reality: to build a family of reality, to live reality.[3]

Oe himself affirms this.

> The baby with the deformity was in reality my son, the fact of whose birth has overshadowed my life and writing.[4]

Now, the question is, what did he learn by 'his decision for reality: to build a family on reality, to live reality'? This question is regarding Oe's understanding of reality. As stated above, his eyes were opened to reality in his dialogue with Dr Shigeto, a witness to Hiroshima, inexpressible, unbearable and unbelievable. Therefore, it is not surprising that his understanding of reality is intimately related to the victims of the Hiroshima tragedy.

> Over the years, I have often written on the theme of living with his (Hikari's) mental handicap, and this same theme also informs my writing on Hiroshima and Nagasaki. I have tried to define the meaning that the experience of these two cities has for people in Japan and elsewhere, and I have been involved in activities associated with what I have written of this subject; but my fundamental perspective has always been that of the parent of a handicapped child. This is the experience that influences everything I write and everything I do.[5]

Yet, in spite of the inseparable relation between Hikari and Hiroshima, the former is fundamental and illuminates Oe's understanding of the latter.

> Thus, for example, my realization that life with a mentally handicapped child has the power to heal the wounds that family members inflict on one another led me to the more recent insight that the victims and survivors of the atomic bombs have the same sort of power to heal all of us who live in this nuclear age.[6]

Accordingly, Hikari in the family and the victims of the atomic bombs in society have a precious and unique position for forming a healing family.

> This thought seems almost self-evident when one sees the survivors of Hiroshima and Nagasaki, by now frail and elderly, speaking up and taking an active part in the movement to abolish all nuclear weapons.[7]

The healing power of the suffering such as that of Hikari and of the victims of the atomic bombs are vital in restoring the normal order, authentic and humane, of the family and society. This is self-evident to Oe. The following statement affirms this:

> They (the victims and survivors of the atomic bombs) are to me, the embodiment of a prayer for the healing of our society, indeed the planet as a whole.[8]

Hikari is so mentally handicapped that he can hardly communicate in words, but when he speaks, he conveys something unforgettable though enigmatic. I will introduce two cases.

> Some time ago, the whole family made a trip back to the village in the woods of Shikoku where I was born. While we were there, Hikari spent a lot of time with his grandmother, to whom he grew very attached. On the flight home, however, I noticed that my daughter seemed upset about something, and it eventually came out that Hikari was to blame. Apparently his rather boisterous farewell to his grandmother had been: 'Cheer up and have a good death!' 'Right you are,' she answered, 'I will, but it's sad to have to say good-bye. . . .'
>
> The point of this story, though, is that some time after our visit she fell seriously ill; fortunately she recovered, but she told my sister, who nursed her, that while she was sick the thing that had most encouraged her to go on fighting it, oddly enough, was Hikari's farewell to her. She remembered just how he had shouted 'Cheer up and have a good death!' to her.[9]

Hikari seems to be an extraordinarily sensitive person. I observed this on the TV screen and on the video. Oe writes on this very vividly. The occasion was Hikari's first visit to the Atomic Bomb Peace Museum in Hiroshima.

> As we were about to enter a room featuring a model of the city immediately after the blast, Hikari seemed terrified, more so than I had ever seen him before. In the end I almost had to push him inside. After the tour, we sat down by a window in the hallway, both feeling drained, but after a while I pressed him for his impressions of what he'd just seen. 'It was all awful,' he said quite forcefully without looking up, the answer half a groan and half an indictment.[10]

Afterwards he composed some music. Its title was 'Hiroshima Requiem'. Hikari's way to music was open at the age of five as Oe reflects on it.

> As I have often written elsewhere, for the first four or five years of my son's life he never once uttered a coherent word, until one day he said 'That's a water rail,' which was something he had heard repeated on a record of a hundred different bird calls we had given him. This first step on the narrow road to communication led almost immediately to music.[11]
>
> I noticed that he was particularly responsive to birdsong, and rushed out to buy a record of a hundred bird calls which I played for him with almost manic frequency. This craze of mine was rewarded one day in the woods surrounding our summer cottage when Hikari, who was five at the time, in a voice that exactly mimicked the announcer on my record, suddenly identified a bird: 'That's a water rail,' he said in the solemn tones of the voice-over — a short sentence that was, in fact, his very first intelligible use of language to communicate with us.[12]

Hikari's music reveals his extraordinary sensitivity. Oe's response to Hikari's music touches on this sensitivity. The following is an extract from Oe's short talk at the beginning of Hikari's concert.

> The person whose works you will be hearing today is someone who has never cried; someone also who may never have had a dream. . . . You will find, however, that among the works included on his second CD is one called 'Dream', a title he gave it himself.
>
> The voice you hear in this work for violin and piano is one we hadn't heard before: a voice I would describe as that of 'a wailing soul'. . . . Where does

> this unhappy voice come from? From deep inside him . . . that much one knows for sure . . . and it can in fact be heard throughout his new collection. . . . Hikari has no verbal means of describing this experience, but it is safe to say that his exploration brought him into contact with a solid core of sorrow that had collected in his heart, and by cutting through it he released this other sound, the voice of 'a wailing soul'.[13]

Reaching out in that darkness, 'a solid core of sorrow that had collected in his heart', Hikari expresses the voice of 'a wailing soul'. This has a healing power, not only for Hikari himself but also for others who are sensitive to the darkness of life with his son Hikari. It is a mystery of art.

> Hikari's recent music, particularly his 'Dream' and 'Nocturnal Capriccio', reveals another truth as well: that in the very act of expressing himself there is a healing power, a power to mend the heart. This power, moreover, isn't limited to him alone but extends to those receptive to what he has to express. And this is the miracle of art. For in the music or literature we create, though we come to know despair — that dark night of the soul through which we have to pass — we find that by actually giving it expression we can be healed and know the joy of recovering: and as these linked experiences of pain and recovery are added to one another, layer upon layer, not only is the artist's work enriched but its benefits are shared with others.[14]

The mystery of art is very much spiritual, being healed through expressing despair, the dark night of the soul, being transformed through healing and sharing the joy of recovery with others.

Oe sees prayers in Hikari's intensive concentration on music. In this regard, Simone Weil enlightened Oe's understanding very much.

> Hikari may not be much good with words, but where music is concerned he has a carefully cultivated ability to concentrate, one that his mother and his teachers have helped him develop but which he himself has also honed by listening to recordings and the radio during almost every waking hour for more than twenty years. The French philosopher Simone Weil has written about this sort of concentration, asking what it is that could link such apparently disparate experiences as 'study' and 'the love of god', and

> concluding that 'the key is in the fact that prayer is a matter of concentration. Prayer is the directing of all the attention of which the soul is capable toward god'. And when I see my son giving all his powers of attention to his music, I am convinced that Weil was right.[15]

Thus, in this context, music is prayer for Hikari.

Finally, music for Hikari is care for others and response to it. Oe is very much enlightened by Simone Weil in this aspect, too.

> In the same passage, she writes of one of the legends concerning the Holy Grail: it seems that a certain knight, coming upon the gravely wounded king who was the guardian of the Grail, greeted him with the question 'In what way are you suffering?', and in that very choice of words revealed himself as worthy of being the next bearer of the sacred vessel. In the same way I feel the people who have most helped Hikari have approached him with the same enquiry. Among them, for example, are the performers in the concert you're about to hear, each of whom, moreover, has that same ability to concentrate on his or her own discipline. And I feel that you in the audience, too, who have gone to the trouble of coming here, are asking him as well, 'In what way are you suffering?' And for each of you, my hope is that his music will serve as an answer.[16]

'In what way are you suffering?' This is again from Simone Weil. Hikari's music itself is also this legendary question. Thus, music reveals the cosmos and humanity as a healing family.

A healing family is sensitive to the voice from deep within our hearts, which is healing power restoring the family and society of joy, prayers and cares. The suffering such as the handicapped, the sick, the victims of violence are the life of the family and of society. Cosmos and humanity is a healing family. Hikari and Oe's family and the prayers of the surviving victims of Hiroshima and Nagasaki are the witnesses of a healing family. The mystery of art reveals this reality.

There is still a bearer of the legendary question, in the world of darkness, 'In what way are you suffering?'

The perspective and experience of the culture of peace cannot be conceived of without a healing family.

References

1. Kenzaburo Oe, *Japan, the Ambiguous, and Myself*, New York; Kodansha International, 1995, pp.27-28 (hereafter referred to as *Japan*).
2. *Japan*, p. 28.
3. *Ibid.*, pp. 28-29.
4. *Ibid.*, pp. 33-34.
5. *Ibid.*, p. 34.
6. *Ibid.*
7. *Ibid.*
8. *Ibid.*, p. 35.
9. Kenzaburo Oe, *A Healing Family*, illustrated by Yukari Oe, translated by Stephen Snyder, New York: Kodansha International, 1996, pp. 87-88 (hereafter referred to as *A Healing Family*).
10. *Ibid.*, pp.136-37.
11. *Ibid.*, p.111.
12. *Ibid.*, p.10.
13. *Ibid.*, pp.139-41.
14. *Ibid.*, pp.141-42.
15. *Ibid.*, p.142.
16. *Ibid.*, pp.142-43

2

The True Meaning of Peace from the Chinese Literary Perspective

Tan Chung

THE concept of 'Peace' in our modern civilization (should I say, Western civilization?) is the facade of war, dominated by the calculations of *realpolitik*. This English word originates from the French concept which denotes 'agreement' — agreeing to stop a conflict or war. When we refer to *The Universal Dictionary of the English Language* we find that the first notion of 'peace' is 'cessation of, freedom from, strife, warfare', and the second notion of it is 'treaty of peace between hostile nations'. Even in the third notion, it is understood as 'freedom from civil disorder, disturbance, agitation' and 'freedom from strife, controversy or agitation'. Only after these notions come 'tranquillity, concord, mental calm, serenity of mind'. This European concept of peace (which is more or less universally accepted) is something similar to the Chinese word *wu* (its palaeographic form shows a combination of denoting 'to stop' and denoting 'weapon'). This *wu* concept was to capture the joyous mood of the soldiers when they heard of the news of cease-fire (stopping the weapon). This was, in fact, the original Chinese word for 'dance'. However, today we use the word for such connotations like 'military', 'fight', 'fighting skill' (as used in *wushu*, etc.) Like the case of 'peace' in the European cultural context, this Chinese concept of *wu* remains a facade of war. I may call this category of thinking the 'red-eyed view of peace'.

In this paper I wish to present the green-eyed view of peace which originates from 'Agroculture'. I have coined this word to avoid using the cumbersome formulation of 'agriculture culture'. When humans came to this earth as a result of evolution, they started making stone weapons to hunt other animals for food. After many thousand years, these primitive hunters transformed themselves into two dominant cultural modes. Some began to tame the animals and graze them on grassland. Some of the animals were kept as their food, but other animals, particularly horses, were used for quick movement and fighting. They finished off the grass in one place and moved to another to graze. This approach amounted to the looting of Mother Earth. Also in the movement they clashed with other nomadic groups and practised the principle of 'might is right'. Nomadic culture is essentially a hunter's culture intoxicated in fighting, looting and warfare.

But there was another cultural mode of settling down in a place and start cultivating Mother Earth for subsistence. When Mother Earth's generosity surpassed their level of subsistence, they domesticated wild animals and fed them — ultimately killing them for food. This mode is the agrocultural mode. Agroculture is a cultural mode that is meant to replace the hunter's culture. Gone are the days when humans tiresomely and cruelly chased and killed other animals on the run. Agroculture is a relaxed mood, oriented in the spirit of peace. It is grown from Mother Earth, and endeared to Mother Earth. Earth is important to an agriculturist (so also an 'agroculturist') who cultivates the good earth under his feet and depends for his livelihood on it. Agroculture thrives on the exuberance of the planted growth, and avoids insensately looting the vegetation in the environment. Agroculture is eco-friendly.

To agroculture, peace is not an aftermath after war. It is an integral part of human existence. The concept of peace takes its birth with agriculture and agroculture. Peace, attachment to Mother Earth, friendship with ecology are essential ingredients for a good agrocultural life. Peace and agroculture are symbiotic. With agroculture there cannot be any concept of peace. For agroculture is a farewell to the hunter's culture, a farewell to arms, a farewell to chasing others — be it a wild animal or a hostile human. The Western way of life has not completely said farewell to this hunter's culture. Western table manners daily practised by the kings and queens, by civilians and soldiers, by the workers wearing white, blue or other coloured collars, by writers, film stars, poets, and so on involves cutting meat with a knife and taking it into the mouth with a fork almost exactly in the same fashion as a primitive hunter did thousands of years ago. But, those who have bid farewell to the hunter's culture have long laid aside, and have long forgotten, knives and forks while eating. For thousands of years, the Indians have put cooked food on leaves and helped themselves with their fingers, while the Chinese have used chopsticks and spoons. These are symbols of agroculture, of non-violence — symbols of peace. For agroculture is born with peace just as peace is born with agroculture.

In this paper I would like to elaborate this concept of peace which has long been forgotten or ignored. As I am not so conversant with Indian agroculture, I shall concentrate on its Chinese counterpart to bring some fresh air to this Unesco-sponsored conference deliberating on the 'Culture of Peace'.

I

What I have said a little while ago seems to have idealized agroculture. Yes, what agroculture is meant to be is one thing, and what reality that agroculture has gone through is another. As agroculture came out from the womb of the hunter's culture, it often reflected the brutal appearance of its mother culture as well. Humans have arrived on our earth to be nobler creatures than brutes, yet, just as Mencius (372?-289 BC) observed: 'How little is the difference between humans and the brutes!?'[1] To carry Mencius' thinking to its logical end, I dare say that he would not consider war decent human behaviour. Mencius and his master Confucius (551-479 BC) talked about *ren* (the normal, also ideal, human relationship) which was penetrated by the spirit of 'love' (*airen*), i.e to love all other human beings. In their schema of *ren* there was no place for war. Peace should be the basic way of life.

The richest ancient treasury of ideas created by Chinese agroculture is the *Book of Change* (*Yijing*, also spelt I-ching), which has two parts. The first part is the 64 *gua* which the ancients used for divination in the dawn of Chinese civilization (from as early as four or five thousand years ago), while the second part is some supplementary commentaries. For each of the 64 *gua*, i.e. omens, there is a separate commentary. Conventionally, people think that there could not have been just one commentator. All these commentaries form a cumulative treasury which must have been contributed by wise thinkers during the course of thousands of years, both before and after the time of Confucius.

In the supplementary commentaries there is a famous observation, 'Tiandizhi dade yue sheng'.[2] The English translation of this should be: '*Sheng* (creation) is the grand virtue of the universe (between Heaven and Earth)'. In the commentary to the 31st *gua*, there is an observation: '*Tiandi gan er wanwu huasheng, shengren gan renxin er tianxia heping*', and its translation is: 'When Heaven and Earth interact there is the creation of all beings. When the sages interact with the hearts of the people there is peace in the universe.'

Here I have translated the term *heping* into peace, but it is a combination of two concepts: *he* (smooth, harmonious and peaceful) and *ping* (even, tranquil, just and peaceful). We can see that 'peace' is conceived of as the law, the rhythm, the logic of the universe. It is conceived of as the virtue, natural feeling, logical mood of humans.

In the commentary of the first *gua*, *qianyuan* (Heaven), there is an observation that the *daren* or great man merges his virtue with Heaven and Earth, merges his brightness with the sun and moon, merges his rhythm with the four seasons, and merges his good and bad omens with the spirits. This term 'great man' is used in the *Book of Change* in such a manner that we see it as a signification of God. The Chinese term *daren* (with *da* meaning 'great' and *ren* meaning 'person') comes so near to the ancient Indian concept of *mahapurusha*.

In the commentary of the second *gua*, *kunyuan*, is praised as the creator of all the things and beings. This *kunyuan* is a reference to our Mother Earth. It is also observed that this Mother Earth interacts with Heaven (*tian*) in the mood of *shuncheng*, i.e. obeying and sustaining.

All this makes it clear that in the wisdom of Chinese agroculture, there is only mutual give and take, sustenance, creation, harmony, tranquillity, and peace — there should not be conflict and war.

Confucius, in his *Daxue* (Great Learning), observed that the learning process began with *zhiyu zhishan* (to stop at the optimum). He continued: 'Knowing how to stop will achieve stability. After achieving stability there is tranquillity. After tranquillity there is peace of mind and ease of mood. After acquiring peace of mind and ease of mood one can think and reflect. After thinking and reflection there is achievement.'[3]

Then, Confucius spelt out the process by which a gentleman could develop his career. First, he should become earnest and sincere; then he should put his heart in the right place; then he should cultivate saintly behaviour; then he should put his family in order; then he should bring his country under a good rule; then he should make the universe a place of *taiping*.[4]

Again, there is some difficulty in translating *taiping*, which is a combination of *tai* (connoting grand, extreme, etc.) along with *ping* (connoting even, tranquil, just, peaceful, etc.). In fact, this *ping* is the same *ping* which we have just seen in the *Book of Change*, and Confucius' *taiping* and the term *heping* we have cited earlier from the Supplementary Commentaries of the *Book of Change* are similar ideas. As I have said earlier, peace was conceived of as the natural law and rhythm of the universe. Now Confucius added a dimension of human dynamism to it. Peace to Confucius was the ultimate goal of human endeavour, in other words.

Our journey starting with the *Book of Change* to Confucius' spiritual world has witnessed a shift of emphasis from the fundamental laws of Nature to human endeavour, suggesting that the peaceful nature of the universe had been disturbed, and should be upheld by human endeavour. This shift does reveal the gap between agrocultural idealism and human reality — peace being constantly disturbed by human activities. However, what I wish to emphasize is that to the Chinese agroculture, peace is no secondary reality, and certainly not an afterthought cropping up at the end of the war or conflict.

To the Chinese agrocultural mind, peace is the reality of the universe, the fundamental condition of human existence: not, as the French and other European definitions suggest, an expediency, a temporary arrangement, or a momentary escape from quarrels, conflict and war.

Peace, as the goal of life, the goal of a political regime and political career, has been ingrained in Chinese thinking. From the Han Dynasty onwards, the Chinese emperors took the lead in codifying the ceremonial music played in the imperial court. The literary text of this music is known as *yuefu* (literally 'music office'). One Chinese ruler who was very diligent in scripting the court songs was the reigning empress Wu Zetian (624-705), who had the unique distinction to be the only woman who sat in the chair of the 'Son of Heaven' (emperor) in Chinese history. In her composition entitled *Huangdi xing* (song of the emperor), she wrote:

> I raise my head to be blessed by the calendar sacred;
> I stoop to appreciate glowing tributes of my subjects;
> Peace in faraway territory, and solemnity around me;
> Society booming, and times in smooth tranquillity;
> Power shines from the jade reigning mirror,
> Our golden law makes the court free from disputes;
> The new ascendance of a majestic ceremony and order;
> Spears and shields are forever placed in disuse.[5]

Known for her Buddhistic inclinations, Empress Wu was using imagery like *yujing* (jade mirror) and *jinke* (golden law) that betray the adaptation of Indian (Buddhist) imagery.

When Confucius talked about peace as a goal it was only from the viewpoint of a teacher and a thinker. Empress Wu talked about peace when she was at the head of a powerful military machine. If she was sincere in the words she had penned (the words which were every morning sung at the court ceremony) — and there is no reason to doubt her sincerity — then we can say that peace had gone into China's ruling ideology in her times and in the subsequent reigns of the Tang Dynasty (618-907).

II

China would not have been on the map of the modern world if there had not been a great politician and tyrant, Qin Shihuangdi (reigning as the King of Qin state from 246 BC and as the Emperor of the Qin Dynasty from 221 BC till his death in 210 BC). This Qin Emperor unified China by means of war, but wanted to rule his empire in peace. He thought of the best way to ensure peace by asking his subjects to surrender all the weapons in their possession during the first year of his reign. After collecting all the surrendered weapons, he melted them and forged them into bells, and 12 giant human figures to be placed in his palace. However, there was no peace during his reign. He was attacked by many assassins, and narrowly escaped death in 216 BC when he and four guards were attacked by robbers in one of his frequent incognito trips outside the palace at night. He was a powerful ruler who could hold his empire together. The moment he died the entire country rose in arms against his regime, and within a couple of years the Qin Dynasty was overthrown.

From the Qin Dynasty until today the existence of a unified (or semi-unified) China was always first wrought by the use of force, and then by maintaining an enforced peace with the help of a powerful army. In other words, throughout Chinese history, the culture of peace has not been different from the culture of war. Weapons have been used to end war and to start peace, to maintain peace. Then, peace was disturbed and war was started by the use of weapons, and a vicious circle between war and peace has been in motion till today.

Chinese agroculture has to address itself to this dichotomy which has been developed in total contravention of the original rhythm of agroculture. Peace and war, it may be said, have been the twins of Chinese politics, and Chinese agroculture has to try for the best. There have been two sources of war: one internal and the other external.

The internal source of war rose from the very fact that the hierarchical mansion of Chinese politics was built upon the self-imposition of the ruling family by means of conquest, all others having been placed under the threat of military might to obey, and maintain peace and law and order. There were always those who wanted to displace the ruling family and come on top of the political hierarchy. A natural source of war was inbuilt.

The external source of war rose from the fact that agriculture had made China a land of affluence in comparison with the homes of the neighbouring races. Adding to this was the fact that China was virtually the only agrocultural society surrounded by non-agrocultural, nomadic societies. I have said at the outset that the nomadic culture has directly inherited the hunter's culture. This was noticed by the famous Tang poet, Li Bai (also spelt Li Bo, 701-62), who observed in his famous poem 'Fighting South of The Town':

> Our neighbours, the Huns, preferred killing to tilling,

The deserts of yellow sands are bleached by skeletons.[6]

As a result, in half of the last two thousand years, China was ruled by foreign conquerors. Foreign conquest and restoration of Han (Chinese) rule formed another vicious circle of Chinese historical development. Both conquest and recovery were by means of war. War, not peace, became the fundamental rhythm of progress and evolution of Chinese history.

Chinese agroculture has mortgaged peace under the duress of the makers of Chinese history who were either the rulers or the destroyers of the rulers of imperial China. Paradoxically, after destroying those who reigned, the destroyers replaced them and became rulers themselves. Their successors would be destroyed by other destroyers. Ruling by military might and destroying a rule by military might became the fundamental rhythm of imperial China, making it impossible to materialize the originally conceived rhythm of peace and tranquillity.

To view it from a different angle, China would have taken a different turn of development (and may not have become what she is today) if the Qin Emperor had not succeeded in unifying China — in other words, if the rulers of six other states (which were there during the pre-Qin period were vying with the Qin state for supremacy) could have prevented themselves from being vanquished by the Qin emperor. This hindsight was provided by a Song scholar, Su Xun (1009-66) in his famous essay '*Liuguo*' (six states). Su Xun commented: 'The six states were vanquished not because of the weakness of their fighting forces. The trouble lay in their appeasement.' He added: 'What Qin had gained was a hundred times greater than the fruits of its military victory. What the states had lost was a hundred times greater than their military defeat.' The six states in dealing with the Qin state (which was the bully), had each tried to appease the aggressor by giving away some territory. This was commented upon by an ancient observer which was quoted by Su Xun as a foolish act, like 'carrying firewood to fight a fire'.[7]

The purpose of this essay was to advise the ruler, Song Emperor Renzong (reigning from 1022 to 1063) against adopting an appeasement policy *vis-a-vis* the aggressive northern neighbour — the Khitan race. Yet it also reflected Chinese intellectual opinion against military conquest of any kind. However, it does not seem to have occurred to Sun Xun that if the Qin regime had not vanquished the six states and unified China, there would not have been the fortune of the Song Dynasty (960-1279), in whose interest he was serving and worrying. There is a dichotomy here, but it is clear that although the Chinese intellectuals have all along been for the stability and strength of their unified motherland, their innate inclination was against military annexation of others' territories.

It was strange that China's territorial expansion was achieved under two different circumstances. The first circumstance was a response on the part of Chinese rulers while dealing with pestering aggressive enemies. The Han Dynasty (206 BC to AD 220) originally adopted an appeasement policy towards the Hun race, which could not stop the latter from repeated aggressive acts, including frequent intrusions and looting of Chinese civilian properties. Finally, the Han Emperor Wu (141-87 BC) made a strong determination not only to fight the Huns, but to fight them to the finish — resulting in driving the Huns away from their homeland (in present Mongolia). The second circumstance was when China herself was vanquished by foreign invasion. But the foreign conquerors of China carried on their expansionist policies beyond Chinese territory. It was under the Mongol and Manchu rules that China had the largest territory of all times. After their rules collapsed, the succeeding Chinese governments inherited the expanded territories as godsend. It was paradoxical that never had Chinese troops gone to conquer the homeland of the Mongols. But Mongolia became a part of China — only as a result of China's having been united with Mongolia by the Mongols.

Chinese agroculture had been pushed to an expansive mood by these two historical circumstances: one reactive, the other passive — never active, let alone pro-active. But, the expansive mood did help Chinese agriculture to achieve a perfect eco-geographic holistic status. We know that China has been heavily dependent on her two major rivers for economic development, i.e. the Yellow River and the Yangtse. While the Yangtse is the fourth largest river of the world (with a length of nearly 6,000 km), the Yellow is the seventh largest (nearly 5,000 km). While no other country in the world possesses the entire length of any of the seven largest rivers on earth, China alone possesses two of them. This is a great gain for China's agriculture and agroculture, objectively speaking. But she has not gotten it by her own merits or efforts. It is a gift bequeathed by the nomadic cultures (of the Mongol and Manchu).

How do China's modern ruling elites view this situation? Their views are represented by three modern statesmen, Dr Sun Yat-sen (1866-25), known as the 'Father of Modern China', and Chairman Mao Zedong (1893-1976), known as the 'Father of Communist China'. The third statesman was Deng Xiaoping (1904-1997), the lately lamented Chinese supremo who had made post-Mao China a very dynamic phase of history.

Sun Yat-sen not only regarded the international boundaries left behind by the erstwhile Manchu Empire as sacrosanct, but wished that the Manchu, Mongol and other races who had joined the Chinese joint family be integrated with the Han-Chinese majority. His ideal state was the United States of America. However, he was also influenced by the ideas of Confucius, as he observed: 'We must revive our nationalism and restore our national status so that we can give good order to the country and bring peace to the universe. We must employ our innate morality and peace as the very foundation to unify the world, to achieve the rule of *datong* (grand tranquillity).'[8] Here, Sun Yat-sen made a reference to the idealism of *datong* which was enshrined in an essay found in *Liji* (Book of Rites) stated to be the observation of Confucius. The *datong* idealism reflected in the passage depicts a society in which no one is selfish, and everyone is selfless, working for the good of the collective. There is perfect order in society, and no intrigue, nor robbery, nor theft (so that people can sleep at night without closing their doors). Then, *Liji* further quotes Confucius to say that such a *datong* society could exist only when the Tao prevailed. 'Now that the great Tao is hiding, everyone takes to one's own family. Everyone endears only his/her parents, loves only his/her children, treating property as his/her own. Thus intrigues and utilitarianism prevail, leading to the breakout of war.' Such a society was defined as *xiaokang*, literally 'small comforts'.[9]

Interestingly this two-stage social development from *xiaokang* to *datong* has become the goal of modern Chinese thinkers. China, in their thinking, has slipped to a state of misery, but the Western societies are in a state of *xiaokang*. However, Chinese thinkers have been wanting to achieve both — first from misery to *xiaokang*, then from *xiaokang* to *datong*. Deng Xiaoping, who put China on the express highway of development, set a target of a per capita income of US$ 1,000 by the end of the twentieth century. He said in 1987 that 'when that time comes we call it a *xiaokang* society — a *xiaokang* society in which people enjoy a universally enhanced living standard'.[10] Though Deng Xiaoping has not made any reference to *datong*, the mention of *xiaokang* puts him in the same traditional mind set being personified from Confucius to Sun Yat-sen and beyond.

Mao Zedong openly said that his ides of 'new democracy' was the adoption of the new version of Dr Sun Yat-sen's 'Three People's Principles' (*san min zhuyi*). He was an ardent patriot like Sun Yat-sen, and his ideal society was communism, as he wrote in 1939: 'The ultimate future of Chinese revolution is not capitalism, but socialism and communism.'[11] Mao's thinking that communist society, in which there is no exploitation but only amity and prosperity, conforms to the ancient Chinese ideal of *datong*.

III

Idealism and reality do not get along well. The makers of China have gotten all Chinese intellectuals in a situation that amounts to helplessness. While one must obey the tide, there can also be a sort of passive resistance — knowing full well that to fail in fighting for one's country would be treason. There is a famous poem penned by a Tang poet, Wang Han (687?-726?), which is worth quoting:

Goblet of black jade, I enjoy my delicious grape wine,
There the alarm sounds, I must do battle in another round.
Don't giggle at me when tipsily I sleep on the battleground,
How many are home-bound since the beginning of time?[12]

What a comic way with such deep sarcasm and pain in highlighting the eternal dilemma of the Chinese people — many of whom did not return home after contributing to the victories of their country! The moral of the poem is: What difference does it make whether wars are won or lost, since the victors don't return home in triumph?

There are others who voiced their sharp criticism against the warlike policies of the Chinese imperial government. Li Bai, in his above-cited poem, went on to describe the horrors of war:

Riderless fighting steeds bellow heart-breaking neighs.
Scavenging vultures busy scooping the entrails of the dead,
Carrying their intestines in their beaks,
Feasting heartily atop the lonely trees,
The leftovers they hang on dry twigs.

The poem concludes with these words:

When soldiers die in the jungles,
Shame to the careers of the generals.
Must realize that war is a deadly solution,
Sage rulers reserve it as the last option.[13]

The third line from the bottom referred to General Wang Zhongsi's refusal to sacrifice ten thousand lives of his own soldiers, for which he had forsaken a chance of his own honour and decoration. What General Wang did constituted a protest in action against the militant policies of the government.

Another famous anti-war poem was written by Li Bai's contemporary, the equally famous Du Fu (also spelt as Tu Fu, 712-70), entitled 'Troops Marching'. The poem protested:

Blood flows like flood on the borderland,
The emperor's unending desire is to expand.

Du Fu concluded his poem on a sad note:

Don't you see, dead bones constantly lie

From ancient times to this day in Qinghai
For those who died no one bats an eye.
New ghosts grumble, old ghosts cry,
Rains boohoo, boohoo, and dim the sky.[14]

Poets could not do much in protest. But they have painted a vivid picture of the tragedies of war. One Tang poet, Chen Tao (812?-85?), wrote about the dead soldiers whose bones lay in foreign lands:

Five thousand braves now miserably lie
Buried in the dust under the alien sky.
The chilly wind makes the skeletons shiver,
Namelessly beside an unknown river.
During spring nights they are still alive
To peep into the dreams of the waiting wives.[15]

Interestingly, not long after Chen Tao, another poet, Mao Wenxi (who lived in the tenth century), wrote a poem which provided the picture from the wives' side in their long wait for their husbands' return from the battlefields. The poem, in the voice of one of the wives, reads:

No, please don't ask!
At your asking I am alarmed,
To ask is to harm, to add pain in my heart,
Water abounds in the pond in an exuberant spring.
A mandarin-duck chasing its mate in a loving game.
.....
I miss my man whose youth sacrificed in the border,
For a long time I haven't received his news or letter.[16]

The culture of peace for the Chinese has now turned out to be a picture of broken families and fractured human bonds. When there was war, those who were not fighting had also to be victimized. A touching depiction of such victimization was depicted by Du Fu in his famous poem 'Officials of Shihao'. The poet was one night staying in this small village (Shihao) when officials raided a house to take away an old man to the front to replenish the depleted fighting force. The old man fled from the back, climbing the wall. His old wife faced the officials and pleaded with them that already all her three sons had been recruited by the army, and two of them had already been killed. Then the officials saw the daughter-in-law, mother of a new-born baby, and wanted to take her away. Finally, it was settled that the old woman would go to the front in place of her husband. After that the midnight stir was quietened, said the poet:

Then the dark night lengthened its silence without a murmur,
I lay awake to an intermittent sob from the inner chamber.
At daybreak I left the village for my onward journey again,
Was waved farewell by the old man who had remained.[17]

This poem has revealed the inner weakness of a great empire when its power was at the zenith. Power to be maintained by military might is always weak as this poem shows. Without the military prop, no regime could survive. How could a state be orderly administered, then? The mighty Tang Empire was internally rotten as the following poem (also written by a Tang poet) has disclosed:

Rats who live in the government warehouse
Are fat like cats and have each a big mouth,
Settled so lordly that they don't run away
Even when the keepers stand at the gate.
Troops in the front have little to eat,
Hungry are the citizens in the street,
Tell me, sirs, where comes all this food
So generously for your greedy brood?[18]

We know that the rat here is the symbol of the parasitic people who battened on the social wealth of the country. With such bad government at the rear, the soldiers at the front also suffered.

All this made the intellectuals and poets long for the natural rhythm of the universe which was by nature to be a world of peace and tranquillity. Let me now return to this intellectual mood to echo what I have discussed at the outset of this essay.

IV

If I don't proceed further, the obvious conclusion is that the 'red-eyed view' of peace is no exclusive property of European culture. When we hear the angry voices of Li Bai and Du Fu, and the lamentation of Chen Tao and Mao Wenxi, we feel that their eyes were red with fury or sadness. But that was only one mood when Chinese intellectuals looked at current developments. Still, the mainstream of the Chinese intellectual mood has been the longing for a return to peace and tranquillity. Still the green-eyed views have not been eliminated or extinguished.

During the Unesco Conference I selected a Chinese poem to present to fellow participants a different Chinese flavour for the conception of peace. This is a poem which was composed by Su Shi (1037-1101) and in 1082, the third spring of his demotion:

Gentle rays cover
The fluvial waves opaque,
Clouds line up
That distant sky —
What a dim sight.
There stands
My sturdy horse,
The saddle still on its back.
I am intoxicated
About to lie on the turf carpet.
The lovely moon
All over the stream
No, stop your hooves
The jade veneer not to crack.
Let the saddle be my pillow
And the bridge
My bed amidst the willow.
I hear the cuckoo.
The day breaks.
In its spring spirit.

I should add that this poem carries a brief preface which reads: 'On a spring night, I passed a restaurant by the side of the Qi River. I went in and had food and drink. After that I was a little inebriated, and rode with the moon to a bridge on a stream. I released the saddle and lay down on it for a while. When I woke up with daybreak, I saw the lush sight all over the hills as if I was out of the sentient world. I then composed the poem and wrote it on the pillar of the bridge.[19]

We see the reference to the sentient world both in the poem and in the preface. There is an unmistakable touch of Buddhist philosophy. In the poem, there first appears the saddle 'soiled by sentient dust', and then the saddle is transformed from the instrument of chasing some target to an implement helping relaxation — the pillow. I have used the word 'sentient' to translate the original word 'zhang' which is the Chinese translation of the Sanskrit word *karmarana* — a hindrance caused by retribution. Clearly, the poet was depicting himself as a man in mundane human bondage. Of course, there was a strong desire in the poet to be free from it.

More important is the imagery in the following two lines:

No, stop your hooves
The jade veneer not to crack.

Apparently, he was ordering his horse not to stir the tranquillity of the stream — a tranquillity that had created a 'jade veneer' on the clean (unpolluted) water under the moonlight, and this 'jade veneer' is the idealism of agroculture.

But there have always been the 'hooves' — both during the poet's time in the eleventh century, and ever after till today. The 'hooves' here are the symbol of the hunter's culture, the culture of human greed, and that of war and conflict. Here, it seems that the poet was conceiving of peace as an escape from war. But he went further:

Let the saddle be my pillow
And the bridge
My bed amidst the willow.

This shows that in the world-view of the poet the hooves are secondary, not any part of the agrocultural world. The true picture of the agrocultural world — the world that was dear to the poet — was what he saw after he woke up: 'When I woke up with daybreak, I saw the lush sight all over the hills as if I was out of the sentient world.'

Su Shi played an important role in creating and preserving a progressive Chinese agroculture. Beginning his life as an ambitious young man, he succeeded in becoming a high-ranking bureaucrat. But there were ups and downs in his career, which helped him to burn out his ego and greed, to blunt the cutting edge of his ambitions, and to see things with blue eyes, not red. As the Chinese saying goes: *Luhuo chun qing*, i.e. the colour of the pure fire is blue. Burning impurities makes the fire red and sparking. Only after burning out the impurities will the colour of blue emerge. In his youth, Su Shi did have his red eyes because of ego, greed, envy, anger, etc. burning within his heart. Only when he viewed things with blue eyes could he see the natural peace and beauty which is the fundamental rhythm of the universe.

The ancient Chinese philosopher, Zhuangzi (also spelt as Chuangtze, 369?-286 BC) once remarked: 'My body does not belong to me. It is a capsule form of Heaven and Earth'. Su Shi paraphrased Zhuanzi's observation to rhyme:

My body isn't of me
(But of Earth and Heaven),
I must forsake and forget
Busy feathering my nest.[20]

In another poem, Su Shi rhymed:

> O, those mountain peaks
> The other lies behind each
> Like folded paintings.
> O, the river course bending,
> Extended screens unending.
> Emperors and their subjects
> Have shared the same dream
> From times olden till now.
> Glorious fame all died out.
> Eternal are the mountains,
> Clouds move in perfect freedom,
> Peaks green under the morning sun.[21]

I have alluded to the poet's Buddhist world-view, which once again appears here. It's all a dream — those glorious careers. What is permanent is the peaceful surroundings of Nature. The moral of the piece: Why strive for the illusory at all?

There is something here abcut the culture of peace through the Chinese prism. Peace is not something that hides among humans. It would be in vain if we try to find peace from the midst of fame-seekers, fortune-seekers, from the empire-builders, from careerists, from millionaires who knock others out on their way to the top of the world. No, all these have gone astray from the right course of life. They have destroyed the natural rhythm of the universe. What they have achieved is contrary to what the Creator has wished.

Su Shi lived nearly one thousand years ago, hence he still had confidence in the peace and tranquillity of Nature. He was sure that the mountains would always remain green, and the clouds never lost their freedom in wandering among the green peaks.

Let me cite the writings of another Song poet, Wang Guan (late eleventh century), who thought life was an ephemeral phenomenon. He said one would be lucky to live up to 70. In these 70 years, the first 10 were childhood, and the last 10 were those of a 'muddle-headed old man'. Then, half of the remaining 50 years was taken away by sleep. What should one do in the real span being left over, i.e. 25 years? He replied:

> *Dui jing qie chenzui, rensheng si lu chui fangcao.*
> (Let us inebriate heavily in the Natural scenery,
> Life is merely a dew fallen on sweet greenery.)[22]

In another poem Wang Guan rhymed:

> There the river lies
> A horizontal wave of the eyes;
> There the mountain peaks go by
> As if all the eyebrows tied.
> Man, won't you tell your destination?
> O, yes, to meet those eyes and eyebrows.
> Spring has bid adieu without hesitation
> And you are leaving all of us just now.
> If you catch up with spring while journeying
> In the southern country of the Yangtse River
> Make sure you stay with her
> For ever and ever.[23]

Here is an exciting if not a melancholy voice in quest of peace — spring being its icon. This peace, as the poet suggests, does not exist among humans, or is forced by humans to bid adieu. But, never mind, one still can try and catch up with it sometime and somewhere in life's journey. The poet also suggests that peace smiles at the humans in Nature. Rivers are its eyes and mountain peaks its eyebrows. And they beckon to those who are longing for peace.

Such old Chinese poems I have just now cited are worthy of appreciation, but they have lost their modern relevance. Today, humankind has almost lost its confidence in the quest of peace. If there were a World War III, there would be no green mountains left. It is as if humans have embarked on a road of slow suicide till one day they finish off all the symbols and icons of peace on our Mother Earth. When we read these ancient Chinese poems, it is no occasion for nostalgia but a time for appeal, for protest, for demanding a stop to the mad, mad ways of our human species which has grown brighter and brighter in scientific knowledge and other faculties, but duller and duller in self-preservation, in sensing the dangers to human preservation.

Peace and Nature go together in Chinese poetic mood. Su Shi wanted to return to Nature when he was longing for peace. We have another poetic mood to look at Nature as depicted by Mao Zedong in 1936:

> Our northern country is a pretty place:
> A million square-feet in deep freeze,
> Over a hundred leagues one sees snowflakes.
> Look at the historic Great Wall,

A dwarf, dwarf, our mighty Nature's thrall,
And lapping, lapping, the Yellow River
Like a lad in the cradle without a murmur.
Mountain ranges the silver serpents
And tablelands the wax elephants
All race to the Heaven's embrace.
Still better on a glorious sunny day
When the landscape is decorated in red
Blossoms with an overcoat in snow-white.
The country is such an enchanting bride,
Numberless suitors have wooed with longing eyes.[24]

Mao Zedong was extremely exhausted at the end of the historic Long March. His revolutionary following had reduced from several hundred thousand to hardly ten thousand men. There was pessimism and blank vision among the rank and file. Yet, Mao wrote in such a mood as if he was descending from Heaven to take the enchanting bride that was China. War (revolutionary war) was his life's obsession. But it was Nature and the vastness of the earth that gave him strength. If we compare Mao's poetic words with those of Su Shi, there is something in common despite the entirely different times and moods. The commonness lies in the grand rhythm of Nature. What Mao saw was not just a docile sleepy Nature, but one full of dynamism. Peace, I venture to think, is not just idleness, actionlessness, changelessness. Peace is creation, movement, and dynamism. When humans imbibe all this from Nature, there is progress, there is mental peace as well.

We have seen all kinds of search for peace on the part of Chinese poets, intellectuals — those who cherish Buddhist or Marxist idealism, those who have learnt from their own experiences that human evolution has not progressed in the proper way, and those who might like to put it back on the right track. Such a search reminds me of another famous poem composed by another eminent Chinese scholar, Huang Tingjian (1045-1105), a contemporary of Su Shi. The poem, entitled 'Music of Tranquillity', reads as follows:

Where is spring?
In vain I try to trace
And I reach a dead end.
Where is spring?
The reply from the knower I seek
To invite her back to stay.
Where is spring?
Let me ask the oriole.

The bird's hundred tunes thrill
But I fail to decipher its signals,
It flies away with the gale
Roses left in its trail.[25]

Like Wang Guan, Huang Tingjian has used the word 'spring' as an idealism. This poem obviously shows the poet's determined quest for it. Today, when we embark on our search for the meaning of peace, for the culture of peace, we are in a similar situation. We are getting nowhere because we are not the makers of the times, because we don't have the power in our hands — the power which can stop the disturbance of peace and tranquillity, the power which can restore the true nature and rhythm of the universe. I have earlier suggested that the concept of peace is the result of human progression from a hunter's culture to agroculture. Now, we see that this original concept of agroculture has been mortgaged by the Chinese political development to the extent that it would be very hard to buy it back — to realize the *datong* society which may for ever remain an illusion. In our modern times, we see agroculture being conquered, flogged, and threatened to extinction by the industrial culture. Today, we have not only lost the true definition of peace, but are made to adopt the French (or English) idea that peace is merely a stop-gap arrangement of cease-fire, merely the absence of war which can return any time. But, even the last poem is not a note of pessimism. As the last line says: there are 'roses left in its trail'.

I must not leave any impression that I put all the blame for war on industrial civilization. I have shown enough evidence that the Chinese agrocultural tradition has been equally at fault. But, the entire humanity should think of peace as a fundamental rhythm of life and try to safeguard it as we safeguard our eyes. Self-destruction has no virtue, certainly not deserving any congratulation. Yet, what we hear these days are nothing but such congratulations. Pray let us stop such stupidity and play the music of tranquillity. Let us look at things with blue eyes instead of red eyes. Perhaps that can change the perspective on peace.

References

1. *Mengzi* (Mencius), ch. 5.
2. *Yizhuan* (Supplementary commentaries to *Book of Change*), Pt. 2, beginning para.
3. *Daxue* (Great Learning), para 1.
4. *Ibid.*
5. *Quan Tangshi* (Collected works of Tang poetry), Shanghai: Zhonghua Bookshop, 1950, vol.1, p. 54.

6. Tan Chung, *Classical Chinese Poetry*, in the *Classics of the East Series*, Calcutta: M.P. Birla Foundation, 1991, p.131.
7. See *Zhongguo lidai wenxuan* (Selected essays of different historical times), Beijing: People's Publishing House, 1980, vol. 2, p. 686.
8. See Wu Hsiang-hsiang, *Sun Yixian xiansheng zhuan* (Biography of Mr Sun Yat-sen), Hong Kong: Far East Book Company, 1982, Vol. 2, p.1654.
9. *Liji* (Book of Rites), ch.9 (The revolution of propriety).
10. *Deng Xiaoping wenxuan* (Selected works of Deng Xiaoping), Beijing: People's Publishing House, vol. 3, 1993, p. 216.
11. Mao Zedong, 'Zhongguo geming he Zhongguo gongchandang' (Chinese revolution and Chinese Communist Party). See *Selected Works of Mao Tse-tung [Zedong]*, Peking [Beijing]: Foreign Languages Press, vol. 3, 1967, p. 331.
12. Wang Han, 'Liangzhou ci' (song of Liangzhou), see Tan Chung, p. 99.
13. Tan Chung, pp.131-33.
14. *Ibid.*, p.153.
15. *Ibid.*, p. 299.
16. *Ibid.*, p. 339.
17. *Ibid.*, p. 155.
18. *Ibid.*, p. 307, Cao Ye's poem 'Guancangshu' (Rats in the Government Warehouse).
19. See Su Shi, 'Xijiang yue' (Moon of the western river).
20. Idem, 'Lin jiang xian' (A saint by the river), see *ibid.*, pp. 246-47.
21. Idem, 'Xingxiangzi' (The one who burns the incense), in *ibid.*, p. 267.
22. Tan Chung, p. 414.
23. *Songci jianshang cidian*, p.185.
24. Tan Chung, p. 515.
25. *Ibid.*, p. 411 (with modifications in the translation).

[illegible]

3

Buddhist Art, the Mission of Harmonious Culture

Jin Weinuo

THE passage east and west of the Buddhist monks of antiquity caused the Silk Road to also become a thoroughfare of cultural interchange.

From the time that Emperor Ming of the Han dispatched Cai Yin and Qin Jing to India and the Indian monks Kashyapa-matange and Zhu Falan came to Luoyang, monks coming east to preach the Doctrine and those going west to seek the dharma formed a continuous procession. Buddhist devotees carried Buddhist scriptures from Gandhara and Kashmir to Khotan, Kucha and on to China in order to propagate the faith. During the Jin dynasty (AD 265-420) the famous Kucha monks Buddhacinga and Kumarajiva came to central China to preach, and Faxian of the Eastern Jin (317-420) and Xuanzang and Yijing of the Tang (618-906) journeyed west to seek the dharma, causing the cultural exchange between east and west to advance a step, greatly facilitating the evolution of eastern thought and culture.

From AD 67 to 220 some 292 works in 395 chapters were translated. In the south, during the Liu Song dynasty (420-78), 465 works in 717 chapters; during the Qi (479-501), 12 works in 33 chapters; during the Liang (502-56), 46 works in 201 chapters, and during the Chen (557-89), 40 works in 133 chapters: so in the south, in all 563 works in 1,084 chapters were translated. In the north, during the Northern Wei (386-535), 83 works in 274 chapters; during the Northern Qi (535-76), 8 works in 52 chapters; and during in the Northern Zhou (535-81), 14 works in 29 chapters: in all during the northern dynasties, 105 works in 355 chapters were translated. When, in 730, Zhisheng compiled his *Kaiyuan shijiao lu* (Record of the Sakya Teaching of the Kaiyuan Era) he listed 1,076 *sutras* in 5,048 chapters. Translations continued to be made subsequently. Further, Buddhist cave temples and monasteries spread everywhere. Indian and Central Asian thought and culture came with Buddhism and art and was influential in the broad reaches of China, and the peaceful contacts among the monks allowed Buddhist theories to develop into glorious achievements, while the Buddhist art which was present everywhere formed testimony to this harmonious friendship.

In the temple murals discovered at Miran, in Xinjiang Province, some at present are in the collection of the National Museum, New Delhi and from these murals one can see the influence of Gandhara art on the temple art of ancient Shanshan. Although some of it is in incised stone and some in stucco sculpture and murals, still in the close connection of the two in subject-matter and in modelling, they present a positive achievement in culture and harmonious interaction. In the murals one sees the depictions of winged angels, the overly generous Prince Sudana, the Buddha and his disciples, which cause one to associate these with the Buddhist doctrine of saving all beings, and the monks who paid no heed to hardships or the long journey, scaling mountains and crossing rivers to preach the Buddhist dharma with devotion and sincerity.

The art work in the Buddhist temples included those the content of which propagated the Buddhist religion, but there were also those which transmitted popular traditional stories. The Khotan painting of the story of the eastern princess who brought the silk cocoons to the western regions reflected regional friendly intercourse, and also marks the desire of the people for harmonious friendship. The princess and her attendant are completely dressed in Chinese attire, and this also from another viewpoint reflects a mutual cultural blending.

Buddhist art disseminated foreign philosophical thought and culture, as well as foreign conditions and customs, and at the same time established its roots in China and flourished, forming in the various areas a distinctive national art. With the propagation of Buddhism, there was an evolution of the cultural traditions of each place touched by the content of Buddhism, and at the same time Buddhist art was also changed by the regional geographical conditions and the aesthetic interests of the people of each place.

The desert region where the cave temples at Kucha were constructed did not have the sort of hard stone used for sculpture in South Asia, and so the local artists carved out forms of caves in the sandstone which were appropriate to sculpture and painting to develop a Buddhist art; and the cave with the central pillar, most popular in Kucha, was the style best suited to the soft sandstone there. The stucco sculpture of the Kucha caves, largely destroyed by natural disasters and by human agency, either no longer survives or has been taken abroad. Fragments of murals, however, still demonstrate the high level of material culture at Kucha and the very distinctive accomplishment of Kuchean art. Kucha dance and music became popular for a time in Tang China, and influenced and enriched eastern art, and what remains of the painting and sculpture demonstrates the high Kuchean artistic standards. The musicians of Cave 38 at Kyzyl and the *bodhisattvas* of Cave 22 at Qumtara are examples of Kuchean art. They reflect the actual nature of Kuchean music and also represent a new regional character in Buddhist art.

Khotan was an ancient state with a high degree of culture, and among the excavated articles of Buddhist art there are murals which are related to the establishment of the Khotanese state. At the site of one temple, to the left of a sculpture of Vaisravana is a painting of Srideva bathing in a lotus pond, and at the side is a small boy; this picture depicts the legend about the time when the king of Khotan had no heir and obtained the son of Vaisravana, who was nourished by the earth (a nipple emerge from the ground), and so handed on the state. The direct use of Srideva bringing up the infant in place of the 'earth nipple' of the legend shows much human feeling and is moving. Further, the beautiful appearance of Srideva in the painting and the close relationship between mother and child is most effective and moving.

The development of Buddhist art in different places and among different peoples of China produced a wide variety of artistic traditions. The temple murals of Guge, Tibet, are among the finest of the Tibetan paintings. The depiction of the celebration ceremony on the establishment of the temple in the Red Hall, Guge, depicts amidst the huge celebration the royal family, the guests and subjects, pictures various musical scenes, and shows the lively customs of the Guge society of that time; this work has the unique characteristics of the folk painting of the Tibetan people.

On account of influences from abroad, there were formed regional styles which created the very rich tradition of Chinese Buddhist art, manifesting endless and radiant stages. Developments over close to two thousand years in the area of art have revealed, in almost every period, outstanding achievements. In the Eastern Jin (317-420) there were Dai Kui and Dai Yu, father and son, whose sculptures, which 'changed the foreign style to a Chinese one', can be seen in gilded bronze examples from the Yuanjia era of 424-53, or Lu Tanwei of the Song (420-77), traces of whose art, characterized as 'fine bones and lucid forms', can be found among the sculptures at Maijishan and Dunhuang. 'Fine bones and lucid forms' did not refer only to the thinness of the images, but rather praised the nobility and purity of their inner qualities, and from this one can note the high artistic standards of the statues of that time. These are all outstanding examples of the adaptation of Buddhist imagery. The four famous schools in Buddhist art (Zhang, Cao, Wu and Zhou) represent the later models of different periods.

The art of the Liang (502-56) was based on that of the Song and Qi but was constantly changing, and the Zhang school which grew out of the Buddhist work of the famous artist Zhang Sengyou differed from the 'fine bones and lucid images', and tended toward plumpness and was considered the model of that age. The Sichuan Provincial Museum has a figure of the Buddha of 522, found at the site of the Wanfo Temple, with the Buddha standing on a double lotus pedestal. The halo is in the shape of a lotus petal, with long robes and broad sash, which flutter slightly to the left, with an appearance of advancing; at the two sides are four *bodhisattvas*, and then four disciples. At the two sides in front of the niche are two *lokapalas*. In front of the image of the Buddha are six musicians. On the mandorla are depicted stories of the Buddha in relief, and below are the names of the donors. The carving is very fine, the form full and rich, and it has a solemn and yet merciful quality. This sort of change in the sculpture and painting of the Zhang school of the Liang dynasty carries with it the influence of that cultural interchange, but even more important was the influence on the artists of actual life and popular taste. The individual styles of the artists, the regional characteristics, the style of the time, and the intertwined geography all combined to produce this richly varied artistry.

The loose and simple lines of the clothing of the images of the Northern Qi dynasty (550-77), the thin robes sticking to the skin, the whole body being smooth and slick, is of a piece with the tranquil and serene expression of the face. From the smooth body or the glossy clothing, it is as if one can feel the body slightly undulating. This lustrous appearance and the downward flowing lines allow the figure amidst a loose dullness to emit an inherent quality. Although the figure has no great dynamism, still it expresses a vigour which can be experienced and felt; there is no ornate ornamentation, and still with a natural and realistic technique, it causes the human image to have an even more realistic feel. This sort of smooth and simple style causes Northern Qi sculptural art to have its individuality and its bright clarity moves one.

The formation of the Northern Qi sculptural style was influenced by the art of earlier periods and there was also an element of regional interaction, but of course what was most important was the creativity of the artists of that time. The Cao school founded by Cao Zhongda of the Northern Qi had even more clearly its own characteristics, and it was said his figures 'were clad in garments which clung to the body as if they were drenched in water'. The Cleveland Museum in the USA has a seated figure of the Amitabha Buddha, of the Sui-early Tang period, with a bare right shoulder, the folds of the robe close together, the variations in the pattern conveying the texture of the cloth, as well as the changing undulations of the muscles, and the body hidden under the thin robes is one of robust flesh and blood. There is a direct continuity between this one and the figures of the Tang period at Tianlongshan, which are clearly standard products of the Cao school. With the large number of Tianlongshan images which have that typical 'clinging wet clothing' characteristic of the Cao school, one has a profound sense that the Cao school's portrayal of the beauty of the human body (both in spirit and in the flesh) has gone far beyond the search for the illusory Buddha nature.

The High Tang is the period of the popularity of the image of the Buddha as made by Wu Daozi; his distinguishing features, what came to be called the Wu school, were of whirlwind energy and vigorous forms which went beyond the ordinary. One can see the effects in the Dunhuang murals and in figures from various places. The depiction of the Maharaja-deva in the murals and on silk from Dunhuang illustrates the appearance of wind ruffled-clothing of the Wu school. The Shaanxi Provincial Museum has a standing figure of a Maharaja-deva in white marble, of which the head, left arm and right wrist are lost. The figure wears armour over a robe which trails behind to the ground. The movement of the figure is robust, its energy awesome; it represents the basic features of the Wu school.

Coming to the middle and late Tang, the creativity of the artist Zhou Fang led to austere but gentle figures which are termed to be of the Zhou school, and which extended to the Buddhist images of the late Tang and later. There were canonical standards and measurements for the making of images of the Buddha, but the influence of the aesthetic views of the time were also operative. The men and women in the paintings of Zhou Fang were for the most part plump, and the Buddhist figures which he made possessed the same characteristic, but he also created a distinctive and very beautiful figure of Guanyin gazing at the moon in the water (i.e., symbolizing the unreality of all phenomena). From the late Tang figure at Dunhuang and other places, one can clearly see examples of this type.

A new sort of figural style which emerged and became popular was the reflection of a transformation in the aesthetic ideal of the time, and at the same time it conversely could affect the common view of aesthetics. The emergence of the Zhou school had a lasting effect on popular taste. The popularity of the Buddhist images of the Zhou school not only met the aesthetic demands of the time but more importantly, Zhou Fang elevated and purified what contemporary society favoured, so that they sought plumpness in the outward form and looked more deeply for an inherent solemnity. He not only depicted the beauty of the *bodhisattvas*' appearance but also concentrated on depicting the inherent benevolence of their attempt to save all living beings. Because of this the Buddhist images which he created were able to be worshipped by the monks and could also be loved and venerated by ordinary laymen. The figure of the Buddha is awe-inspiring and sacred, and its kindness is moving. The artist must deal with its awesomeness and its kindness or benevolence, which are completely different, and even mutually cancelling elements, and still meld them together, so that the Buddha has an external image of gravity and an inner store of kindness. Therefore gravity should not be fearful, and the kindness cannot be offensive. In depicting the ideal Buddha one must be good at embodying the Buddha nature and good at depicting that sort of extraordinary sacredness which is yet able to move the heart of man. The ability of the images of the Zhou school to be moving perhaps was precisely that while seeking to bring out Buddha nature, they created a type of Buddha image in which benevolence was nestled within the beauty of its solemnity.

A standing *bodhisattva* of the middle Tang (766-820) in the collection of the Lushun Museum in Liaoning, of wood and painted, has a lotus crown. Swirling sashes hang from the shoulders, there is a full chin and thin eyebrows, and a downward glance. The upper torso is bare, it wears a brooch, the left hand holds a fluttering heavenly robe in two fingers while the right hand is raised upwards, the thumb and middle fingers forming a circle (the *vitarka mudra*). The figure has graceful and elegant secular female characteristics, and yet it has a solemn and quiet religious mood.

Buddhist images are required to display the thirty-two *lakshanas* and eighty notable physical characteristics of the Buddha, to seek dignity, a singular superbness, in order to embody all excellences and good fortune and virtue, and still to give shape to one's own individual aesthetic view. The Buddhist idea of aesthetics, during its two thousand years of development, was enriched continuously by the artists of each period. The outstanding artists then maintained the admirable tradition of the previous age and went on to turn their minds to expressing a specific aesthetic ideal in the process of seeking to paint or to carve different personalities. And these aesthetic ideals were manifested precisely in the dialectical process of displaying the Buddha nature by the sculptors or artists who were imbued with those ideals.

The attempt to paint and sculpt the many types of human characteristics among the Buddhist images on the one hand reflected the perceptive observation of society by the artists, an intimate knowledge of customs and practices, and this circuitously reflected ability of realism which enriched Buddhist art caused the it to permeate society even more. And so the rich images in the caves and temples of China reveal a tangible view of the development of Buddhist art over more than a thousand years, and the age-old examples of this exquisite art are an extremely important treasure for searching out the artistic creations and experiences of men of the past.

Peace and friendship are important topics within Chinese Buddhist art. For example, the depiction of the Western Paradise reflects aspirations for a peaceful and prosperous life; the depiction of society's hardships then reflects the search for peace and stability.

In cave 127 at Maijishan, of the Western Wei, there is a Western Paradise scene; aside from the three holy ones of the Western Paradise (Amitabha, Guanyin and Mahasthamaprapta), *lohans* and disciples, and the populace listening to the dharma, in the painting there are also pavilions and kiosks, balustrades and pools, dancers and musicians. At Dunhuang, in a Sui dynasty depiction of the Western Paradise, aside from the Buddha preaching beneath the jewel-tree and canopy, in the Seven-Jewelled Pond lotus flowers open wide, youths born of the flowers pay homage, while ducks frolic in the water, heavenly musicians soar about, it is a joyful scene. With the spread of Pure Land Buddhism among the people, many murals depicting the Western Pure Land appeared in cave temples and monasteries during the Tang — at Dunhuang these are the most numerous among the murals which are based on the *sutras*, over a hundred. Depicting what is said in the *Amitayus Sutra*, 'There are the Seven Jewel Pool, the Water of the Eight Lakes of Meritorious Deeds, the Golden Sands which cover the earth, and the gold, silver and coloured glazed stairway. . . . In the pool the lotus flowers are as large as wheels, all sorts of exotic multi-coloured birds, a breeze rustles the Treasure Trees producing a marvellous sound.' This sort of picture of the Western Paradise 'without the sufferings of all, only receiving the many pleasures', came to completion in the early Tang. In Cave 220 at Dunhuang, dated AD 624, in front of Amida Buddha, Guanyin and Mahasthamaprapta, who sit in a pavilion at the Jewel Pond, is outlined a balustrade with worshipping *bodhisattvas* paying homage. In front of the pond on a coloured glazed surface are symmetrical groups of dancers and two *apsaras* dance with orchestral accompaniment opposite each other, their movements are lively, and their robes swirl about. At the top of the painting is a decorated hall and a jewelled canopy, with drifting clouds and flying flowers, and heavenly drums harmonize, presenting a propitious atmosphere of dancing, singing and peacefulness. This dated early Tang depiction of the Pure Land paradise is the largest mural preserved in the Mogao Caves, and it is typical in the beauty of its composition and the fineness of its drawing. The depictions of the Pure Land paradise reflect the aspirations of the people of the time for peace and happiness.

At the time of the popularity of scenes from the Lotus Sutra, at the Mogao Caves there appeared individual mural panels which depict a single chapter of the *sutra*; the 'Guanshiyin pumen pin' on the south wall of Cave 45 is one of the most typical of the Tang. In the middle of this mural is painted a standing figure of Guanshiyin *Bodhisattva*, and on both sides are small paintings in many layers, illustrating the 33 incidents of Guanyin appearing to save others from dangers and difficulties. Among these are depicted how merchants upon encountering bandits escaped the danger, or those placed in cangues were freed, or when boats encountered an evil wind the seas were calmed, and so on, and the depictions of the people were so vivid. These pictures of calamities and dangers on the one hand depicted how helpless one was in the face of real difficulties and yet reflected how at the time one could only place all one's hopes on an entreaty for harmony and stability.

Harmony is that for which man in every age has hoped, and to obtain peace it is necessary that people the world over strive for it together.

Chinese Buddhist art was affected by influences which came from the east, and at the same time there were also influences from neighbouring states; and these influences greatly enriched and broadened the content of eastern culture and art and at the same time achieved great success. The effect which the Buddhist monks had on cultural exchange might serve precisely as a model for the exchange of peace and friendship of the people of all countries. In these new times how we might advance cultural exchange between the various countries and bring ever-increasing progress and prosperity within a peaceful environment is that to which we ought to strive all together.

4

Satyam, Shivam, Sundaram

Natalia Kravtchenko
Vladimir Zaitsev

From ancient, miraculous stones build the steps of the future.

Nicholas Roerich

WHEN one considers the problem of peace, immediately we think of its opposites, aggression and war. It is a cornerstone dilemma of many generations: What are the roots of violence? What are the reasons for human impatience and cruelty? What is the way to protect ourselves from violence and preserve peace? Is peace an unfulfilled dream of humanity? In the ancient texts of Hinduism, Jainism, Buddhism, Christianity and other world teachings we find very profound considerations and real concern about peace. Presently we would like to suggest that we take a look at the problem of peace through the spectrum of beauty, creativeness and art. We regard beauty and art as the most powerful mediums in the process of mutual understanding of different nations and their peaceful coexistence.

In the recent past noble and lofty ideas of art and beauty were considered idealistic, superficial and abstract conceptions. Human consciousness, narrowed by modern technocratic civilization, moved back the achievements of culture maintaining an idea of its material impracticality. In spite of this in human history we observe another process — everything striving towards cultural constructiveness and unselfish knowledge created brilliant epochs of renaissance, and on the contrary every departure from the foundations of beauty, from culture has always brought destruction and decay. It is also a fact that old, forcible methods do not solve present conflicts and contradictions, they only increase tensions and the threat of war.

It seems to us that the present scientific and technological development took the form of a desert mirage: when it is far it gives the impression of prosperity, stability and development, but when we reach it this disappears and in front of us is the whole range of modern problems. The most serious and crucial amongst them is the threat of the use of nuclear weapons. In this reality all our present achievements, innovations and progress look meaningless unless we approach the real understanding of peace.

One would be able to reach it when the difference between mechanical civilization and the coming culture of the spirit is realized. 'For man intellectually developed,' writes Sri Aurobindo, 'mighty in scientific knowledge and the mastery of gross and subtle nature, using the elements as his servants and the world as his footstool, but undeveloped in heart and spirit, becomes only an inferior kind of *asura* (demon), using the power of a demigod to satisfy animal nature.' Observing the historical panorama one may find that civilization is created during a few decades, while culture is based upon achievements of thousands years.

At present we have what painters call mistake in perspective. Instead of going on the *vertical level*, in other words the change from within, spiritual development and growth, the modern way of progress turns towards the *horizontal plane*, change from outside, the way of material prosperity and widening of technocratic might. The last does not fulfil the qualitative role in the change of human society. It does not reach the depths of consciousness and spirit of man. It was never said, 'the hand kills not, but the thought'. It is true that the idea of killing another living being is already its potential realization. As a matter of fact a war is not outward disaster, it is an expression of ignorance and of the absolute absence of the culture of the heart.

The continuous process of man's isolation from nature, increasing of emotional, personal gaps between people, the loss of cultural and spiritual values of past generations, have reduced the capacity of man in sensitiveness and receptivity. He misses the sense of beauty of being (existence), no more does he consider himself a part of infinite creation. Hermit Zosima in Dostoevsky's *The Brothers Karamazov* contemplates: 'What is hell? It is inability to love, to feel unity with the world in all its forms.' Thus the link between different worlds is distorted.

From childhood the sense of unity is a natural feeling for man, there is need, thirst in a child for communication and friendship with the outer world. Slowly his mind impresses on its screen all prejudices, conventional divisions: political, social, religious, national, domestic, all the atavisms of society; he becomes a certain screw in a grandiose machine. In hierarchy, where people are separated between one's people and strangers, rich and poor, etc., a man completely loses feelings of community and identity with his environment. The serene world of his childhood is revealed to him as strange and hostile.

Heaven in its rapture dreams of perfect Earth,
Earth in its sorrow dreams of perfect Heaven,
They keep their oneness by enchanted fears.

The profound thinker Tagore wrote that the present 'civilization expects its great fulfilment and the expression of its soul in beauty'. From Russia the voice of N. Roerich sounds — 'Realization of beauty will save the world'. They are convinced that realization of this very principle brings the solution to many diseases of human society.

Without exaggeration one may say that the treasures of culture were the strongholds of nations. The entire upbuilding, all enlightenment, all spiritual inspiration, all happiness and salvation will be born upon the foundations of cultural treasures. Likewise, it will not be an exaggeration to say that the language of the heart has many times proved in the history of mankind the most convincing and attractive as well as unifying.

Not only are the names of Rubens, Velazquez, Griboedov and many others immortalized in art, but also for their unforgettable advice in the field of statesmanship. Objects of art themselves very often were the best ambassadors, introducing peace and friendship. It is known that the exchange of art treasures prevented misunderstandings and was ahead of verbal agreements.

The remarkable results of art in education were proved by the experiments of Tagore in his university, Visva Bharati. All the programmes of this institution were based on unity and harmonious relationship with nature and development of the sense of beauty. A great deal of art and creativity is involved in the educational process of Sri Aurobindo Ashram, where it is considered the foundation for the intellectual and spiritual development of man. Here art is part of integral *yoga* and creativity is the active power in the evolution of man.

Considering the 'culture of peace' one should not forget the original experiments in the field of culture conducted by the great peace-builder Nicholas Roerich. At the end of the 1920s he established in the United States an international institute of art named Corona Mundi and a museum which were prototypes of contemporary academies of fine arts. Musicians, painters, poets, writers, architects, scientists were united in these creative communities under Roerich's slogan 'peace through culture'. Later this idea was extended in artistic activity in the preservation of cultural monuments and treasures of art. It finally materialized in the international memorandum, the 'Roerich Pact', signed by 54 countries in Gaag after World War II. For the first time cultural heritage was recognised not as a luxury, but as a necessary foundation for the spiritual being of mankind. For its humanism contemporaries named this project the 'Red Cross of Culture'.

In the service of peace and spiritual principles, art and creativeness reach their highest self-expression. For the spiritually alive human being the value of art lies in its beautiful existence, in its great mystery, in its mighty transforming and purifying power (catharsis). Through art one discovers the whole universe of the human spirit, limitless spaces of human thoughts and feelings. At one moment through the charming sounds of music or rhythm of ancient chants one may be united with events going back to thousands and thousands of years ago. Art in its sublime forms and expressions gives us an opportunity of unforgettable experience, it reminds us of a different kind of reality, the origin of existence.

The process of creativity is comparable with the spiritual path (*sadhana*). In all fields of art meditative disciplines are a normal part of human experience and have a profound effect on artists. The insight born of these disciplines inspires a sense of participation, of identification with all life. In Russia there exists a system of inner discipline of the artist formed during the centuries. Most powerfully it was expressed in the art of icon painting.

Long before starting a painting, artist practises prayer and silence and maintains mental and emotional purity. These helped him to achieve the resonance, like a musical instrument, to be one with the subject of his painting.

There is a certain duty and responsibility of the artist towards his invisible ideal. In icon painting the main stress is on the expression of inner beauty, spiritual power, where they are considered limitless love and compassion. In the instructions to the artist we read: 'Maintain the unity of your will. Do not listen with your ears but with the mind. Do not listen with the mind, but with the spirit. The spirit is an emptiness ready to receive all things.'

By stilling his heart, that is, shedding thoughts and emotions of his personal life, an individual can reflect on his heart-mind the power of High Consciousness (the holy spirit, tao, *atman*, etc.). The sense of another reality within allows the artist to find out new artistic and technical solutions. So in some old Chinese paintings one may discover that what seemed to be empty was never vacant. Obviously the artist was able to suggest aliveness in unfilled surfaces and employ empty space in ways which are extremely daring. Poetically it can be illustrated in the following lines:

Stillness — a transparent mirror for celestial reflections.
Stillness — a morning song forgotten by mankind.
Stillness — the sound of eternity amidst the cries of the earth.
Stillness — the invisible door to the silence.
I shall try to unlock it. . . .

in art of this subtlety there are qualities that go farther than naturalness or realism. The process of communication between artist and object creates specific relationships between them; the artist is much more attracted to the inner content of the subject than to its external attractiveness.

There is always difference between likeness and truth. 'Likeness could be obtained by shapes without spirit, but when Truth is reached, spirit and substance are both fully expressed.' Evidently, beauty does not necessarily spell perfection of form. This has been one of the favourite tricks of artists in Japan and in some Scandinavian countries — to embody beauty in the form of imperfection or even ugliness, or asymmetry. All these methods of creativity served one main desire of the artist — to reveal another nature of the subject, to express its inner cosmos.

Thus in the art of icon painting we are moved first of all by the unspeakable beauty of the artistic image, which is transformed from the personal into universal. We completely agree with the opinion of Nalini Kanta Gupta who wrote on the *Upanishads*: 'Art at its highest tends to become also the simplest and the most unconventional; and it is then the highest art, precisely because it does not aim at being artistic. The aesthetic motive is totally absent in the *Upanishads*; the sense of beauty is there, but it is attendant upon and involved in a deeper strand of consciousness.' Indeed, at its highest, art does not tolerate any conventionality, nor violence. In the very foundations of being lives the concept of beauty, and where there is beauty, there is peace.

> In Beauty we are united!
> Through Beauty we pray!
> With Beauty we conquer!

References

Bose, Nandalal, *Shilpa Kalpa*, Shantiniketan, Visva Bharati.

Dostoevsky, F., *The Brothers Karamazov*, Literature, Moscow, 1976.

Ghosh, Sri Aurobindo, *Savitri*, collected works, Sri Aurobindo Ashram, Pondicherry, 1970, vols. 28 and 29.

———, *The Future Poetry and Letters on Poetry, Literature and Art*, S.A.A., Pondicherry, 1972, vol. 9.

———, *The National Value of Art*, vol.17.

———, *Foundation of Indian Culture*, vol.14.

Morris, Desmond, *The Naked Ape*, London, 1978.

N. Roerich and Banner of Peace, New York, 1940.

Parekh, J., *Nandalal Bose Memorial Lectures*, Pondicherry University, 1995.

Roerich, H., *Collected Letters*, Riga, 1939, 1940, vol.I, vol.II.

Roerich, Nicholas, *Gates into the Future*, Riga, 1936.

———, *The Blessed Ways*, Riga, 1932.

———, *The Realm of Light*, Riga, 1938.

Raine, Kathleen, *India Seen Afar*, Green Books, London, 1990.

Tagore, Rabindranath, *Collected Works*, 12 vols, Moscow, 1974.

5

Creative, Hence a Peaceful Society

Devi Prasad

The kind of sadness and destructiveness we are experiencing all over the world is due to the increasing power of man's distorted intellect and selfish attitude. Economic or political steps may seem to bring change, but they are temporary. Change will be permanent only if steps other than those leading to physical indulgence and self interest, can be taken and practised.

Music, literature and art provide those kinds of possibilities. Healthy human attitudes are built by them. Rhythm and harmony between the specific and the whole — one and many — is their gift to humankind.

Nandalal Bose[1]

WHILE travelling in Sweden in 1966, I met in a training camp for conscientious objectors nearly a hundred draft-age men who had declared themselves against military service on grounds of conscience and opted for alternative civilian work. That year nearly six hundred draftees had declared themselves conscientious objectors. Towards the end of the meeting I asked the group if they knew the total number of conscripts that year. 'Over twenty-five thousand', one of them answered. Then I asked if they could explain why on earth only six hundred out of twenty-five thousand had opted for C.O. status, specially as life for a C.O. in Sweden was easier than that of a conscripted soldier: they could go home every week and their girl-friends and relatives could visit them every now and then.

The answer to my question came after the meeting, when ten or twelve of them suggested that we continue the discussion in the bar. What came out of this discussion was, as one of them said: 'The fact is that they are afraid of making their own decisions'.

Another said: 'Most young men dislike military service, yet to write "No" on the form is difficult. After a period of dilemma they just sign "Yes" on the form, designed precisely in a manner that will put the draftee in that particular dilemma.'

In most countries with military conscription, draft-age men receive orders to personally report for registration, a constitutional requirement. A man who would like to be a C.O. has to submit a special application for obtaining that status. The mechanism for obtaining C.O. status is such a deterrent that most young men decide to go in for military service. It is the easiest way to escape the unpleasant experience of going through the exercise — filling up forms, producing proof of their pacifist convictions and facings tribunals, etc. They console themselves by thinking that after all life in the military, specially in peacetime, is not too bad, and it is four months shorter than alternative service. The essence of all this is that in one case the decision is made for you and in the other you have to make it yourself.

I have described only one situation, i.e., in regard to compulsory military service in some countries. However, in nearly all the countries of the world there are traditions, laws and practices which train and condition the individual not to be able to make his or her own decision on many issues that he or she faces in day-to-day life. The crux of the matter is that in spite of the claims of modern upbringing and education that they prepare the individual for facing life sensibly and courageously, men and women are the least prepared to confront the challenges and dilemmas of life intelligently and with courage. Similar to the young men who put 'yes' on their draft forms, most people do not know what actually they want and must do.

There is a beautiful anecdote from the seventh-century philosopher Azid ibn Muhammad al Nasafi. When Ali asked Mohammad, "What am I to do that I may not waste my time?" the Prophet answered, "learn to know thyself".'[2] The tragedy is that modern education spends most of its time and resources in teaching facts about the universe and going into space, etc., but totally ignores the need for self-knowledge, which alone can help in resolving the dilemmas that are presented at every step. Those who opted for military service remained victims of the situation created by the State using the narrow concept of nationalism and lack of a sound educational system. If they had learnt and practised the art of knowing oneself, many more from among the twenty-five thousand conscripts would have refused military service. The same applies to many other aspects of life in most regions of the world.

The awareness of the need for self-knowledge is further scuttled by the introduction of fear in several ways from the beginning of one's life as a child. Educational principles such as reward and punishment and the emphasis on performance rather than on creativity do more harm than good to the growing individual. They create fear in several forms: fear of failure, fear of losing position, status, property, fear of death, etc. It need not be so always. Fear sometimes may have an important role to play in one's life. I remember the Greenham Common Protest Camp initiated by a small group of British women who felt desperate about the prospects of the U.S. cruise missiles being sited in their country. These women acknowledged their fear of nuclear weapons and tried to gain the confidence to take action against them. They said, 'Fear is the starting point' and succeeded in overcoming it and undertook creative action. For them their action was 'for building a life worth living'. However, the role of fear is of little importance in the present context: we are dealing with the role of fear in destroying spontaneity and the freedom of the individual to act courageously and for doing good.

It has been experienced time and again that fear is not a reliable factor in motivating people to act. I shall give two examples to illustrate this. I am reminded of Bernard Shaw's play *The Black Woman in Search of God.* There is a description of a man sitting under a tree talking to the black woman. He tells the woman that he does not know how to climb trees. Suddenly the black woman tells him in a panicky voice that he is sitting on a crocodile. The log of wood on which he was sitting looked like a crocodile. He jumped up and found himself on the tree. Now he could not climb down, even after being convinced that the log on which he had been sitting was not a crocodile. He had to be frightened again, this time of a poisonous snake hanging over his head, so that he would jump down in desperation. Fear worked wonderfully, but the responses of the man were reflex actions. In short, extreme behaviour has no use for consciousness or conscious processes.

The other example is from my own experience. Bengal suffered from very severe floods in 1943. As student volunteers some of us went to a nearby village for relief work. Two of us reached a house of which the courtyard was already under two feet of water, which was rising very rapidly. A young couple — handsome and strong looking — were standing in the courtyard, and a cart and two bullocks were also there. The whole place looked like a huge lake. Two small children were eating the last remaining grains of rice, sitting in the verandah with their grandfather. The verandah floor too would be under water in no time. Like most of the families of the village, this too could have loaded its possessions on the bullock cart in less than fifteen minutes and left for a safer place, but they had done nothing of the kind. They were standing like two pieces of sculpture with totally blank expressions on their faces. They did not utter a word in response to any of our questions.

At first I thought that they looked so stunned because they were worried about their possessions. They probably could not cope with the fact that they would lose everything if they left the house. We entered the house and saw twenty or so largish earthenware containers (*gharas*). I thought that these containers must be full of clothes, pots and pans, etc. But to my great surprise and sadness, I found that there was nothing, literally nothing, in those containers, not even a grain of rice. Their inaction could not have been a result of the fear of losing possessions or property. We tried to persuade them to come with us to a safer place. There was still no response from the young and hardy man and wife, used to poverty and deprivation. Their children and the old grandfather did not grasp what was happening. The grandfather and the couple remained nearly lifeless. The couple stood completely stunned and with no wish left to move. Fear of death for them had reached such a height that all the motivation to save even their innocent children from drowning in the deadly flood had disappeared. We had to actually drag them away, which was easy enough because they had no resistance and energy left in them. I must say that this was not an isolated phenomenon: it was a result of the social structure that was created by circumstances.

Why is it so? It occurs to me that there must be a borderline somewhere in the middle of the scale of fear which kills motivation, and beyond which there develops a mechanism against any thought of fear. At that point one loses all initiative. I can, though, understand making use of fear for therapy, in which case it will be a matter of deciding the maximum degree of fear that can be used to motivate those patients who have lost initiative or hope due to some neurological or other reason. In such cases, which will be relatively few, it is a matter of discovering and deciding the position of that borderline. But the fact is that for the majority of people there is some force different from fear which is more positive and lasting and which comes from within one's self. The case of the Greenham Common women's anti-nuclear campaign is an example.

I am convinced that the most crucial role in the present context is that of education. What is education, after all? Before dealing with this question I would like to put before you a problem. For many years scientists and so-called enlightened people have been talking about the question of environmental pollution. Take for example the degree of pollution in Delhi. In the last five years or so the environment has become more and more polluted. It is difficult to see even an object like a tree clearly in late afternoon. A large number of people have started suffering from throat diseases and lung problems. But neither the administration nor the public has been able to do anything to overcome the problem. I am extremely impressed by the qualitative and quantitative information that scientists are providing to show the dangerous aspects of the situation. And yet, when it comes to taking drastic action against the dangers that hang over our heads, most of us lack the inclination and courage as individuals to say: 'I shall not allow it to happen'.

Why isn't all that information, indisputably true and efficiently conveyed, making the impact that its gatherers and disseminators aim at? The answer lies somewhere in the inner layers of the human personality and its developmental processes. It seems quite obvious that more information need not necessarily create motivation. Information can be of different types, quality and importance. For instance, if *A* has no particular thing to do and is lazing in the evening and *B* drops in with the information that a good film is being shown on TV or at the local cinema theatre, *A* may be tempted to say: let us go. Here, the given information may provide motivation to *A* for overcoming laziness. It will depend, of course, on many other factors, e.g. whether *A* is fond of films in general or only a particular type of film and whether *A* likes the judgement and the company of *B*, etc.

If the information received should involve a major decision-making process its impact might be different. Moreover, if action upon the information received means risk — to life, money or image, etc. — the result may be entirely different. What would determine *A*'s response would be his predisposition to act (or react) in a given situation. The degree of this predisposition would depend upon the level of cognitive development of *A*, and his or her capacity to make judgements as well as the capacity to take social responsibility, the urge to exercise one's power and the preparedness to face suffering or punishment if taking a particular kind of action is considered illegal in a court of law or socially unacceptable.

To put it briefly: a person may have the knowledge of how to act in a given situation but be unable to control his or her impulses and desires. Knowledge, which is understood today as the accumulation of information and self-discipline, is therefore two different virtues. The point is that most individuals are unable to internalize the information which they find intellectually sensible and useful. Why is that so? The answer lies in the modern system of upbringing and education. Most educational systems begin and end with the pursuit of intellectual growth of the individual, and knowingly or unknowingly distort the emotional side of the personality. Education today stresses the development of logical faculties, which are functions of the part of our psychic apparatus which is called the ego and which represents reason and common sense. The emphasis is on rationality, forgetting that human behaviour is not always inspired by rationality. There are other supra-rational factors that play an equally or more important role in building a good and liberated personality.

I would like to give the old-fashioned simile of the human mind being like an iceberg of which only a tenth is visible and nine-tenths remain submerged under water: The one-tenth being the conscious mind and the nine-tenths the unconscious mind. Present-day education handles the conscious and totally ignores the unconscious, the id, which contains the passion and the source of all energy. 'The id contains everything that is present at birth, that is fixed in the constitution — above all, therefore, the instincts, which originate from the somatic organization and which find a first psychical expression (in the id) in forms unknown to us.' According to Freud,[3] 'the id is unorganized, the ego organized; the id observes the pleasure principle, the ego the reality principle; the id is emotional, the ego rational; the id conforms to the primary processes which ignore differences and are oblivious of contradiction and of space and time, the ego conforms to the secondary processes which are analytical and respect the principle of contradiction and categories of space and time'. Under the impact of present-day educational practices and also due to upbringing, the id, the unconscious, does not only remain unlived, it is also repressed and regressed. Education slows down and distorts the process by which precepts are converted into images forming part of our mental furniture and structure.

Herbert Read explains it very well:

> The whole ideal of education is intellectual. It tends to become even narrower than that: the ideal . . . is scientific. Even in subjects which used to be described as 'liberal' — philosophy, literature and history — the spirit of teaching becomes increasingly 'objective' or 'positive' and all questions of 'value' are rigidly excluded. . . .
>
> I do not deplore the time given to games in our schools — on the contrary, it is often the only time well spent. But the moral discipline thus inculcated is of very limited duration — it has no depth, it does not involve the imagination or the emotional life in any profound sense. Games morality, the team spirit, has become indeed just one more social convention, though to be 'a good sport' generally means to behave like a human being rather than a conventional citizen — in other words to disregard 'morality'. But 'morality', in the sense of a code of right and wrong, has to be distinguished from the moral values of good and evil. Morality itself has been intellectualized, codified, and made a matter of rational judgement instead of spontaneous action. Moral education in the ancient world, when Plato and Aristotle handled the theme, meant the learning of something like good manners or good form, good doing and good making; it was a dynamic concept, a concept of mobility, of wisdom, of courage . . . but I am quite sure that our existing systems of education lead right away from social union, and dissolve the subtle bonds of love and fellowship, and leave us a nerve-ridden aggressive herd.[4]

The present system of education is partitive. Instead of uniting, its tendency is to divide. Instead of fostering mutual aims and love, it generates competition and hatred. It is based on a caste system and hierarchical divisions, not only in age and professional groups, but by deciding that certain tests should determine the right of an individual child to proceed beyond a particular stage. Within each group, similar tests and examinations determine the place of the individual child. The procedure has the effect of pitting child against child in an unhealthy struggle for places. This process accentuates the sense of social disunity.

An education which accentuates disunity cannot foster a sense of community, and where there is no such sense, no sense of belonging, it cannot be expected to give any importance to social responsibility or to those values which recognize the needs of human beings living with one another in a community based on sharing and mutual help. Fullness of life cannot be realized in a disunited society, and where there is no evidence of fullness of life there cannot be real knowledge, that is, of the integrated self.

I do not need to elaborate the development of the individual's personality during the first three or four years of life. Freud and his followers and many psychologists have convincingly pointed out some facts about the existence of aggressive and destructive instincts in human beings. We are not born with these instincts, but they are an inevitable consequence of the infant's adaptation to external reality. The strength of these instincts depends upon the degree of severity of experience beginning from that of birth and the early months and years of one's life. These experiences of infancy get buried in the unconscious and are 'forgotten'. But they find their way out in disguised forms in adult life. Unless these instincts have the right outlets at the right time they turn inwards, with destructive effects. The period of infancy is a difficult one in the relationship of the infant with its parents, which again can result in problems of adjustment with the world around. But I shall not go further into that discussion here.

The problem is twofold. One aspect is concerned with the need to liberate the personality from those fears and complexes which have accumulated during infancy and the early years of life. The other aspect is related to the orientation of the personality in the direction of social integrity. One demands healthy outlets for the energy which has regressed into destructivity and the other requires growing in the direction of creativity and social good. Again, it is the task of education and educators — I do not leave out parents from this category — to see that in the process of growing up and in the environment, the individual develops all his or her faculties that make the life-journey fulfilling and socially constructive.

Rabindranath Tagore once wrote: 'We have come to this world to accept it, not merely to know it. We may become powerful by knowledge, but we attain fullness by sympathy with all existence.' Tagore is asking for a programme of education which is based on unity and harmonious relationship with nature, and in which intellectual understanding and rationality will naturally be by-products. He insists that one can reach truth only through sympathy. 'The world of senses in which animals live is limited. Our reason has opened the gate for our mind into the heart of the infinite. Yet this freedom of reason is but a freedom in the outer courtyard of existence. Objects of knowledge maintain an infinite distance from us who are the knowers. For knowledge is not union. Therefore the further world of freedom awaits us there where we reach truth, not through feeling it by senses or knowing it by reason, but through union of perfect sympathy. . . .'[5]

The human individual is by nature an artist, a creator. Whatever he/she receives is not with passivity and in the mind it is not an accurate physical representation of the objects around. In the subconscious we go on adapting it, transforming it into human imagery, tinged with the values we hold to be part of our sentiments and imagination. Plato writes: 'For rhythm and harmony penetrate deeply into the mind and take a most powerful hold on it, and if education is good, bring and impart grace and beauty, if bad, the reverse. And moreover, the proper training we propose to give will make a man quick to perceive the shortcomings of works of art or nature, whose ugliness he will rightly dislike; anything beautiful he will welcome gladly, will make it his own and so grow in true goodness of character; anything ugly he will rightly condemn and dislike, even when he is still young and cannot understand the reason for so doing, while when reason comes he will recognize and welcome her as a familiar friend because of his upbringing.'[6]

As a teacher I observed that children who engaged in spontaneous creative activities were happier than those who did well in their intellectual performance but who did not take part in either sports or creative activities such as growing plants, craft work, painting and music. I have also found that children's drawings which are the results of spontaneous activities, are direct evidence of their physiological and psychological disposition. These spontaneous activities of self-expression create a great deal of self-confidence, a healthy self-image, in children. After all, self-expression is self-improvement and self-realization.

Self-realization does not mean merely the discovery of one's intellectual capacities and other skills. It is a process of discovering oneself as a free and fearless individual at peace with oneself on the one hand and on the other an integral part of and in harmony with the larger reality, social as well as universal. This harmony is developed in the individual not by the imposition of law from the top but by that discipline to which the senses naturally submit. Creative activities are that discipline in which the senses quite intuitively seek harmony, proportion and wholeness of any experience. The use of media and tools such as clay, cotton, wool, leather, wood, stone, brushes, potter's wheel, saws, impose this discipline by their very nature. Moreover, it draws us closer to nature, which alone is the supreme example of harmony, sympathy and union. These are the same laws on which the human community depends for its own unity and integrity.

Freedom to be close to nature — to be one with it — is to gain one's own freedom, to grow in fullness. Child art not only allows but also encourages the artist to enter the world of freedom, to the fruition of all his gifts and talents, to his true and stable happiness in adult life. Art leads the child out of himself and helps him in becoming an integral part of not only the community but also of the larger unity between nature and human society. From my own experience in the field of child art and education[7] I have seen that art activities in general also have a therapeutic quality which liberates individuals, to a great extent, of their aggression and other repressed instincts accumulated from childhood onwards. I shall give here two simple examples from my own experience.

In the Sevagram school we had a boy from a tribal area. His father was a nationalist rebel during the Quit India struggle of 1942 and was waiting for trial in solitary confinement. The Gonds are a hardy and warring people. The boy, ten-year-old, was not only endowed with his Gond characteristics, he was also emotionally highly tense, mainly on account of the suffering caused by his father's being imprisoned as a freedom-fighter. He used to get violent with other children. I took him in my class and gave him the freedom to spend as much time as he liked in art and craft activities. He liked it. Interestingly, he often drew pictures of historical heroes. He was also encouraged to join in doing hard physical work, such as chopping firewood for the community kitchen. To cut the story short, in a year or so he was a different person, responsible and active in a constructive sense, and he became a popular child artist in the community. What worked to bring about these changes in him? His need was not only to give vent to the extra energy, frustration and anger he had accumulated during months and years, but also to sublimate them, which creativity generates.

The other case was of a girl of fourteen who had not grown mentally beyond eight or nine. She always sat in a corner in every class and did or said nothing. Her teacher considered her socially useless and ineducable. In my art class also she did nothing for months, although when she came to the class I greeted her as I did the other children, and often asked her if she would also like to make some pictures or clay models or do anything that she liked. One day a piece of paper reached my desk from behind. I turned back and saw that it was the same girl — Malati was her name. This piece of paper had a bright cadmium yellow figure which looked like a man. This was her first attempt to say something, probably a thank you to the teacher for having treated her like any other child in his class. Later she told me that it was my portrait. In the next class I requested her to make a picture for me to keep. The result was a drawing of an elephant in the folk style, the style of work she must have seen in her village. I was astonished at the imagery and aesthetic sense of this girl. At last she discovered herself. It is a long and interesting story. Here I shall only say that in a year or so she became a popular child artist and one of the best in the community. She was now a self-confident, active and responsible member of the community.

My experience with our rural population has also convinced me that people who live on the land, farming and gardening, people who earn their livelihood through art and handicrafts, making things of daily use for themselves and their communities, are, by and large, more peaceful and disinclined towards war and warlike activities than those who do only intellectual work in both rural and urban areas. This disinclination towards war in peasants and artisans can be attributed to two factors. The work that they do provides them with healthy outlets for their emotions and violent urges, probably because it sublimates their aggressive instincts. It may sound simplistic, but it is true that after doing hard work in weeding out unwanted growth in the field one may feel liberated from the violence accumulated within on account of other factors.

Another important aspect is that their activities make them one with nature and the natural material they handle. However, it has to be admitted that this phenomenon is no longer as powerful as it was before society was as materialistic as it has become today. Today's artists have become as self-centred and competitive as people in other professions. Yet the truth of the matter is still relevant, as can be observed through children.

I can give endless examples of children's capacity to get totally absorbed not only in the act of painting or doing any other art activity, but in the drama that is the subject-matter of the picture or model. A child of ten years once made a picture of a landscape with a bullock tied to a tree across a brook and a boy trying to cross the brook to go and bring the animal to the shed, as it had started raining. He was holding an umbrella. The boy slipped and fell and the umbrella flew out of his hand. Just before the young artist was going to give finishing touches to his painting he put it at a distance so that he could have a good look at it from the other end of the room. I was quietly watching his movements from the window. After placing the picture against the wall he started moving backwards. His right hand was in a position as if he was holding an umbrella. All of a sudden he acted as the falling boy and moved as if to catch the umbrella which, as in his painting, had flown away. As an artist myself, and having known many serious artists, I was able to fully understand the need of this child to feel that what he was representing in his painting was his own reality.

The crucial point here is that unless we as individuals feel ourselves parts of the whole we cannot experience the whole, which is the ultimate aim of humanity. And without that personal experience we cannot be happy and feel fulfilled. Art assists the individual in creating the desired unity with the universe. Let us see how the dynamic works.

According to Indian and Chinese aesthetics it is of supreme importance that the maker should identify completely with the object that he or she makes. Writing on Chinese painting, Ananda Coomaraswami states: 'The Chinese artist does not merely observe but identifies with the landscape or whatever it may be that he will represent. The story is told of a famous painter of horses who was found one day in his studio rolling on his back like a horse: reminded that he might really become a horse, he ever afterwards painted only Buddhas. An icon is made to be imitated, not admired. In just the same way in India the imager is required to identify himself in detail with the form to be represented. Such an identification, indeed, is the final goal of any contemplation reached only when the original distinction of subject breaks down and there remains only the knowing, in which the knower and the known are merged. . . .'

'If', Coomaraswami continues, 'what seems at all strange to us (the Western and the Westernized), whose concept of knowledge is always objective, let us at least remember that an identification was also presupposed in medieval European procedure; in Dante's words, "he who would paint a figure, if he cannot be it, cannot draw it".'[8]

At this juncture I must make a point which I think is of some special importance. Art here does not mean what it is often understood to mean. 'Art today', wrote Herbert Read, 'is too often a wayward, partial, even perverse expression of universal harmony. It is too often but an expression of personal fantasies, of egoistic and aggressive impulses. It is prostituted to purposes which destroy aesthetic nature'.[9]

The idea here is to experience and develop the unity in which we are born, by learning from nature; in the process of creation all the necessary information and knowledge is gathered. After all, creative activities are related to the external world. To make an efficient table, pot or house, or to make music, it is necessary to know arithmetic, history, geography, science and what not. The natural way to acquire that knowledge is through the unconscious discipline that is possible by way of aesthetic activities. It is this procedure that makes education an unconscious process, therefore natural.

What I am trying to convey here is that to be able to experience and act, and act creatively and constructively, one has to be predisposed to taking such steps in one's life. These steps are not just occasional ad hoc acts in the life of the individual. The whole of life itself is a series of these steps. I am asking no more than what Maria Montessori suggested in her message to the international congress against war and militarism in Paris in August 1937. 'If at some time the Child were to receive proper consideration and his immense possibilities were to be developed, then a Man might arise for whom there would be no need of encouragement to disarmament and resistance to war because his nature would be such that he could not endure the state of degradation and of extreme moral corruption which makes possible any participation in war.'

I am only asking for an educational programme that would teach and motivate the individual to make constant efforts to know himself or herself and to act and behave fearlessly. I am actually pleading for a lifestyle and educational programme that would make individuals predisposed to a beautiful and peaceful society — a society made up of fearless and liberated individuals. It is exactly what Nandalal Bose says in the quotation given at the beginning of this paper. 'Music, literature and art provide those possibilities which build healthy human attitudes. Rhythm and harmony between the specific and the whole — one and many — is their gift to human kind.' I interpret the term art in the sense that classical India did, and which Nandalal Bose himself propagated, without making any distinction between fine and applied arts. In today's situation and mental make-up one may call it a utopia. But let us not forget that every time in history a revolutionary idea was born, it was first labelled a utopia. Haven't we seen that only utopias have succeeded?

References

1. Nandalal Bose, 'Shilpa Katha' (Bengali), in *Drishti Au Shrishti*, Viswa Bharati Publications, Calcutta.
2. Quoted by E.F. Schumacher in *A Guide for the Perplexed*, p.78.
3. Sigmund Freud, 1940.
4. Herbert Read, *Education For Peace*, Routledge and Kegan Paul, London, 1950, p. 49.
5. Amiya Chakravarty, ed., *A Tagore Reader*, Beacon Press, Boston, 1971, pp.218-19.
6. Plato, *The Republic*, trans. Sesmond Lee, Penguin Books, 1980, p.163.
7. Devi Prasad, *Child Art and Education* (Hindi), 1959); *Art — The Basis of Education*, in press, National Book Trust, India, New Delhi.
8. Ananda Coomaraswami, quoted by Roger Lipsey in *Coomaraswami: Selected Papers*, Vol 1, Princeton University Press, 1977, p. 309.
9. Herbert Read, *Education For Peace*, Routledge and Kegan Paul, London, 1950, p. 49.

6

Peace as Theatrical Experience

Bharat Gupt

Introduction: Conflict as a Modern Value

THERE are three main features of modern culture which distinguish it from nearly all the ancient cultures: individualism, presentism and agonism. These are values initially fostered by modern Europe and America and are now being foisted on all other cultures of the world, sometimes blatantly as in economic and military affairs, and sometimes surreptitiously through the export of new ideologies.

Individualism, presentism and agonism are intrinsically promoters of conflict. They create an environment in which peace becomes the first casualty, which otherwise could have been an easy fruit of modern science along with opulence and leisure. Whereas in ancient societies higher personal fulfilment consisted of achieving a position of transcendence such as 'an existence of fame' (*yasassarira*) through heroism or martyrdom, in modern times fulfilment resides in the achievement of material power which is regarded as synonymous with immortality. The individual now does not wish to subdue or abnegate but mostly to aggrandise himself, and hence is placed in unending competition with others.

Presentism, which is a natural corollary of the myth of progress, takes it for granted that only those aspects of ancient cultures are worthwhile which have supposedly led to the development of modern civilization. For instance, Periclean Greece has been graded as the golden age because it formulated democracy and rationality leading to modern parliamentary democracy and the natural sciences.[1] Presentism having given a new shape to historiography, studies of past societies tend to become exercises in reconstructing the past according to the prejudices of the present. History becomes a myth retold (projected as a fresh discovery of facts) to serve new values. Historical developments are seen as an evolution in which the present age is the best. Whereas the ancients held their ancestors in unquestioned veneration and treasured their past with obstinate pride, the moderns are raised to hold past people in axiomatic contempt.

Since the theory of evolution postulated the survival of the fittest, conflict has come to be regarded by the West as a basic virtue, indeed the prime mover of life. Contest, duel, struggle, agitation, protest, fight, these are the fundamental paradigm for achievement in any field. Like other ideologies of European Romanticism, the theory of evolution also postulated that man is intrinsically good and not a fallen creature with evil within him. He is chained by other men or the outer environment, be it nature or social hierarchies. He has hence to fight, not with himself but with the outside constraints. Conflict with the other or the outer, not with the self, was therefore the road to freedom. With this attitude, modern civilization got far removed from peace, in faith as much as in action.

For ancient and even medieval cultures, conflict was an intervention (a *vighna*), or for the very unlucky ones their unhappy portion (*moiras*), thrust upon them by the gods or by fate. One who was able to overcome conflict and win was proud of his conquest, but never claimed the credit all to himself as he could not ignore the element of what was believed to be divine grace. But in our purely anthropocentric world all conquest is a logical culmination of a well-planned contest. Everything depends upon man and man alone.

Seeing the parameters of our thought today, how can there be peace unless there is a major shift from the value of conflict and acceptance of a different perception of the nature of things? For this we may need to revisit some older cultures and understand their philosophical tenets.[2] Through the focus of theatre one may now analyse three older visions: of Renaissance Europe, which retained some medieval Christian concepts, of the classical Greek period which had just begun to emerge from the Indo-European sacrificial religion of the Olympian deities, and of ancient India of around the second century BC, when iconic worship was yet to start in a big way.

European Theatre: Peace as an Argument

Shakespeare set the tone for the thinker-playwright-reformer tradition of Europe, prevalent to the present time, in which the dramatist projects the futility of war and heroism as an argument for peace. In *Troilus and Cressida* he took an episode from the siege of Ilium, recasting the ancient heroic myth into a story of degenerate behaviour. Here is a vision of gloom, concentrating on the worst aspects of human nature. Shakespeare consigns all idealism to transitional brilliance that has no chance of survival in a brutish world. Love is shown here to be no more than lechery, and honour a cover for plunder. There is no extolling of peace but a strong argument in its favour is made through the devalorization of war.

Although in the history plays there is hardly a Shakespearean character who vaguely resembles a glorious hero, in *Troilus and Cressida*, while portraying the Greeks as an alien and heathen race, the playwright speaks out against war with full frankness. What the modern classicists[3] allege through a historical analysis (that the Greek-Trojan conflict was primarily a strategy by the Western Hellenes to capture the trade routes of Asia Minor), Shakespeare depicts dramatically as lust for plunder and sexuality cloaked under heroism. Those who believe in honour and the rules of the game are condemned to defeat. Here, in contrast to the Homeric account, an unarmed and unarmoured Hector is killed by Achilles, not in single heroic combat but by a crowd of warriors. Earlier in the play, Achilles is shown refraining from battle and ditching his fellow Greeks because he was lusting after one of the daughters of Priam. Troilus, the faithful lover, has to face disappointment on seeing his fickle beloved going into the arms of an enemy with irresistible passion. War is shown as murderous waste; and heroes are downright immoral, like Menelaus and Paris, the 'cuckold and cuckold-maker'.

The direction pointed out by Shakespeare by deglamourizing war and deconstructing the hero was taken up by many playwrights in Europe from Dryden to Shaw, whose work I have no time to discuss here. But the important point to be noted is that peace in this theatric tradition is argued for as a value, not portrayed as a presence. The dramatic action hardly ever shows an experience of peace.

Greek Theatre: Peace as Epiphany

It has been customary to state that Greek drama, particularly the tragic, was devoted to the portrayal of the conflict between the human and the divine. But on closer scrutiny one realizes that this is a simplification under the impact of the modern fascination with conflict. This understanding of Greek drama is based upon the habit of looking at the Greek plays singly and not as trilogies. It is well known that in actual performance at a Greek festival, not a single play but always a set of three tragedies were performed; and the playwright presented them as three parts of a single opus. A single play like *Oidipous Rex* or *Bacche* does not represent the totality of the Greek tragic form and experience. The ninety-odd plays extant are only parts of trilogies. Each trilogy, like the only surviving one called *Oresteia*, was more concerned with showing mutability as the essential human condition. While starting on the course of agon, it worked towards creating a balance. It depicts two murders but avoids the death of the hero Orestes, and instead of ending in horror and deprivation arrives at reconciliation and harmony. Its last prayer-song sounds surprisingly similar to the concluding benediction of ancient Indian plays.[4]

Consequently, we see that in tragedy, conflict is not the essential human condition, what is more important is mutability. As in many tragic plays, change of fortune could as well be from bad to good, but always emphasizing mutability and working for a happy balance. However, as tragedy was always keen to point out, both the balance and the ensuing peace are extremely precarious. In the cycle of mutability, this peace is fragile and is a momentary manifestation. But none the less it is real and worthy of celebration. It is a promise and a resurrection and a recognition of the possibility of happiness, no matter how mutable. In the tragic plays it is recognized with awe, in comedies with wanton gaiety, as in Aristophanes' *Peace*.

However, in Greek theatre, over and above the arguments given for peace, the tragic and the comic genres created through myth and fable (paramyth), respectively, an emotional experience of peace for the audience. The plays, particularly as trilogies, such as *Oresteia* or the tale of Oidipous, were made to ritually enact, after the suffering (*pathos*) and the tearing apart (*sparagmos*), the process of restoration and purification (*kenosis* and *katharsis*), which was reinforced through dance, music and festive participation. Peace, here, howsoever short-lived, was known as an epiphany.

Indian Theatre: Peace as Benediction

In a somewhat similar way, theatrical activity in ancient India created an experience of peace through emotional purification and elation (*satvodreka*), which led to the deeper aesthetic experience called *rasa*. Whatever may be one's view of the cause (*karana*), arising (*nispatti*) or nature (*padarthatva*) of *rasa*, it is universally agreed that it is a profoundly peace-giving experience. Nor is this aesthetic experience an escapist or individualistic enterprise, as was sometimes projected by the Marxist critics of regional Indian literatures. It was aimed at elevating a whole community, not only theatre lovers. It began by inviting the gods to protect and watch the theatrical performance and ended with a benediction (*bharatavakya*), presuming that the sacred act of enactment ensured the well-being of all sections of the audience. What is more important, it aimed to elevate both its divine and mundane audiences into a pleasure (*rasa*) which, more than merely bringing peace to the soul, also made the onlookers more sensitive to the pain and suffering of others. It also pleaded for an acceptance of suffering by bringing most tales to an auspicious (*subham*), not necessarily happy, conclusion. But it always, as in *Svapnavasavadattam* or

Mricchakatikam, gave a deeper understanding of individual desires or personal love reconciled with social and spiritual responsibility enveloped by the new peace in the land.

Theatre of the Future: Peace as Consonance

The theatre of the future, though not required to be committed to peace in a propagandist manner, needs to work for it in a major way, for peace is now more than ever a global need. Though theatre in the future shall have to be created and performed locally, it must reflect global movements and events. The perception of 'global' is, however, a matter of bitter controversy because of the differing traditional (pejoratively called 'ethnic' by the West) identities of the perceivers. In fact, there seems to be a widespread fear among many circles, particularly of the White majority nations, that the twenty-first century will witness an extensive 'clash of cultures', of ethnic groups.

In such a situation theatre has to alter its approach to artistic truth. From agonism and presentism it should turn to consonance between cultures. Instead of continually emphasizing the differences between civilizations and cultures, their history and their development, which has been the thrust of social and cultural anthropology for nearly a century, theatre should go on to discover the similarities beneath the cultural diversities.

Theatre can begin by locating the common ground between cultures, because commonality and not differences are the need of the hour. If culture is to be something more than the exchange of goods, then we may benefit most from turning to an old definition of human communication called *samvada*. '*Ekatrasya tu anyatra darsanam samvadah*' (When something existing at one place is also seen at another, this phenomenon is called *samvada*). This is done by locating a core of vibrant similarity between the two objects, a similarity that exists beneath all differences and which, instead of being wiped out by the individual differences, sustains itself and the differences as well. To provide a simile, it is like the consonance between two musical notes, which are always independent yet capable of generating a mutual resonance by virtue of their common grounding in a given scale. Within our pluralism we need to explore our common scale. Theatre, as the oldest art of communication, is best suited to highlight consonances between cultures and promote the common scale of peace.

References

1. In his *Early Greek Philosophy*, first published in 1892 and reprinted till 1930, J. Burnet says, '. . . a new thing came into the world with early Ionian teachers — the thing we call science. . . . Science has never existed except among people who have come under the influence of Greeks' (p.31).

2. We now need to turn away from the modern habits of individualism, sensationalism and mass indulgence. In this endeavour of forging new values, nothing can be more helpful than pre-Aristotelian Greek thought and Upanisadic Indian thought. These philosophies can help us prepare a new ground through ethical courage (*areetee*), metaphysical humility (*eulabeia*), self-analysis (*atmanavesana*), and unpossessiveness (*aparigraha*). These are the values most needed to evolve new cultural constructs and balanced social structures.
3. 'The Trojan war is historical, and whatever the immediate cause may have been, it was a trade war' (Robert Graves, *Greek Myths 2*, Penguin, 1955, p. 302).
4. For a detailed discussion on this, refer to my *Dramatic Concepts: Greek and Indian*, Delhi: D.K. Printworld, 1994, p. 216.

Part - II

Examining the Emperical Reality of Beauty and Peace

7

A Dehumanized Environment

Keshav Malik

This is my third day in Rampur, a small hill town in north India. It is the prototype of similar hill towns all along the Himalayan foothills. Like others, I too at times go to the Mall, but oftener to the more secluded forest roads. The fatigue of the Indian plains that has accumulated these many years comes unstuck, here where nothing much happens except when the football of the schoolchildren overshoots into the *khud*. Down in the dusty town where I live I can rarely hear the sounds of the earth. Oh, I know you can hear them even there, but the effort that one has to make is prohibitive. Nature, or what to me are the distinct individual voices, of running water, the clear ring of a single human voice, the fall of a stone, a footfall on the gravel, and so many little things, these cannot be heard, just as the colours on the mountain tops, the contrast of the bottle-green with the azure, the lights shimmering in the valley, these and many other things get lost in the cry of humanity and the crazy traffic down below.

But now at last I can hear the running water in the pipe, and the *bansee* down in the pines. The water's sound changes ever so often: at first it is like an engine letting out steam at a wayside station at night; at other moments it climbs purposefully, at still others it compares well with the crickets' sound beyond the fence.

It is night, and very quiet outside. As my eye lifts I see a moth by the wooden ceiling, flitting about in abandon. Yes, the plains, in psychic terms, are far away.

And now remember too, with me, the sounds from, and the shapes of, the mountains during the day: then, as I recline in my armchair, my eyes open up at the thickly wooded hill parallel with the eyes. I watch the lights change every so often; there are the greens, the dark shadows and an eagle or two circling above, round and round. The clouds are bathed in the autumn sun. I hear the cows' bells tinkle on the slopes of the hill to my side. The fern-covered oaks near the fence, these I stare at for minutes on end; I notice each curve of each branch and the movement of the leaves in the lightest of breezes. I watch the clouds' surgical white float by and the grass by the old threshold stir. I breathe a deep sigh of relief. And why?

This is a escape, a necessary one, I tell myself. Where I live and work, down in the big mega-town in the plains, the silhouette of personality is lost. I have no clear idea what the Indian was like before the machines came, before the British came, before the Moghuls came. But perhaps this Indian's was a well-defined world with its particular harmonies, its peculiar refinements, with little of the ugliness and hopelessness that invests such a large part of life at least in my big town on the northern plain. Oh yes, there are good things: there are electric light and the flush system, two admittedly very important acquirements, which can extend one's day and conceal a tell-tale object of organic origin. I'm all for these and for all the other inventions. But no, these are only good means, now unwittingly made out as ends. What I assert is that civilization, its gadgets, its assets, serve better if they help serve one fundamental primary end. The end has not changed, it has not changed since the pastoral age with all the vicissitudes of complex civilizations and cultures. This all-important end is the flavour man gives to his life, or to put it better, the consumption of beauty. This end is quite unrelated to the accumulation of the skills of civilization. This end is achieved through a certain simplicity, open eyes and ears, and the receptivity of the skin's surface to the phenomena of nature. What I say is that nature, rather our receptive attitude to nature, has been lost in the plethora of our skills; we have brains, but those of shopkeepers, accountants, clerks, so we can see nothing save with a view to profit and loss. What has happened, may I ask? Was it always like this? I do not know.

But too many people, and it is only from them that one hazards generalizations, and especially those like myself of the middle strata, are lost in the worship of means; there is such grasping for things, for power, that no time, no possibility, is left for the human in the machine. How then can we have peace? For we do not listen but are driven, and so the internecine conflicts between competing individuals wanting the same object, an object perennially in short supply. This is a strange fate for a culture that prided itself on deep meditation. But perhaps it is not so strange, for the meditation in question has itself for long been put at the service of salvation, that is, as a means to the furtherance of the defensive or offensive self. This is the way I look at it. Most of present-day religion, a good deal of what is called our current spirituality, serve non-contemplative goals. All we have ended up with is a sort of ancestor worship. The perpetuation of the line, a natural enough end, appears to have become the chief goal. It may not even be that, but merely each for himself or herself. Meditation or *yoga*, or whatever, to men already cast in this form, becomes no more than a technology, a magical means of emotional control over others. But there is no inner tranquillity.

A growing will to power, yes, but a rapid loss of the sense of beauty — and therefore no peace.

8

Modernity and Individual Responsibility

M.M. Agrawal

IN today's world, the consolidated effect of modernity, the picture of man as the rational autonomous individual endowed with free will, is complete. The individual is individualistic: self-interested, egoistic, clamouring for more and more power, wealth and social status. He has stopped thinking about life considered *as a whole*. There is no overall spiritual meaning to life. His life is divided between purposes which are contingently thrust upon him by his environment, requiring fulfilment with a speed and efficiency which occlude any evaluation of their meaning for life as a whole. Indeed, he finds it difficult to apprehend life as a whole, to consider it as a unity, except chronologically. As MacIntyre in his most perceptive discussion of the contemporary scene observes:

> Modernity partitions each human life into a variety of segments, each with its own norms and modes of behaviour. So work is divided from leisure, private life from public life, the corporate from the personal. So both childhood and old age have been wrenched away from the rest of human life and made over into distinct realms. And all these separations have been achieved so that it is the distinctness of each and not the unity of the life of the individual who passes through those parts in terms of which we are taught to think and to feel.[1]

Moreover, the very character of the social has changed so much, as many post-modern thinkers have emphasized, that the individual need not even bother about the unity of life and its overall inclusive end to provide a teleological framework for his endeavours. The social no longer demands conduct in which human relationships are informed by *virtues*. Indeed, most social institutions of the past which provided for the cultivation of virtues and qualities of character in the individual have either totally disappeared or have been rendered underdetermined by the vast changes in the character of relationships sought by individuals. This is the age of shifting relations of interdependencies, where even the most basic forms of human bonds — pair relations, sexuality, family, kinship and friendship, for example — have become institutionally underdetermined. The individual is faced with the stark reality of a communitarian alienation and competitive insecurity. The notion of rational autonomous subject has been taken to its ridiculous limits — freedom into anarchy, individualism into self-centred egoism, rejection of the substantial self into total fragmentation. The blemishes that have warped our ethical consciousness and disfigured our conscience are many, but perhaps the most serious one emerges, ironically though unselfconsciously, from what must be considered the virtue of modernity. Modernity which brought *freedom* from the unthinking callous authority of various non-secular traditions went too far and liberated the hidden greed lying curled up in the human heart.

But surely, in the culture of greed-satisfaction there is no hope for *peace* — peace as a cultural realization must manifest itself first in the social spaces of interpersonal attitudes, intentions and relationships.

The extent of degeneration in the values of interpersonal relationships is obvious when we realize that today we have come to need a *justification* for treating others equally and impartially — the rational precept which could provide the underpinnings for law. And philosophers have discussed the question 'Why should I be moral?' And if we need to discriminate protectively in favour of those who are severely marginalized, we need a veil of ignorance about their real human status so that we can be convinced in our hearts that we are not being unfair to ourselves in going out of our way to help the needy. In this extraordinary situation we find that the ethics of compassion, love and caring has suddenly ceased to be relevant. There may be no basic 'given' (eternal) structure of human relations but, under the surface of sophistication, it certainly seems to have *become* what Hegel's famous image of 'master-slave' anticipated. Even the most ardent believer in human freedom, Sartre, succumbed to its temptations.

> While I attempt to free myself from the hold of the Other, the Other is trying to free himself from mine; while I seek to enslave the Other, the Other seeks to enslave me. We are by no means dealing with unilateral relations with an object-in-itself, but with reciprocal and moving relations . . . within the perspective of *conflict*. Conflict is the original meaning of being-for-others.[2]

We need not accept this verdict upon the nature of interpersonal attitudes as a description of the fundamental, ontological structure of human relationships, but as a correct representation of what has *become* of it, it is surely undeniable. We face one another with the motive to prevail over the other, in a moving situation of perpetual conflict.

The individual is oriented towards ends which are discrete, unrelated, making for no coherent ethos or even style of life. But what is most frightening is the ethical and aesthetic dislocation of sensibility. The aesthetic consciousness is ingrown, has lost communion with nature and the life of the universe as a whole. It is churning out stuff in the name of self-expression, as though self-expression were the highest form of a characteristically human achievement. It has forgotten to take note of what has *become* of the human self (a social product, conditioned in its virtues and vices), which has grown on the stage of conflict and which has accumulated all the filth of consumerist modernity. There is a point where the line between life and death is too thin, just as the line between art and vulgarity, but the line all the same is there. That we fail to recognize it only shows that we have forgotten what it means to be an Artist on Life.

The world of human relationships has lost its intrinsic worth. The world is *my* world in which everything is organized instrumentally for the satisfaction of some undefined, intangible need of personal security and individual fulfilment. The fragmented life of this divided individual is glowing with the feeling, the fear, of being left out of the race — an insecurity whose origin and character he is blissfully totally ignorant of. Man is lost in the wilderness of a civilization of his own cultivation.

The loss of the ethical perspective upon life both in thought and in social action is evident enough. For the former, modernity having admirably freed the moral agent from the stifling hold of the esoteric authority of 'revelation' and the blind precepts of superstition, landed him into the hands of another, equally esoteric authority of 'rational intuition'. God may have died (as per Nietzsche) but man could not have killed him. Perhaps He committed suicide in utter disillusionment and frustration over his proud creation. And again, having unhooked the understanding of the moral agent from the mysteries of 'foundationalism' and 'essentialism', modernity has thrown him into the hands of the unmerciful loneliness and uncertainty of his *subjectivity*. The modern moral agent, devoid of any inner spiritual strength, dependent upon externals and lacking reference to the ultimate worth of his activities, is constantly afraid of losing, or being too late to collect, the visible and immediately affective pleasures of life. He is left with no choice but to continue to struggle in the pursuit of his own personal achievements with a sustained drive, greed and competitiveness so characteristic of the contemporary engagement with life. And such choice, in turn, has landed us into deeper crises. The by now familiar environmental crisis is nothing but an outer aspect of an inner crisis of meaninglessness in the ethical consciousness.

As for the loss of the ethical perspective in social action, the degenerate state of the relationship between culture and politics is amply in evidence. Cultural politics has turned into the politics of culture. Moreover, the fragmentation and short-sightedness of political enterprise the world over exposes the ethically ambivalent inner state of mankind.

On the one hand being egoistic, and realizing that everyone is trying to get *there* (God knows where) first and possess as much as he can, he must submit, in a quasi-Hobbesian manner, to the rule of law, apparently based on the moral idea of equality. On the other hand, being impelled by the desire to dominate over others, (as we saw in the primary structure of human face-to-face) he must try to seek power in all forms and ways accessible to him. He must then (unconsciously perhaps) introduce loopholes in the systems of society, in particular in the laws, and hope to retain control over them through a system which has all the pretensions of equality but is inherently open to subversion by the cleverer and stronger. He thus submits to the rule of law (allows the law to take its own course) only to ensure a smooth transition to his desired inequality. His purposes are perhaps best served in the installation of modern liberal democracy.

The social ideals of justice and democracy which the Western Enlightenment admirably struggled to realize is inherently aporetic, based upon a deep contradiction in the modern consciousness. We are content to believe that though liberal democracy is not perfect, it is the best that can be realized. Or those who are not so pessimistic contend with the thought that human rationality will one day find a solution. But even if a rational solution could be found it will be limited and short-lived, we cannot install the gains of reason into new institutions. The old institutions are fast losing their grip on reality, if not already dead or rendered ineffective. And the new would need infinite flexibility and versatility to cope with the infinite disorder in the fragmented but fast reshaping river of *all* consciousness. Shattered beings can best represent reality in bits and pieces.[3] The resolution of the conflict cannot come from the ready-made 'objective' social morality, from determinate moral rules to be followed or virtues to be cultivated, or from the calculations of the 'greatest good of the greatest number'. For, as Zygmint Bauman has observed,

> morality is endemically and irredeemably non-rational — in the sense of not being calculable, hence not being presentable as following impersonal rules, hence not being describable as following rules that are in principle universalizable. The moral call is thoroughly personal; it appeals to my responsibility, and the urge to care thus elicited cannot be allayed or placated by the awareness that others do it for me, or that I have already done my share by following to the letter what others used to do. Being moral means abandoned to my freedom.[4]

Today we are faced with making a resolute choice between getting swallowed up by a culture thrust upon us by the dictates of a technocratic capitalism, and working towards creating a culture sensitive to the spiritual dimensions of human existence which respects nature and life in all things. This choice cannot be made by the collective: it is not a politico-economic choice. It can be made only by a 'true' individual, who, unfortunately, somehow lost his way in the new industrial metropolises.

Contemporary critics tend to overidentify the ills of capitalist modernization, which encouraged monopolization and misuse of power, which distorted knowledge to suit manipulative techniques for economic subordination, with the rather honest and noble intention of intellectual modernization to create a rational and scientific approach to knowledge and social progress, and consequently wrongly identify the aggressive individualism encourage by the former with the essentially ethical individualism of the latter. The intellectual modernity rejected the grounding of practical reason in blind 'authorities' of occult subjectivity both in matters of morals and in objective truth. And by and large it (notwithstanding the claim of 'rational intuition') placed a premium on the honest, dispassionate and unprejudiced judgement of the individual, *in the final analysis*. But the spirit of the enterprise left all judgements open to revision, though no doubt always aiming at objective finality. In this attempt they, perhaps inappreciatively, invoked the authority of the 'ethical' in final adjudications of all truth claims. The individual had to feel responsible for his truths and social commitments, and had to arrive at them through honest impartial consideration. Such individualism is not dictatorial or idiosyncratic. It is another matter that this healthy individualism lost its battle for humanizing culture against ruthless capitalism, and irresponsibly grew into a 'fat and selfish' egoism.

The upshot of this brief reflection on the odds and evens of some contemporary myths and insights is to invite us to give the devil his due, to face ourselves to realize that any programme of social action for cultural regeneration stipulated by seminarists curls up upon the participants considered as individuals. It is the individual human being in whom alone there lies, first and foremost, the creative energy needed for cultural transformation. He must somehow realize that *he* is responsible for the way the world is today — violent, uncaring, unsharing and unloving; not he alone nor he collectively, but he individually. And this means that social action must begin from action upon himself, the action of making ourselves integrated beings, whole and true individuals. This would require the discipline of self-knowing, of understanding oneself as a *total process*.

The process-view of the self that I am invoking here recognizes that the self, though a unitary centre of consciousness, is not a totally separate psychological or psycho-physical entity, cut off as it were from the rest of being. At every stage of the living process, it is embedded, sustained and carried over by the extraordinary life of the whole. Today this view has been made available to us by the insights of scientists into the way living systems sustain themselves and support one another and move forward together in evolution. Their participation in the whole is a form of mutual cooperation. The realization of total interconnectedness and interdependability can promote an almost mystical sense of unity with the whole, with the consequence that the consciousness of separateness is rendered insignificant and is even ontologically incinerated. But perhaps more to the point is the fact that the sense of unity with the whole is sufficiently real for the individual.

What we are saying is nothing but a retrieval of an aspect of the Indian spiritual heritage central to which is a holistic perspective upon life. In the holistic vision of life there is also the ending of the fragmentation of life. And in the ending of fragmentation there is the ending of conflict within. Such a conflict-free individual, the true individual, is the proper foundation for peace in the world. We have experimented with impersonal objective approaches to ending conflict 'outside', but without success. It is not enough to see conflict 'out-there' and offer pragmatic solutions for immediate relief. Such an approach can only control tensions temporarily. But a non-erupting volcano is not a land of flowers. If the individual is conflict-ridden on the inside, if he is fragmented and feels separated from the world, he is bound to project it upon the collective. Greedy, envious, egoistic, pleasure-hunting individuals will inevitably produce wars and fragmentation. Only conflict-free individuals can neither be manipulated not will desire to manipulate others.

The ever-present feeling of insecurity due to the consciousness of separateness on the one hand and the consciousness of the essential unabidingness of the self on the other, constantly pushes the individual to seek salvation in various forms of the collective. The being of the individual needs to be protected. But it is not easy to do so when each one has set himself in competition with the others. The collective offers the power of the state, of legislation. But who is to wield this power? Obviously, individuals of the same kind as those who need protection — scared, insecure, lonely, and therefore aggressive, possessive and manipulative. Is it surprising, then, that everywhere in the world state power tends to acquire an oppressive personality of its own? In the typical consciousness of oneself as a necessarily acquisitive and consumerist self — an essentially separate entity which nevertheless continues to retain its personal identity throughout its history of seeking satisfaction of the vagaries of desire — there can be no peace.

To transform the acquisitive culture of conflict and aggression into a culture of peace and care, man must return to himself, perceive the hidden motivational springs of his action and in knowing himself thus and so, discover the sacredness of life, of nature and the wholeness of his interrelatedness with it. As it is, the culture we have created, which in turn has conditioned us, is the result of our constant endeavour to succeed and dominate, to acquire personal power in one form or another, as separate beings. It is a sad story of human misery and suffering and endless conflict. Each one of us is composed of these cultural universals. One has to realize, not only intellectually but experientially in the structures of one's consciousness, perceive the truth that 'we are the world and the world is us'. 'The world is in each of us; to feel that, to be really committed to it and to nothing else, brings about a feeling of great responsibility and an action that must not be fragmentary, but whole.'[5]

The culture of peace is the way of life of individuals who have put themselves on the road to total freedom — freedom from the conditioned dictates of the acquisitive culture. Such individuals do not succumb to pressures for the blind run for what glitters like gold but *alas*! melts away like wax. The promised land of happiness through single-minded devotion to material (industrial) growth is a mirage whose true nature one fails to see in the culture which has given us the unquenchable thirst for more. We must assume the responsibility for regenerating the culture of peace through re-making ourselves into integrated wholes, beings that are at peace with themselves; and then the spiritual quality of the feeling of the unseparateness of the 'me' would enable us, naturally and quite spontaneously, to relate to others in love, freedom and understanding.

Epilogue

This is not to suggest that no institutional action is needed on the 'outside', in society. Creativity is necessary for a robust culture of peace. Such a culture must keep blossoming, comprehending the contemporary ethos, it must be reappropriating its resources towards a meaningful *telos*. In its aspect of creativity, a living dynamic culture, as I have argued elsewhere,[6] must be seen as a *quest* for (to put it generously) the 'holy trinity' of Truth, Goodness and Beauty, which signify the three *generic* perspectives upon life available to man. The goals of a 'quest', in contrast to those of a 'search', cannot and should not be given determinate definitions. We understand them and move towards them through the negation of what are empirically known to be their opposites. For example, we embrace non-violence by the negation of violence. 'Non-violence' does not represent *a* being, but violence is recognizably actual. Non-violence is a way of *being* in the world without violence.

If cultural processes signify a creative quest for the meaning and truth of life, then their logical relationship with educational processes is evident enough. Holistically speaking, education must awaken the integrated intelligence of the learner rather than encouraging conformity to patterns of canonised knowledge, education should enable the individual to comprehend himself as freedom, understanding and creativity. Educational processes have lamentably become merely *informative* processes. True, there is always a considerable amount of technical, factual data and concrete utility-skills to be transferred from the teachers to the taught, but surely to exhaust the meaning of 'education' in solely 'that', is a vulgarization of a form of life which the ancients rightly considered sacred and which they approached with great humility.

But today educational institutions have turned most violent — the violence, for example, of ideological brain-washing and the marginalization of those who refuse to surrender to power relations of dominant epistemic discourse, or of those who simply cannot afford to buy it. The system and its operations are imbued with the egoistic, acquisitive and domineering character of modern man so characteristic of the 'liberal individual' of contemporary culture. His ruthless pursuit of a notion of truth which is laboriously constructed on utilitarian foundations, on what may be called the 'pragmatics of material advancement', and the notion of goodness signifying manipulative success, and of beauty that lures and earns, offers only a sad caricature of the educational process.

Surely it will be generally agreed that when we behold education in all its beauty, depth and richness, we see it as the power which liberates, and enables and inspires man to live creatively. This power is *freedom*—freedom from the fear and insecurity of non-conformity and non-'success'. Education, particularly in the humanities, must awaken the integrated intelligence of the learner; instead of encouraging conformity to patterns of canonized knowledge, education should enable the individual to comprehend himself as a total process. Thus, self-knowing must be a simultaneous and non-cognitive (i.e. without the subject-object separation) accompaniment of knowing the external, the objective.

To live creatively, no doubt one needs a matrix of facts, knowledge and techniques. But though such a framework is logically necessary, it is not sufficient. To live creatively one needs to be perpetually transcending the 'given', the conditioned and determined. In the spontaneity of freedom and the insights of understanding of life as a whole, one is always going beyond the literal meanings of traditions, enriching them with newness and thus carrying them forward. Creativity is the very dynamic of living, and living is an artful quest of the meaning of life.

References

1. Alasdair MacIntyre, *After Virtue*, Duckworth, 1981, p.190.
2. J.P. Sartre, *Being and Nothingness*, New York, 1956, p. 474.
3. To echo Rainer Maria Rilke: 'Shattered beings are best represented by bits and pieces'.
4. *Postmodern Ethics*, Blackwell, 1993, p. 60.
5. J. Krishnamurti, *Unconditionally Free*, KFI, 1995, p. 34.
6. *Manascharya*, Vol.1, No.1, 1995, pp.1-10.

9

The Illusion of Seeking Peace

S.C. Malik

A human being is a part of this whole, called by us 'Universe', a part limited in time and space. He experiences himself, his thoughts and feelings as something separated from the rest — a kind of optical delusion of consciousness. This delusion is a kind of prison for us, restricting us to our personal desires and to apportion for a few persons nearest to us. Our task must be to free ourselves from this prison by widening our circle of compassion to embrace all living creatures and the whole of nature in its beauty.

Albert Einstein

The Crisis of Fragmentation

MODERN civilization, since the sixteenth-seventeenth centuries, has persistently been subscribing to propositions which have logically led to the atomization of the whole fabric of human existence, experience and being. Analytic dismemberment has certainly produced enormous material wealth, but with it immense suffering, both physical and spiritual. However, it is evident that the hegemony of material and intellectual vested interests seems to preclude a basic reappraisal of this suicidal specialization, this mechanical model of thought which has long outlived its usefulness. The old paradigm continues to merely reinforce dormancy on a major part of the brain. It is time to end the stranglehold of linear, causal, mechanical orientation over the intellectual culture of our times. Any attempt to overcome this conditioning requires, primarily, a serious engagement with one's self.

Some examples of the seminal concepts which have dominated our times, and which appear as self-evident axioms, are the various binary opposites (spirit *versus* matter, individual *versus* society, subjectivity *versus* objectivity, sacred *versus* secular, you *versus* me); the notions of linear time, the idea of development and progress, and the importance to techno-economic models. It was hoped that this fragmentary and mechanistic approach, along with science and technology, would usher in an era of plenty, followed by peace and happiness — a transformed quality of life for most of humankind by the end of the twentieth century.

Today, we know very well that these dreams and prophecies are true for only a few in the material sense, leave aside the unprecedented barbarism we see all around. Only a few have dared to question the underlying assumptions of modern society. It is crucial to closely scrutinize this kind of 'unthinking thinking', since that is where the cure for the contemporary malaise may be discovered. Unfortunately, those who control power, wealth and knowledge — whether in the East or the West — are not willing to give up the outdated formulations since, generally speaking, vested interests are seldom known to give up power to others. The pity is that those non-Euro-American civilizations who do have alternate world-views and life-styles available — such as cyclical time, a different notion of knowledge — are losing touch with their indigenous cultural psyches. The 'modernized' elite groups within these civilizations are equally responsible for ignoring contemporary scientific developments which in many ways indicate a convergence towards ancient speculative thought.

The causes of the contemporary crisis do not lie solely in the external world. It is abundantly clear that the psychological crisis (of loneliness and alienation) has entered into the very psyche of modern man. He has lost the ability to be in touch with the existential-experiential ontological states of human existence. The issue of fragmentation is in fact a psychological problem since it is like a crossing of wires in the brain which is at the root of the issues which one faces all around. The deep-rooted conditioning within the framework of confrontational dualities has resulted in contradiction and conflict not only in external situations but in the brain itself. Meaning thereby, the brain-mind complex is being pulled in two directions, not knowing which way to go; there is a dominance of the rational analytical half of the brain which is governed by language and semantics, which of necessity must create such confrontational conflicting dualities. In other words, while symbols and images are necessary for the universe of discourse in an intellectual sense, this is only half the story. This analytical approach is not sufficient to get one into the experiential right brain way of intuitive or holistic knowing — another kind of knowledge — and it certainly does not by itself lead to any experiential states of 'happiness', of any states of feeling like an integral being, of peace. Evidently the intellect by itself cannot create love, peace and harmony.

Cognition — how do we know what we know?

Normally, most of our lives are governed by unconscious implicit assumptions received from the socialization process which we take for granted. These premises are what allow us to know what we know, but not how we know it. In order to move in this direction we must have an encounter that delves deeply into some epistemological-ontological issues. This becomes imperative if one is to correct the suicidal path along which humankind is heading. Here one can only deal with it briefly, less in terms of academic philosophy and more as a personal encounter, a serious engagement with one's self, within the context of 'experiencing', as has already been said. This brief exploration is crucial since it allows us to ponder over what and how we perhaps communicate, feel, think, experience and so on in everyday life. The three interrelated spheres are as follows:

(i) Abstractions — concepts, symbols, images, thought.

(ii) Experiencing — feelings, emotions, intuition.

(iii) The overarching Be-ingness.

In a holistic functioning, the three categories are totally integrated as one, in the full functioning of the mind. In normal functioning, operations are limited within the first category which is governed by the linear-hierarchical model. It is also dominated by causal concepts, of cause and effect logic. The second level also operates covertly and implicitly within the first sphere, i.e. feelings and sensations are triggered by thought, words, semantic categories; even though initially it appears as if this sphere is quite distinct from the first. The reverse is also likely, i.e. it is emotions and stimulus-response functions which stored as memory create thought statements — symbols and images which are considered crucial for the 'survival' of the individual and the collectivity. The linear model of course emphasizes the need for achievement, in order to reach a goal in the future — there is the domination of becoming over Be-ing. However, in this mode, there is a recurrence of similar problems that are recreated in new garbs — new structures, forms and contents that are rearranged every now and then — and thus, basically nothing new is allowed to manifest itself, i.e. holistic ideas and those about peace and harmony. This sphere of linearity and hierarchy only makes us believe we are making contributions.

As long as thinking is confined within old concepts and paradigms, it is an illusion to believe that transformations are taking place, whether 'progress' or 'peace'. Since all ideas of change and transformation are confined within the old paradigm of 'survival', thinking about newer paradigms remains confined to the old box. Nothing new is possible, since one in fact is the paradigm which runs one's life. It is like living in a prison, imagining creating peace and freedom outside, by painting pictures within the prison, without leaving it.

So, how is it possible to do away with this conditioning? The first step is to be aware of this primary problem, since it is in the very understanding of this dilemma — the very limitations of the box, this paradigm — that will allow one to step outside the limits. It lies thus in the awareness that the box may disappear, by not getting lost in the operationally created limits of the self and society. It implies being open to uncertainty, it is the wisdom of insecurity which helps create the possibility of the impossible. In fact, the new and limitless cannot be understood intellectually. All this is only possible by dropping the old, which functions by re-cognition. Only creativity is true cognition. In this sense of re-cognition, all knowing of the new once again becomes the old. To be open is to be beyond boundaries, to accept the idea of no-thingness. Here, thingness is equated to thinking, which as stored symbols is an object, a thing. Thus, the old way is to be comfortable in the knowledge of the known. It is this moving from something to something is limiting known to the known — whereas moving from something to nothing — known to the unknown — is to be living, i.e. dying from moment to moment, to all of yesterdays, is to be open to psychological uncertainty and hence it is a movement towards peace, harmony and true creativity.

Certainty is not creativity, it refers to security and survival. In its very effort to go beyond it creates more of the same, albeit it is shifted every time to another 'higher' level. It does not allow one to be in touch with the Source, the Be-ing, the Universal Oneness which allows one to share, to be equally related to all of Creation. On the other hand, becoming arises from a position which one wishes to defend, to be in the safe box believing one is secure in it. This kind of living is mere conceptual living, since the ego is all of these concepts, abstractions, reactions. These are the limitations which do not allow one to be in touch with one's Be-ing, and therefore it causes incessant insecurity. The more one avoids insecurity, in trying to be secure, insecurity is only strengthened. One might well remember that there is no such thing as security psychologically, and certainty in other areas. In short, thinking about life is not living it, and one thus has to remind one's self that thoughts have to be seen as subsets — material manifestation of Be-ingness — of the larger overarching category of Be-ing, and not the set.

Thoughts are about the past and future reconstructions, about the becoming, which make us believe that we are alive. It is this becoming, this movement of thought, which causes restlessness, this incessant seeking of what one has not got — away from 'what is'

— this wanting, desiring, searching for certainty since *per se* abstractions and concepts are residues of incomplete experience, or 'inexperienced-experience'. For example, this is why most of us easily recall painful and unpleasant experiences rather than good and beautiful times; because the latter are complete experiences by themselves and have little residue as thought (merely stored as information, and not as a recall system). Hence, by this very inherent logic, i.e. concepts are about something, and therefore in most of our lives it is thoughts that trigger off feelings and emotions — linguistic memory — is a kind of experiencing which becomes a secondary feature, not a primary or original experience. For example, the word anger triggers off the concomitant emotions. Thought then wishes to do away with anger, etc. in the future — 'tomorrow and tomorrow we will make it better, more and more. . . peace. . . .' This is the becoming game of thought in which one is caught up, and this indeed is the ever-receding mirage-like illusion. This seeking itself is what causes insecurity. It is in this way that modern man seeks goals that are perpetually about yesterdays and tomorrows and seldom about any experiential-existential states of the present or 'now'. But can insecure individuals who make up society create a secure, peaceful and harmonious society?

Thinking, limited within the paradigm stated above, has only led humankind to do all kinds of 'going through the motions' with regard to its intentions for goodness, charity, peace and harmony and the like. This unconscious thinking — reactions — has only further increased disorder and chaos. Of course, for a while there appears to be satisfaction, a feeling of achievement. But soon the old problems return, despite reaching the moon — so to speak, humanity continues to wrestle with the same old problems. But what, one may ask, is Be-ingness? It is not a thing, it is manifested in things. It may not be known conceptually, but experientially-existentially by a Self which transcends the boundaries of the limited person, a shadow of the Be-ing. So, how do we know of it? It is like electricity, or light which is known through its effects, functions, use and behaviour. These, like Consciousness, are not known or seen empirically, directly, as an object. Be-ingness is the witnessing Consciousness, Self; it allows us to be aware, to 'know' choicelessly while at the same time allowing one to participate in the world. Each one of us knows it, as it is in the universe of experience of all of us.

The reference here is to primordial reality, experiencing *per se*, which does not arise out of any person. It is an impersonal experiencing that transcends both the experiencer and the experienced. The latter are peripheral and arise secondarily as shadows of the former, such as that these are commentaries afterwards on and about the unspeakable, the action. It is like listening to the commentary on a tennis or cricket match and believing it to be mistakenly to be the match — where action is taking place. Hence, what one speaks about the action is mostly taken to be the experiencing. This is where discrimination is required to be able to distinguish between these two distinct spheres, not confusing one for the other.

It is in this confusion of the different spheres that the error is further compounded when out of the long range of memories, thoughts of particular sets become the thinker, and this commentary is what says that there is a thinker separate from thought; forgetting that the experiencer is the memory itself — the thinker is thought itself. The problem is really of knowing who one is, not who one thinks one is; an identity problem. In this false identity, he/she seeks an experience, identifies with psychobiological reactions, arising out of previous knowledge only. These reaction are the 'me' and its extensions which incessantly move for endless goals, arising out of past experience. Normal actions are thus only reactions, and create in fact the illusion of action. This 'acting' is in fact inaction. True action lies in a kind of choiceless awareness. This implies the total functioning of all the three spheres, to be in the 'here and now' with no other purpose than to be aware, to be conscious, to be 'awake', to be 'alive'. This perception itself is action. This itself is the transformation which arises out of the eternal 'now'.

Nevertheless, even intellectual acceptance by a few puts pressure to work towards it by asking such questions as 'how' and why' about holism, viz., 'while I understand it intellectually, what is the practical way of doing it, going about it, and what is the discipline or path to tread whereby I may live this integral life so as to contribute to society, to go beyond personal-selfish goals?', and so on. These apparently serious rhetorical questions seem very justifiable, yet they are still framed within the old ways because there is no philosophy or an ism to this holistic way of life; there is no new renaissance 'out there' to be achieved — another 'heaven on earth', another utopia.

This movement of thought from 'here' to 'there' is linear time, it needs to be remembered. The old conditioning functions very subtly, by means of such 'logic' and 'rationality' that it is not easily discerned in the new garbs that once again surreptitiously take over the new alternative. Within the paradigm of 'survival', it is necessary to preserve the old psychological security, of moving from the known (past) to the known (it is not really unknown since it is a projection from the past and is re-cognizable in a sense of what it ought to be like so that one is comfortable in these expectations that function strongly both at the personal and social levels) albeit modified (appearing as if 'new') in order to be 'understood'. These are the assumptions on which most of human existence is maintained, giving a kind of security and familiarity.

But have we ever questioned all this, given the recent advances in the sciences, given the mystical insights, that this movement, this becoming, is always a repetition of the old, both psychologically and socially? The old perspective is deadly in its literal sense. Unless this false security is questioned, brought in front like a mirror in terms of one's personal-existential-experiential lives by being here and now, no breakthrough is possible.

Peace — Integral Listening and Communication

The emphasis in this section is on communication and integral listening, it is about the silence which forms the background of true human communication. The context of this discussion is the beginning of the modern era, which starts from the seventeenth century. It is also important in an evolutionary sense, since during this period language along with all other associations begins to dominate human behaviour. It reflects an over-specialization of a distinctive area of the brain. In this way the positive advantages have also become detrimental to the further evolution of the human species. It is important to note the role of the cerebrum, which consists of two distinct halves. Each functions autonomously in sorting information received, i.e. the left side is more logical, rational and involved with the use of language, the right being more intuitive and syncretic. This is part of the evolutionary growth of bilateralism which gives success and survival advantage to the species, to get around, for animal species in general and man especially, in this integral development of the nervous system. But when the two halves, it has been studied, do not exchange information and get severed for one reason or another, then a dualistic or split personality is formed. This oppositional duality psychologically is the state man is in today; this neurotic, schizoid life, of saying one thing and doing another, etc.

To illustrate, one of the most conspicuous indications of this functional asymmetry, or laterism, is the phenomenon of 'handedness' (right or left). Dramatic evidence has come through the observation of the effect of damage to the respective hemispheres. If a part of the left hemisphere is affected by accident or disease it can seriously impair certain higher intellectual faculties such as speech, in a way that seems not to happen if the damage is sustained in the corresponding part of the right side. Today it is recognized that both hemispheres are involved in higher cognitive functioning, but there are a division of labour and fundamental modal differences between the two sides. The two hemispheres process information differently and are organized differently. It is not surprising, in view of the fact that they are separate entities, that they should have differing views of the world.

In spite of their marked differences there is a modal complementarity in the functions of the separate hemispheres: one could generalize and say that the left tends to think in words and the right in images, but the division and specialization of their respective talents go much farther than this. For example, the left side is associated with logical, verbal, rational, analytical, convergent, sequential and linear order of thinking: the right with intuitive, emotional, non-erbal, syncretic and divergent, simultaneous and spatial behaviour.

There are fairly obvious risks attached to a brain that operates on a double-plan system, the most outstanding being the danger that the two separate mental domains might vie with each other for control over the organism. The most important bridge to avert this is the massive bundles of nerve fibres that establishes reciprocal connections between corresponding centres in each hemisphere — this is the corpus callosum that carries something analogous to a telecommunication system of the order of 200 million lines of cables. It is well to remember that the combination of the two systems are far more effective than one on its own. Even if one may see with one eye our stereoscopic vision is essential, so also is stereocognition necessary to function fully, in harmony and creativity. This is the only way one may respond to a universe and nature which is similarly organized but which may never be revealed except in its own style of dynamic functioning, in all its various dimensions.

Every individual brain is subtly organized in different ways, its psychic configurations creating unique patterns of ability and personality. Each individual psyche makes its own response to the inherent dualism of the mind/brain just as it responds to the cultural dualisms that are a feature of all social structures. In general these preferences are made as unconsciously as those of the left/right dominance determining reflex itself: we are quite 'naturally' of an artistic or scientific cast of mind, or, for that matter, political orientation. The divide between the East and West may also be seen, beginning with the seventeenth century, to be the dominance of the left brain activities as against the non-verbal, nonlogical and 'fluid' methods of eastern philosophies — the likes of which have disappeared in Western thought but are surprisingly perhaps making a return via the new vision of science itself. At any rate, it is worth mentioning that psychologists have noticed that the left brain has a distinct tendency to 'take over' and feel itself responsible for all the actions of an individual, even to the extent of rationalizing those decisions made by its right partner which it has played little or no part in making. There is surely an analogy in the functioning of modern society, of rulers, political and other authority — the experts and their systems — who claim to know that they know what is best and have an overbearing attitude. One of the philosophical problems thrown up by the confirmation of the dual mechanism of the brain concerns the nature of consciousness. If modern science — relativity and quantum theory — has cast doubts on the nature of space, time, matter and energy which are no longer tangible, solid 'things', then what is the self, if neither of the hemispheres are the separate selves that they pretend to be, nor can it be the corpus callosum, then what is it, this Self and Consciousness?

The over-specialization of cerebration restricted to the reptilian-mammalian areas of the brain is the source of a great deal of anguish and sorrow for humankind. This is obvious from the fact that one sees the tremendous need of so many to take to drugs, alcohol, sleeping pills, tranquillisers and so on. It is a clear indication of the urge to stop this incessant restlessness and agitation further provoked by the consumerist overkill of advertising. However, all external remedies of the serious crisis are futile, as we see from the self-evident destruction which is going on in the world despite all good intentions. The fundamental issue is an internal, psychic one. It may be called psychological or spiritual, but it is closely linked to the development of language and the framework of philosophies governing it. Modern man has lost the ability to listen, he simple hears; like he simply looks and no longer sees (as an insight).

This non-listening has given rise to two types of conceit, one of nations and the other of scholars who believe that what they know is as old as the world. The tacit, ubiquitous belief that recent Western logic represents the most reliable cognitive standpoint appears to characterize world wide culture. Has not listening, as ancient art, being gradually lost in the noisy inflation of discourse and by the infestation of pseudo-symbolic language, this constant chatter of thought uncontrolled? Or, conversely, could it be that the vital, ecological rationality has exhausted itself in its overwhelming production of talking since it is more interested in hunting than in cultivation? Has this intellectual heritage not caused the conceptual connections of other traditions to disappear? Has it not given rise to an idea of truth which is fitting for the vacuum it has produced?

In this more or less shared hegemonous cultural structure, the problem therefore is that of creating sufficient silence to at least hear the incessant rumbling of a cultural machinery — thought — that seems to have lost its original vitality as a result of its enormous success. No longer able to hear the noise it makes, there is alienation and a sense of desolation because of this logocentric dominant-orientation which denies even the earlier, the minor or unsuccessful traditions — that they ever existed, or have become totally irrelevant. No real dialogue is possible in this blindness. But the same holds true if there is an over-evaluation of the tradition that leads to cultural games and presentation of the real, or even imaginary cognitive values of that tradition. This approach is framed within the same game, and debates which are yes-and-no games within the dichotomies of rational and irrational, coherent and absurd. In this way one negates life itself by being dogmatic about such yes-no states. The question is not of making every tradition equal, or allowing everyone access to the highest knowledge; it is the domination of one form of knowing, a single way only, that is the problem. The balance of Yin-Yang is missing.

The creation of an empty space, or distance, within a dialogic relation might be the only way of letting the deeper meanings and implications of that relationship emerge. The nature of silence is as a gap or distance in which germinal meanings can be developed. (The hollow of the drum, the spokes of the wheel around nothing). This no-thing, this emptiness, can be compared with silence and is probably called 'no-thing' because it is not manifest or immediately perceptible: it is not a question of thoughts or emotionally tangible events but, possibly, only of that which organizes them from within and allows their springing to life. Silence is not an interval but that which unites sound.

It seems that civilized humans are no longer capable of a cognitive propensity for inner time as they are constantly suffering either from boredom or else from haste. Possibly much of the total yield of 'cultural' messages seems to be an antidote to the ever more serious problem of boredom in the sense that we are now inextricably tied to media of all kinds, everything becomes a performance intended for a show. It even becomes 'necessary' to change things into a show so that humans can have some di-version and thus de-flect attention from themselves, turning centrifugally toward external stimuli of any sort. Technological advances, for example, are geared to develop instruments designed to make everything faster — growth, exchange, elimination — and thus to 'save' time or delusionally even 'produce' it.

The technology of informatics and the achievement of 'real time' constitutes precisely the annulment of the time spent in waiting. In this way one moves even further away from biological time, undeniably contained within the limits of birth and death time and scanned by such rhythms as sleeping and waking, diastole and systole. Modern 'time' of rationality has lost all rhythmical flow and only speeds up in a planar, uniform and unhalting way. It is a notion of time that can be integrated more easily with a technology of treatment than with the prevention of pathological states. In a practice that is incapable of abbreviating, economizing or annulling time, the listening approach comes across with even greater relevance in the context of temporality. A listening dialogue is fertile inasmuch as it is willing to ignore time measures. In the absence of such an approach, cultural constraints do not allow creative thinking, and the human being can no longer really live his own awareness of time; the experience of death inevitably assumes the stereotypical appearance of the absurd. Thus the knowing subject is reluctant to let himself 'die' even when cognitive 'death' is equivalent to relinquishing familiar models in order to be able to seek models elsewhere, in a creative knowledge rather than in the mirroring of standard rationality. We palm off 'having' for 'being'.

A Question of Identity

Sometime after World War II there was a great deal of assurance for humankind of the practical dimensions of the notion of 'progress' on a global scale, equated with high technology. It has not only led to a crisis of confidence but also to unprecedented barbaric inhumanities everywhere. Humankind is in the throes of a deep crisis not only externally but psychologically. The modern world's predicament lies in the many unexamined assumptions that continue to govern its way of life, e.g. linear time, progress towards a certain state. However, there is the transformational world-view which the new science and ancient insights suggest, i.e. of a friendly universe, to be accepted, experienced and celebrated: Nature is an evolving eco-system of which you and me, the human species, are a part. This quest for seeking a unified field — scientific or otherwise — begins with one's self, with personal yearning.

But is it possible in this search to make a peaceful whole from the parts, given the assumptions of separateness — dualities — to begin with both intellectually and socially? This 'objective' distancing has made man least responsible for nature and the planet, or for creating any overall harmony despite statements to the contrary. At the physio-psychological level the body-brain mechanism, being already a totality, is being hard put to understand all these goings-on. This conditioning is so deep-rooted, especially the identity as a separate self, that it causes agony and alienation, an empty feeling. Can this so-called separate self really discover any solid, stable 'me' or an answer to 'who am I?', leave aside peace? Nevertheless, the brain struggles to search for its real identity, and not finding one in what it has learnt within that limited dimension, it is thoroughly exasperated.

The inner psyche is still looking for its true identity, and no amount of external solutions will bring about any lasting peace or contentment. The organism is receiving contrary messages, or at least it knows that what is given is not so. But in the present trance-like conditioning one continues to grope in the hope of 'tomorrow and tomorrow', little realizing that mirages continuously recede and will never materialize. The first sign of awakening is to be aware of this false image, the false changes, this hope against hope, this untruth. This is the first step towards a new dimension which without being stated may bring about the 180-degree transformation that is so imperative in bringing about the shift in global consciousness. In the dynamic universal of perpetual motion, there are only moments of one state to another in the sense of a totality of NOWS, whichever way this may be defined. This enquiry and search is not to be subsumed in terms of a linear-time, linear-mind, framework, and not even the liberal cyclical time-framework, i.e. the search will lead one to in time, to the peace, love and truth when it will all be revealed once and for all!

In other words, in the process of discovery there is no ego just as is the case in any experiencing or a creative moment like an aesthetic one where the discovery and the experience are simultaneous. But the subsequent operation of putting the experience into words, to communicate it even for one's self, these are all entrapped in the language and symbolism of the socio-cultural milieu one lives in. Even more so is this true when the psychological entity of the 'me' seeks explanations or gives a commentary on the experience of discovery; all this movement is that of time, thought, the me and the ego. The continuous one process is thus split up, fragmented; since language and symbols intrinsically as abstractions must do.

This saying one thing and doing another is the split-brain symptom of the current crisis which dominates modern times. The singularity of this state implies that the ego, the commentator believes, not lives, in knowing and searching, in sincerity, love and action — all of which it shall achieve soon in this manner of dangling the carrot in front of the donkey, and striking it from behind. Then, it says, it will all be over and finally there will be peace. Mostly, one is not even aware of such double-speak statements. Obviously, nothing will ever be right, specially reaching any of the goals mentioned so often: peace, love, and harmony. But this only perpetuates the known past that is projected into the future which is therefore the same as the past, of chasing a mirage. The only alternative is to stop this split between perception and action. The unity of the timeless and time must be seen not as any concept but as an awareness of waking up to 'what is'. The game of splitting reality is then over. Then change of perception itself is action. The search in the present, NOW, is the important dimension. To see this game of one's self and of the universe, is the awakening from the somnambulism of the split-brain fragmentation with which humankind is confronted today.

For the linear-mind, which is the me — ego — the question will arise, is this not another goal, to move beyond the duality by evolving yet another high-sounding philosophy of detachment, of being an observer, and suggesting one ought to be some kind of *yogi*? And if one agrees to all this, how does one achieve this state of awakening; what are the methods, and how, when, where does one know of it? These questions arise from the split linear-mind itself and the intellect has to realize its limitations without wanting to achieve any state. If there is any such state, it is beyond the intellect which the latter has itself to see. The awakening is of a larger context that sees the duality as a manifestation, as a dialogue, as an indicator of the non-dual, i.e. the linear dual aspect to be the shadow of the non-dual as one sees one's own body's shadow and therefore knows of the existence of the body which one cannot perceive physically as a whole as one sees another — the other being also a reflection of one's self in another sense.

The point is that the shadow must realize that it cannot possibly become the substance, which it is struggling to become in this unconscious conditioning. The shadow perpetuates the dilemma by asking questions of how, when and where along with why; all this seeking, appearing very significant, creates the illusion of hard work, of a destination to be reached and taking one's self very seriously. This is the nature of the finite self; these several selves in the world are trying to seek unity by false notions which only accentuate, reinforce its earlier states and conclusions. The psychological process is the same as that of an 'expert', who asserts authority — whether within the dialogue that is taking place most of the time in one's head or outside — and all this is only a commentary on or about the actual, the experiential, and acts in terms of thought as a 'censor' which forms a socially conditioned personality, hardened as one grows up from the already given genetic and mental *samskars*, potentialities.

The personality, this 'expert', is basically lazy since it functions by being the authority that is constantly attempting to dominate both within and without. But it is an incomplete structure, and is therefore also inevitably dissatisfied, incomplete and wanting-desiring at the same time more and more without actually completing anything. The personality is like a bucket with a hole trying to measure the ocean without being aware that its handicaps are in-built. But all these games are basic to its existence, even its own denial, since all this splitting and duality perpetuate its self and are not merely seen as manifestation of the ONE. The split is from here to there, from the self to the other, of saying one thing and doing another, and separating perception from action. If this was not so, how would it perpetuate itself?

All that needs to be done is to drop the glasses, or the split mind, by simply being aware of the split and not doing anything about it. This is to state that one needs to know the limited role which the 'who I think I am' plays, and instead be aware of — be with it — a 'who I am'. Most of modern man follows the former rather than the latter, wherein lies one's Be-ingness. The crisis is that this split-level paradigm operates all the time, since who one is becomes this paradigm itself, at all of the inner and outer existences. The way to hell is paved with good intentions, one well knows. The above intellectual statements are meant as indicators for one to notice — the finger that points to the moon is not to be mistaken for the moon — to observe choicelessly, and it is this witnessing is what may create a sense of authenticity, sincerity, and creativity. The awareness, the awakening itself is the action; perception itself is action — when the split-eye glasses are removed, metaphorically speaking, everything becomes clear and transparent. This once again is nothing to be reached for, because this initial or first step is the last step. The impact is tremendous as the hold of the old paradigm diminishes. Now, to put it simply, everything, you and me, are okay. It is to be Here and Now, for the sake of the search, for joy, in whatever one is doing, or not.

All the external threats of ecological and nuclear disasters are symptoms of a deadly psychological disorder in the human brain itself which is the covert culprit that one is seldom aware of. It is clear that this awareness is necessary, and to see that modern civilization has continued in fact at a petty pace, with the illusion of 'tomorrow and tomorrow', even though it may appear as if giant steps have been taken. The giant step has to be radically different from what went before, i.e. it is a breakthrough from the past, a discontinuity, since creativity is of that order. When reptiles flew it was a clean break from this earth in a sense, suddenly new, not clinging to the old consciously. Psychologically this is what man has to do. Revolution is creation in this sense, a newness; the chick has to break the shell to come into its own, or the butterfly has to emerge from the larvae stage to become so. Are the stages connected? Yes and no!

Is Reality a paradox? From our limited angle and viewpoint it is, yet not by itself. It contains all the possibilities present in the universe at any given moment right now. It has always been so, except when we walk around in our boxes, with blinkers on. Like electricity, it is always available, except when it was suddenly discovered. There never was a time when it was not. The time has come in all walks of life to create a breakthrough in all spheres and this comes out of the uncertainty and insecurity which alone demands a new creation all the time. The dynamics of the universe and nature demands this, not being certain with one single notion of reality, of the past. It is not out of the past, yet emerging from it as if by standing on it and not being an effect of it. The need is to transcend duality, to a dimension which is unthinkable, so to speak, for that is the unknown. It is to make life a mystery once more, to live in uncertainty.

Life is living it, not thinking about it. Thinking about it is only part of it, and thinking, feeling, and experiencing are one process which we may classify separately but which are subsumed under a larger whole of Being. The falseness of the triad of known, knower and knowing needs correction. The constant need to be secure comes from Be-ingness, of the Self, of some inner unnameable core of existence, an effable experience which each one of us had even for a moment. This is what one wishes to seek, repeat, but which is not repeatable; these moments of aliveness when that 'I' is not. It comes and it is a discovery of one's self only. This is the Oneness of the universe, alone, without a second that has to be discovered a new each moment like breathing afresh every time; that is, knowing-living moment to moment. We seem to forget that life is larger than its contents, it is not simply its contents. It is this shallow thinking that is causing incessant problems, and that is why not all the desire to create peace brings nothing but more wars, killings and violence. It is this wrong thinking which changes nothing externally. It is like trying to get love through the conditions of love, i.e., doing steps to know loving. But one knows that there is no mechanical way of knowing love; it happens and is then manifested as feeling and knowing, into action instantly and spontaneously. Nobody can know peace, love and harmony through doing, having, achieving it. It is by knowing it in a deep sense, thinking without duality, as one's inner being, that creates it by itself because both body and mind have their own intelligence. The universal 'I' is intelligently manifested in the body, it is a holograph of the brain. It is not limited human thinking that is going to create peace and love, through some separate narrow view of each one of us as an island.

If our basic assumptions are not changed, we will continue to reinforce pre-existing notions, within the framework of the survival paradigm that dominates our psychological make-up. It continues to be so despite all attempts to change it, since we function within the old paradigm 'box' which one becomes. So that all attempts to refine, elaborate, modify are mere superficial movements governed by the underlying and hidden rules, say that of linear hierarchy and other notions which form the main focus of the reptilian-mammalian brain that is interested only in itself or its notion of survival. In short, the paradigm of survival, inheritance of the biological ancestral notions of survival, of scarcity with which we began in our evolution at some point of time, haunt us today. We may say that the reptilian and mammalian brain, which forms a small fraction of the human brain is still what dominates our thinking even though this is no longer necessary for a large part of humankind. But the older notions today are deeply culturally entrapped within the framework of the same hidden reality, and nothing radically different, a breakthrough, a mutation takes places. The search for 'peace' and 'freedom' remains thus a dream, since that is what everyone is pursuing, each one in his/her own way, in order to contribute to life, to make a difference. So, why does not anything happen? Because, the ultimate 'urge', 'source' has been forgotten, because all this is not considered 'rational', 'reasonable'. But creation is out of no-thing, not something; peace and love come from such a creation, not by having it or doing it.

References

Artigiani, Robert, 'Thermodynamics and History', in Kishore Gandhi, ed., 1990.

Bateson, Gregory, *Mind and Nature: A Necessary Unity*, London, 1984.

Bohm, David, *Wholeness and the Implicate Order*, London, 1980.

———, and J. Krishnamurti, *The Ending of Time*, New York, 1985.

Cassidy, David C., *Uncertainty: The Life and Science of Werner Heisenberg*, 1990.

deChardin, Teilhard P., *The Phenomenon of Man*, New York, 1959.

Dirac, P.A.M., *The Principle of Quantum Mechanics*, O.U.P, 1958.

Dossey, Larry, *Space, Time and Medicine*, London, 1982.

Ferris, Timothy, *The Mind's Sky; Human Intelligence in a Cosmic Context*, Bantam, 1991.

Fiumara, Gemma Corradi, *The Other Side of Language: A Philosophy of Listening*, Routledge, 1990.

Gandhi, K., ed., *The Odyssey of Science, Culture and Consciousness*, New Delhi, 1990.

Harris, Errol E., *Cosmos and Anthropos: A Philosophical Interpretation of the Anthropic Cosmological Principle*, New Jersey, London, 1991.

Heisenberg, Werner, *Physics and Philosophy — Glifford Lectures*, George Allen and Unwin, London, 1959.

Kothari, D.S., 'Science, Culture, and Values', mimeographed, 1986.

———, 'Complementarity Principles: Physics and Beyond', in *N.R.L. Technical Bulletin*, special issue, New Delhi, 1989.

———, 'The Perception of Truth in Science and Philosophy', in Gandhi, k., ed, 1990. *The Odyssey of Science, Culture and Consciousness*, New Delhi, 1990.

Lester-Smith, E., *Intelligence Came First*, Illinois, 1975.

Lovelock, J., *Gaia: A New Look at Life on Earth*, Oxford, 1979.

———, *The Ages of Gaia*, London, 1988.

Malik, S.C., *Indian Civilization: The Formative Period—A Study of Archaeology as Anthropology*, Shimla (reprinted, 1987), 1968.

———, 'Human Evolution: Some Reflections on Its Philosophy', *Eastern Anthropologist*, 1972.

———, 'Models and Social Relevance of Indian Archaeology', in D.P. Agrawal, ed., *Radio-Carbon and Indian Archaeology*, Bombay, 1973.

———, *Understanding Indian Civilization: A Framework of Enquiry*, Shimla, 1975.

———, 'Dual Nature of Thought', *Vishwabharati Quarterly*, Santiniketan, 1987.

———, *Modern Civilization: A Crisis of Fragmentation*, New Delhi, 1989.

———, 'Holism and Life Style Studies: The Civilization Context', *Eastern Anthropologist*, 1990.

———, B.N. Saraswati and Madhu Khanna, eds., *Art: The Integral Vision*, D.K. Printworld, New Delhi, 1994.

———, ed., *Intercultural Dialogue and the Human Image: Maurice Friedman at the IGNCA*, IGNCA, New Delhi, 1995.

———, *Reconceptualising the Sciences and the Humanities: An Integral Approach*, Manohar and NMML, New Delhi, 1995.

Prigogine, I., *From Being to Becoming*, San Francisco, 1980.

———, *Order out of Chaos*, New York, 1984.

Schroedinger, E., *What is Life?*, Cambridge, 1948.

Sheldrake, R., *A New Science of Life*, London, 1980.

Weber, Renee, *Dialogue with Sages and Scientists*, New York, 1986.

10

Man in His Becoming
A Change of Perspective

Mira Aster Patel

As we stand poised at the end of this century, we are conscious of being on a significant threshold — a threshold which spells major changes: changes in the very process of man's becoming, in the evolution of his consciousness. The problems emerging in the wake of the great achievements of this period are proving to be intractable. Something in the very *nature* of man and his quality of *functioning* and dealing with his environment — this is what comes in for serious questioning.

Man, in his being, does not seem to measure up to the structures of life and civilization that he has created. He has released potencies of a tremendous magnitude but does not have the wisdom to utilize them for the good of all. He has penetrated into the secrets of matter and discovered therein a core of 'wholeness'; but in his own being he knows only fragmentation. He does not correspond, in quality or dimension, to the essential nature of the universe in which he lives. The imbalances are marked — and a grievous sense of disproportion lies heavy on our spirit.

In the early years of the century, Sri Aurobindo had foreseen that such a situation would come upon man, when he wrote:

> At present mankind is undergoing an evolutionary crisis in which is concealed a choice of its destiny: for a stage has been reached in which the human mind has achieved in certain directions an enormous development while in others it stands arrested and bewildered and can no longer find its way. . . .
>
> Man has created a system of civilization which has become too big for his

> limited mental capacity and understanding, and his still more limited spiritual and moral capacity to utilize and manage, a too dangerous servant of his blundering ego and its appetites. . . . Reason and Science can only help by standardizing, by fixing everything into an artificially arranged and mechanized unity of material life.
>
> A greater whole-being, whole-knowledge, whole-power is needed to weld all into a greater unity of whole-life.[1]

As the curve of the century comes full circle, we sense that these changes are already beginning to take place. They appear as inevitable landmarks in Nature's own process of evolution. New movements are afoot, new experiments attempted, to cross this threshold consciously and discover what lies beyond. The future beckons powerfully and sometimes reveals itself in flashes of experience which serve to give a new sense of direction. Another perspective altogether begins to emerge. In this brief paper we shall present this perspective as it unfolds itself, in stages, remaining as close to experience as is possible.

I

We habitually use the mind as our instrument of knowledge and make it serve as the tool for the organization of life. This primacy of status as mental beings has now to make way for another status — that of beings poised in the Spirit and living and acting from that dimension of consciousness. The transition must be made from the state of extreme fragmentation in which we live today to a future possibility of re-creating life on the basis of a concrete experience of wholeness.

From mind to Spirit is the threshold to cross in the immediacy of our consciousness. A shift of level, a change in status and poise. From the analytic, divisive, discursive, organizational approach to life to a more comprehensive one of wholeness, in which the 'inwardness' of the real has primacy of status. And the conscious being, thus poised, reaches out into the realms of life and matter in one single, swift movement of intuition, of an immediate and direct awareness of what they contain. Such a movement seizes the whole in its essential unity as also in the dynamism of the play of forces acting within it.

From 'within' to 'without' is the innate movement of the spiritual consciousness till, in its own unfolding, it reaches a point where the 'without' ceases to be, for all is contained in the One Whole.

The mind fixes itself on the 'without', on the outer surfaces of things, in the first place, and tries to organize the same at the linear level of its existence. Then it does attempt to look 'within', senses a presence, tries even to reach out to it, but is firmly held back by its own organizational obsession with all that is external. The mind *seeks* the 'inner realm' but cannot enter it, because it follows, by its own characteristic action, a reverse process — from the outer to the inner. It is unable to move from within outwards, in a direct and intuitive manner, as the Spirit does.

The sense of being on such a threshold of change is palpable in our consciousness. Not only as individuals perhaps, but as a species. Therefore is the difficulty of the present moment so great. We carry the weight of an evolutionary charge! It is the very nature of the universal process that is changing.

At the level of present experience, however, we find ourselves unable to detach the totality of our being from the mental consciousness which stands at its apex. This latter forms one piece with the external surfaces of life and matter. Though we are keenly aware of the confusion and conflict this externalized consciousness leads to, we are unable to draw back from it and plunge into the rich profundities of the inner consciousness — with its golden-hued warmth, its supple interwovenness, its innate intuitions and spontaneously right actions. We sense this realm, we feel it throbbing in our depths: but the separation, the detaching from that surface mental involvement is hard to achieve. We do not know how it will eventually come about.

The difficulty of present times lies in being able to 'cross over', to 'go through': to be able to dive into these inner domains of conscious living and arrive at a steadily maintained poise in that status of being. This latter is important. And, then, to look afresh at the 'without', at the structures of the world, at our pattern of civilization and culture and see how they can be created anew, in the light of this level of experience and by the energy thus released.

Shall we reaffirm, however, that the hold of the mind is not easy to shake off — but there is no other way. For, at the present stage of evolution, the characteristic action of the mind is proving to be a great limitation, one which needs to be surmounted so as to arrive at the greater and far richer possibilities that the Spirit holds for us. We are on the move, from the lesser to the infinitely greater, in which all other levels of existence are integrated and each finds its own rightful place, of both being and action. Nothing is left aside of the long evolutionary progression from matter to life to mind. The Spirit includes all and accords to each its fullest value and true sphere of action, leading to the realization of a complex harmonic existence. Only the limitation of each level is surmounted in this ascending order of evolution.

Let us draw the needed energy from Shri Aurobindo's own experience:

> If mankind could but see though in a glimpse of fleeting experience what infinite enjoyments, what perfect forces, what luminous reaches of spontaneous knowledge, what wide calms of our being lie waiting for us in the tracts which our animal evolution has not yet conquered, they would leave all and never rest till they had gained these treasures.[2]

II

In this evolutionary endeavour, the people of Asia would have a special role to play, with those from India taking a certain initiative, if they are able to seize upon the significance of this period of transition, marking a change from one level of consciousness and corresponding action to a greater possibility of consciousness ahead. The long history of these people is witness to the sustained explorations in the realms of the Spirit that have been made by them. Modern times have further enriched these cumulative gains of the past and added new dimensions to this existing storehouse of treasures. They are there for us to draw upon in our present effort. In this regard, our best help, we feel, can come from the experience and work of Sri Aurobindo and Swami Vivekananda.

The West was the cradle of the Renaissance of the sixteenth century. The curve of knowledge that began at that time has brought us to the frontier where we stand today. Stupendous have been its achievements. Incredible its knowledge of the laws and processes of Nature. Formidable, in its impact, the utilization of matter and the resultant technology.

But, *alas*, this magnificent curve of knowledge has made man bereft of a name, of an identity. His own being has become denatured in the process. The obsession with matter has worn off on him!

Man has to become wider, vaster, richer and more complex in his consciousness to be able to *effectively* master this greatly increased field of knowledge and the potencies this knowledge gives access to. A corresponding growth in the quality, the extent, the power of consciousness that wields this knowledge needs to take place. The imbalance between the two, as of now, is too great and dangerous; and all the tension, the chaos of today is only an expression of this disequilibrium. Man as he is in his consciousness and the world of structures and forces he is called upon to guide and control are not commensurate.

The course of growth seems evident. Man must measure up in power, in consciousness, to this external reality he lives in and make changes in it where needed. This movement is not impossible, not unnatural. In fact, it is inevitable and, logically, must constitute the next step in the universal process.

In helping man to chart this course, we would need to look for, discern and gather together the concrete, psychological processes that can lead to a change in the quality and level of consciousness. Well-tried and practised methods would be needed to serve as a basis. This knowledge and experience form part of the ancient and continuing heritage of the Asian part of the world. The term 'yoga' broadly covers this domain.

It is important here to note that Sri Aurobindo offers a detailed delineation and elaboration of these processes, issuing from his own direct experience. And, in a special measure, he makes extensive explorations into other realms of the Spirit, not yet revealed to us. The most significant of these he terms the 'Supramental'. It is a dimension of consciousness in which the mind exceeds itself and arrives at its own fullness in the Spirit. The Supramental is a consciousness of the Whole, the dynamic concrete Whole. Its power is that of a self-effectuating Force that acts on the Whole. This level of consciousness, he adds, is pressing upon man to manifest itself. Such growth seems to be the next logical step in the unfolding of the evolutionary process.

Sri Aurobindo, in his own experience — and that of the Mother, his collaborator in this endeavour — has worked out and clearly identified, in fine detail, the psychological processes that lead to the realization and manifestation of this level of consciousness. He terms this body of processes the 'Integral Yoga'. Of special significance here are those processes which are in a kind of 'proximity of experience' to the Supramental level of consciousness and power. He presents them under the fascinating title 'The Yoga of Self-Perfection'.

Here are some indications of the future — a future to be lived, but already permeating the air around us!

The play of man shifts to another scene — and to another goal. The being of man is in question. What are the qualitative and dimensional changes that can take place in his consciousness? And *how* can they be effected? The discovery of the method is important.

The method which served to unravel the processes of physical nature will not prove to be of help here. Another method more evocative than analytic, more supple than trenchant, more harmonizing than divisive would be called for. A method essentially psychological in nature and progression, for the subject to be addressed is that of consciousness, at the many levels at which it has its modes of formation and corresponding quality of action. The hierarchy of all these dimensions has to be explored — from matter to life to mind, and specially from mind to spirit. An exploration of these dimensions of consciousness as they exist in our own individual beings and as they are experienced in the unfolding process of the universe around us. The cumulative energy of India, in this regard, is ours to tap.

III

A new perspective stretches out, offering another curve of becoming and of action. We wish to reproduce a passage from Sri Aurobindo which gives a dynamic thrust to such a movement of growth.

> Therefore the individuals who will most help the future of humanity in the new age will be those who will recognize a spiritual evolution as the destiny and therefore the great need of the human being. Even as the animal man has been largely converted into a mentalized and at the top a highly mentalized humanity, so too now or in the future an evolution or conversion . . . of the present type of humanity into a spiritualized humanity is the need of the race and surely the intention of Nature. . . .
>
> They will adopt in its heart of meaning the inward view of the East which bids man seek the secret of his destiny and salvation within; but also they will accept, though with a different turn given to it, the importance which the West rightly attaches to life and to the making the best we know and can attain the general rule of all life. They will not make society a shadowy background to a few luminous spiritual figures or a rigidly fenced and earth-bound root for the growth of a comparatively rare and sterile flower and ascetic spirituality. They will not accept the theory that the many must necessarily remain forever on the lower ranges of life and only a few climb into the free air and the light, but will start from the standpoint of the great spirits who have striven to regenerate the life of the earth and held that faith in spite of all previous failures. . . .
>
> The thing to be done is as large as human life, and therefore the individuals who lead the way will take all human life for their province. These pioneers will consider nothing as alien to them, nothing as outside their scope. For every part of human life has to be taken up by the spiritual — not only the intellectual, the aesthetic, the ethical, but the dynamic, the vital, the physical, therefore for none of these things or the activities that spring from them will they have contempt or aversion, however they may insist on a change of the spirit and a transmutation of the form. In each power of our nature they will seek for its own proper means of conversion;

> knowing that the Divine is concealed in all, they will hold that all can be made the Spirit's means of self-finding and all can be converted into the instruments of divine living.[3]

He offers a clarification:

> Divinization itself does not mean the destruction of the human elements; it means taking them up, showing them the way to their own perfection, raising them by purification and perfection to their full power and *Ananda* and that means the raising of the whole of earthly life to its full power and *Ananda.*[4]

A far-sighted goal of perfection could be ours if we had the vision and the courage to pursue it.

Such a perspective of man's becoming as is unfolding itself before us, can be daunting, to say the least. But are there other paths to travel? We do not think so. Everything has been tried — and nothing works. We try re-fitting the jigsaw bit but the picture doesn't come together. It gets more and more awry. The signs are clear: there must be another way. And there is probably another picture. Let us then look for them. They may not be all that remote.

In fact, the feeling grows that a radical kind of breakthrough, or change, is imminent. Something just round the corner and pressing down on our consciousness. A little more, and the consciousness may go through to another dimension and recover the wholeness that is in its depth. The 'wholeness' within rushing out to meet the wholeness discovered in matter's secret core!

New spirals of evolution are marked by audacity. The greater the audacity, the more promising the new spiral must be.

References

1. *Sri Aurobindo*, Sri Aurobindo Birth Centenary Library, Sri Aurobindo Ashram, Pondicherry, 1972, Vol.19, pp.1053-5.
2. *Ibid.*, Vol.17, p. 79.
3. *Ibid.*, Vol.15, pp. 250-51.
4. *Ibid.*, Vol. 22, p.125.

Part - III

Working Towards the Restoration of Peace

11

Vipassana and the Art of Peaceful Living

S.N. Goenka

EVERYONE wants peace and harmony, everyone wants happiness. I feel deeply pleased that the theme of this gathering accords with the noblest aspiration of man: to search for the knowledge which can lead to peace, harmony and happiness.

The twentieth century has witnessed tremendous advances in science and technology. Immense avenues have opened up for material comforts and ease. Yet we find man's mind is not at ease. High tension is the hallmark of modern man.

As we stand at the threshold of the dawn of the twenty-first century, the stark reality is that humanity is facing a grave crisis. The deep erosion of moral values, the paradox of affluence and abject poverty coexisting, pervasive violence and crime, ethnic, racial and religious conflicts, and deep antagonism between man and man — all thwart the very existence of human civilization. We see conflicts everywhere — between individuals, families, communities and nations — and no one seems to be at peace.

Confronted with an almost similar situation about 26 centuries ago, Prince Siddhartha Gautama made a supreme effort, unparalleled in the annals of human history, in the quest for a solution to the all-pervading phenomenon of misery. In that process he rediscovered the ancient technique of *vipassana*, the most sublime and noblest heritage of India. Through its practice he eradicated all his defilements, achieved purity of mind, and became a *sammasambuddha*, a fully enlightened one. Then with love and compassion he started distributing the technique to suffering humanity.

Millions of people in India benefited from this technique. The benevolent message of *vipassana* went beyond the shores of India and made a deep impact in neighbouring countries. The great emperor Ashoka used this technique as the principal instrument of his public policy in the governance of his vast empire, as his rock edicts clearly amplify. India achieved a high degree of progress in all spheres of life, material and spiritual, and was hailed as the 'world teacher'. Indeed, the contribution of India to the cause of peace, harmony and good order was profound.

About 500 years after Buddha passed away, the technique of *vipassana* was lost in India. But fortunately it was preserved in its pristine purity in Myanmar by a chain of teachers. Sayagyi U Ba Khin, my distinguished teacher and a renowned exponent of *vipassana*, has the desire that the jewel of *vipassana* should go back to India, the country of its origin, and spread to the whole world for the peace, good and happiness of suffering humanity. *Vipassana* has thus come to India. With this brief historical background let us understand what *vipassana* is.

At this stage let us be clear that in our quest for peace and harmony in society, the individual is the key. Man matters most. For society to change for the better the individual has to change. When the entire forest has withered, each tree has to be nurtured — its roots cleared of disease and then watered. Then the entire forest will bloom again. Similarly, for the betterment of society each individual has to improve.

Now, let us reflect. What is the cause of the lack of peace and harmony in the individual, and therefore of peace and harmony in society? If one investigates the problem, it becomes clear that whenever one starts generating any negativity or defilement in the mind, one is bound to be agitated. A negativity in the mind, a mental defilement or impurity, cannot coexist with peace and harmony.

How does one start generating negativity? Unwanted things happen and create tension. Wanted things do not happen, or obstacles come in the way, and one generates tension. One keeps on tying knots, Gordian knots, and makes the entire mental and physical structure tense and full of negativity. Life becomes miserable.

One way to get rid of negativity and achieve peace and harmony is to divert one's attention to any object of sensual pleasure. But this gives only temporary relief as the peace one experiences is limited to the surface level of the mind. The behaviour pattern of the mind at the root level does not change.

Therefore the great explorer of inner truth went still further in his search. By experiencing the reality of mind and matter within himself, he recognized that diverting one's attention is only running away from the problem. Escape is no solution. One must face the problem. Just observe the negativity that has arisen and it will be eradicated.

But it is difficult, nearly impossible, for a common person to observe abstract negativity and get rid of it. Hence one who reached the ultimate truth found a real solution for everyone. He discovered that whenever any defilement arises in the mind, two things start happening at the physical level. One is that the breath loses its normal rhythm — one starts breathing slightly harder at the gross physical level, and at a subtler level some kind of biochemical reaction starts within the body manifesting as some sensation. Every defilement generates a sensation of one kind or another in some part of the body.

This mental-physical phenomenon is like a coin with two sides. On one side is whatever thought or emotion that arises in the mind, and on the other side are respiration and sensations in the body. Any thought or emotion, conscious or unconscious, and any mental defilement, manifests itself in the breath and bodily sensations of that moment. Although it is difficult to observe abstract negativity, one can easily learn how to observe breath and sensations. Thus by objective observation of these corporeal phenomena one is observing mental defilement. Instead of running away from the problem one is facing reality as it is. One soon finds that the defilement loses its strength, it can no longer overpower as it did in the past. If one continues the practice, the defilement eventually disappears altogether. One becomes peaceful and happy. This peace is not temporary, because with repeated practice one is able to change the habit pattern of the mind at the deepest level and thus get liberated from the misery experienced due to negativities.

When one reaches this stage, the entire pattern of one's life starts changing. It is no longer possible for one to do anything vocally or physically which will disturb the peace and happiness of others. One realizes that the entire cause of misery lies inside. Similarly the entire cause of happiness also lies inside, not outside. Just as man matters most in the quest for peace in society, similarly the mind matters most in the quest for peace in the individual. The root of every unwholesome action, vocal or physical, is the mind. One cannot kill unless one generates anger, hatred, ill-will or animosity. One cannot steal unless one generates greed. Sexual misconduct is impossible unless one generates passion.

Before one harms others, one actually harms oneself. As soon as one generates negativity in the mind, one becomes miserable. One becomes the first victim of one's own negativity. The law of nature is such that one is punished, there and then. It takes time for the laws of government to ensure that one is punished for a crime, but the law of nature does not wait.

A negative mind not only becomes agitated and miserable in itself, it causes misery for others. The atmosphere surrounding such a person will be permeated with agitation and tension and this will start affecting others. Similarly a balanced mind not only becomes peaceful in itself but helps others also to become peaceful. The atmosphere surrounding such a person will be permeated with peace and harmony and this will start affecting others too. It is this experiential understanding that will lead to improvement at the level of the individual and consequently at the level of society.

This is what Buddha taught, an art of living. He taught the technique of *vipassana* to observe nature as it is by observing the realities inside. Out of ignorance one keeps reacting in a way which is harmful to oneself and harmful to others. When one ceases to react blindly, then one is capable of real action which is always positive, creative, helpful to oneself and helpful to others.

By this technique of self-observation, introspection, one learns to stop reacting blindly, to stop creating defilements. Naturally, old defilements are gradually eradicated. One comes out of all miseries and experiences lasting happiness.

To learn this technique one has to join a residential retreat of ten days. There are three steps to the training. The first prerequisite is that one has to observe five precepts. One has to abstain from killing, stealing, sexual activity, telling lies and taking intoxicants.

Observing these precepts, one is in a position to explore the truth as it is within the framework of one's own body. Sitting down with eyes closed, the aspirant directs his attention within the framework of the body and observes the natural breath as it comes in and goes out. One does not regulate the breath, it is not a breathing exercise or *pranayama*: one just remains aware of the flow of the natural breath. If it is deep, one is aware that it is deep; if it is shallow one is just aware that it is shallow. Mere observation, bare observation, without any reaction, without giving any valuation. The technique is to observe the reality manifesting itself from moment to moment without any reaction.

A wonderful beginning is made. One has started observing the truth pertaining to oneself — the truth of the functioning of mind-matter phenomena. With one's own experience one will find that as and when a defilement arises in the mind — anger, hatred, passion, fear — the breath loses its normality. It becomes hard, fast. And when that particular defilement has passed away the breath will again become normal. So breath is strongly related to one's mind and mental defilements.

The practice doesn't involve any blind faith or sectarian philosophical dogma. There is no verbalization in this technique, no visualization, no imagination. One is working with reality; one is exploring the truth that one experiences. Practising thus, one sees that the mind is calming down, getting a little concentrated. It is quite true that by using words or by imagining a shape or form along with the awareness of respiration, it becomes easy for the mind to get concentrated. But the final goal of this technique is not mere concentration but actually the purification of the mind. The mind may become fully concentrated on craving, aversion, illusion or delusion. But the aim of *vipassana* is to make it free from all of these.

Observing moral precepts and achieving a modicum of control over the ever-fleeting mind are the first two stages of training. The student of *vipassana* then embarks on the third stage, deeper investigation of mind-matter phenomena.

Focusing on a small triangular area with the base at the upper lip and covering the area of the nostrils, the mind becomes more sensitive and subtler realities start manifesting themselves. One starts feeling different types of sensations. They may be sensations of heat or cold or perspiration, they may be throbbing, pulsating, vibrating, or tingling, they may be sensations of expansion, contraction, or maybe dryness. One has not to look for a particular sensation. It is a choiceless observation. Let nature play its role, one has just to observe.

As the practice develops the student starts scanning the entire body from head to feet and from feet to head, surveying each and every part of the body, each and every particle of the body. One finds that there are sensations everywhere — some biochemical reaction or the other, some electromagnetic reaction or the other — every moment on every little part of the body. One starts experiencing it, and the technique is just to observe, never to react. Awareness and equanimity are the crux of the practice. So for the rest of the ten-day period the student trains himself to observe sensations objectively.

What does one attain by this? How is it beneficial? One starts exploring the truth pertaining to oneself by direct experience. One starts realizing the truth about the working of mind-matter phenomena: how mind and matter interact and influence each other. How mental impurities are generated, resulting in misery, and how they can be eradicated. The meditator realizes that as respiration and mental impurities are strongly related, similarly bodily sensations and mental defilements are strongly related. The so-called unconscious or subconscious mind remains in contact with the body sensations day and night. The unconscious mind reacts whenever there is any sensation in the body, pleasant or unpleasant. If it is pleasant it reacts with craving and a clinging *raga*. If it is unpleasant it reacts with aversion, *dvesha*. It has become a prisoner of this habit pattern.

One has to go the depth of the mind, the so-called unconscious mind. In the language of India of those days, it was called *alaya chitta*, the storehouse of the mind. All our mental complexes, conditioning, and behaviour patterns are stored there. They keep on flowing with the flow of the mind, and from time to time they come to the surface and overpower us. The impurities, the defilements, the negativities stored there were called, in the language of those days, *anusaya kilesa*, latent impurities like sleeping volcanoes. At any moment they can explode and overpower. So long as one harbours these impurities one is not free from misery. One has to train the deepest level of the mind not to react with craving or aversion in spite of feeling pleasant or unpleasant sensations. The barrier between the conscious and unconscious minds is broken by *vipassana*, by this technique of observation.

As one starts observing the reality pertaining to matter and to the mind, it becomes very clear that whatever arises, arises just to pass away. One observes that a sensation which has arisen, whether pleasant or unpleasant, will sooner or later pass away. Ignorantly one keeps on calling one's physical structure 'I', 'mine', and develops so much attachment towards it that it becomes a real bondage. If it is indeed 'mine' then one should have control over it. But one has no control. Things just happen, due to the universal law of cause and effect. What is this physical structure, after all? It is nothing but a mass of subatomic particles. By experience one finds that the entire physical structure is nothing but tiny little particles, tiny little wavelets, arising and passing with great rapidity.

So also mental structure, which is nothing but wavelets arising and passing, constantly changing. This is what the Enlightened One found — that the entire physical structure, the mental structure, and the combination of the two is nothing but vibrations. *Sabbo loko pakampito*: The entire universe is vibrating.

At the experiential level, when we start understanding the law of nature, we realize that the moment we generate any negativity there is an unpleasant vibration which makes us unhappy and agitated.

Outside objects are not the real cause of suffering — they are only apparent causes. Whatever we experience in life is encountered through our six sense doors. When the six sense doors come in contact with their respective sense objects — vision with the eyes; sound with the ears; smell with the nose; taste with the tongue; something tangible with the body; or a thought with the mind — a sensation immediately starts in the body, either pleasant or unpleasant, according to the evaluation we have given to the objects outside.

If the sensation is pleasant we start reacting with craving and become miserable. If the sensation is unpleasant we start reacting with aversion and become miserable. This is what the words of the Enlightened One refer to *Vedana pacchaya tanha*: with the base of sensation, craving and aversion arise. The missing link that was discovered by the Buddha is *vedana*, the sensation in the body. If one is ignorant of this, one directs all efforts to rectify things outside. One does not rectify things inside, where the root cause of the misery lies.

With the practice of *vipassana* one understands the interaction of mind and matter within oneself. One realizes the whole process of the arising of misery and the eradication of misery at the experiential level. It is so scientific. Whenever any negativity arises in the mind there starts a secretion of an unpleasant flow of biochemical substances in the blood vessels. This helps to increase the negativity, which in turn increases the flow of biochemicals. Thus the vicious circle continues to multiply the misery. In the ancient language of India this flow of unpleasant biochemicals was called *asava* or *asrava*. Buddha found the technique of *vipassana*, through which one can become *anasavo* or *anasrava* — that is, free from the misery of this biochemical flow of negativity.

Vipassana is a technique of truth realization, of self-purification through self-observation. By practising *vipassana* one eradicates defilements from the deepest level of the mind. The mind becomes pure, full of infinite love, infinite compassion, infinite sympathetic joy, infinite equanimity. These are the basic characteristics of a pure mind, and all actions which emanate from a pure mind are full of peace, harmony and goodwill.

Dhamma, or *dharma*, means truth, the law of nature. *Vipassana* helps one to realize this universal law of nature and get tuned to it. This is how one learns to live peacefully and harmoniously. Each and every member of human society can practise *vipassana* and get the same benefits. The technique is universal and non-sectarian. One may be from any religion or any country, it makes no difference. The human mind is the human mind. *Vipassana* can become an instrument in generating human values and integrating human society by eliminating all racial, ethnic and communal conflicts and other disintegrating factors.

People from every caste, community, religion, and background are taking part in *vipassana* courses. There are even courses for children. And courses are being organized for prison inmates and members of staff in several states, including Tihar Central Jail in the capital city of India. The impact has been profound. Within the prisons, hardened criminals, drug addicts and habitual offenders are coming out with deep remorse and a resolve to change their habits and lead healthy, peaceful, harmonious lives.

Furthermore, leaders of various religious systems and social groups — monks and nuns, *munis*, *sadhvis*, *sannyasis* and *yogis*, Christian priests and nuns — are joining in large numbers. And senior government officials, members of public and private sector organizations and institutions of higher learning are taking advantage of the technique as an effective instrument of education and reform.

In view of the magnitude of the problems that human society is confronting today, a very small beginning has been made. *Vipassana* beckons to all those who are dedicated to the noble pursuit of peace, harmony and human welfare. Let them try this wonderful technique of human development.

May you enjoy peace, may you enjoy harmony, may you enjoy happiness.

12

Buddhist Doctrine and the Culture of Peace

Pataraporn Sirikanchana

PEACE is the essential teaching of Buddhism. As the means of practice, peace cultivated in a person's mind is a source of an act of peace and a moral deed. Only a peaceful mind can originate a peaceful act. Many passages of the Buddhist teachings encourage a person to keep his/her mind in peace and demand peace from others. A passage here may illustrate the point:

All men tremble at punishment,
all men fear death;
remembering that thou art like unto them,
do not strike or slay.

He who, seeking his own happiness,
does not injure or kill beings
who also long for happiness,
will find happiness after death.
All phenomena (originating from a sentient being)
— *dhamma* — are preceded by (the activity of) the mind,
have as their chief agent the mind;
and are made up of the mind.
If one were to speak or act
with a pure mind,
happiness follows one as a consequence,
even as the shadow that never leaves one.

The Dhammapada

Like Mahatma Gandhi's *ahimsa*, the Buddhist loving-kindness (*metta*) and altruistic practices should be cultivated internally. It is not proved to exist by means of a helpful act, white or yellow clothing, a smiling face, and so on. It is essentially the sincerity and purity of a person's heart. It cannot exist without a peaceful mind.

A peaceful mind yields wisdom and all virtues. Thus, in Buddhism, meditation is a crucial means to attain a peaceful mind. The principle of meditation is the training of mindfulness. Whenever we pay attention to our own thoughts, words, and deeds, we are conscious of ourselves and are aware of our movements. Being aware of our own selves, we feel ashamed of doing evil and thus do not let ourselves go wrong.

There are many places in Thailand which offer free courses in meditation to Thais and foreigners. For example, the meditation teaching at the Non Pah Pong Monastery and meditation lectures and training at the World Meditation of Buddhists headquarters are well known to a considerable number of meditators.

In the view of Ajahn Chah, the former abbot of the Non Pah Pong Monastery, meditation practices are the cultivation of mindfulness and insight. First, we must find a meditation subject which is suitable to our particular tendencies, a way of practice which is right for our character. For example, going over and over the parts of the body: hair of the head, of the body, nails, teeth, and skin, can be very calming. The mind can become very peaceful from this practice. If contemplating these five things leads to calm, it is because they are appropriate objects for contemplation according to our tendencies. Whatever we find to be appropriate in this way, we can consider to be our practice and use it to subdue defilements.

If such practice does not work, we may try again with another meditation subject, e.g. the recollection of death. For those who still have strong greed, aversion, and delusion, it is useful to take this subject of personal death for meditation. We shall see that everybody must die some day. Developing this practice, we find that an attitude of dispassion arises. The more we practise, the more we find peace. This is because it is a suitable and appropriate practice for us.

According to the Buddhist Scriptures, the *tipitaka*, the Buddha searched for peace and enlightenment in the forest. Thus, it is a tradition and preference for monks to go to the forest and live in solitude. There they practise meditation and find peace in their ascetic lives. In addition, the Buddhist discipline prescribes that monks should live not too close to and not too far from a village so that they can live a peaceful life, find some food, and preach the doctrine to lay people.

Since, in Buddhism, the meditation subject can be anything suitable for each meditator, the meditation practice is beneficial to all, even to non-Buddhists. It is the universal way of peace. Christians may concentrate on Jesus as their meditation subject. Hindus may meditate on Shiva or Vishnu and Muslims on Allah. If all human beings practise meditation everyday, the world will be free from wars.

Apart from being the means of practice, peace is also the goal and the ideal of Buddhist life. The final goal of Buddhist moral practices is the attainment of peace both worldly and other-worldly. The goal of the monastic life is *nibbana* or the ultimate peace as follows:

> The bhikkhu (monk) who lives in loving-kindness,
> and is pleased in the Buddha's teaching,
> attains the peaceful state (*nibbana*),
> which is happiness at the allaying of conditioned things.
>
> *The Dhammapada*

> And the goal of everyone, monks and laity, in this world is *nibbana*.
> Those whose minds are rightly trained in the factors of enlightenment, and
> who changing to nothing,
> and delighting in such dissociation,
> they — the resplendent ones — attain *nibbana* even in this world.
>
> *The Dhammapada*

In order to form the habit of peace offering, Buddhists are taught to diffuse loving-kindness to all beings as often as they can everyday. For example, before they go to bed at night, Buddhists recite the verse from the Buddhist Scriptures as follows:

> Let creatures all, all things that live,
> All beings of whatever kind,
> See nothing that will bode them ill!
> May naught of evil come to them!
>
> *The Culla-Vagga*

Having the habit of peace offering, one's mind always rests in peaceful happiness and in peace with others. Buddhists who reject peace and do not try to live in peace with others are wayward followers of the Buddha and can hardly be called Buddhists.

Buddhadasa-bhikkhu (1906-93), an eminent monk of Thailand, once gave a lecture on the subject 'Till the World Is With Peace'[1] asserting that peace should be fulfilled through qualified peace-makers as follows:

1. Peace-makers should be well educated and moral people. Education here aims at

spiritual growth and moral wisdom. On the contrary, education today emphasizes only academic knowledge, intellectual capacities, and technology. Thus, it rouses desire and selfishness and ignores the religious truth guiding human beings to right thought and right conduct. Ideally and properly, education should cultivate our basic human-ness in order to make humankind righteous and peaceful.

2. Peace-makers should be physically, mentally and spiritually healthy. In order to be healthy physically, one should be free from all excessive enjoyments and indulgence. To be healthy mentally is to be free from all defilements and fetters. To be healthy spiritually is to be free from false conceptions and blind faith. The unhealthy are those who are slaves to their own selfishness, defilements, worldly enjoyments and other trivialities of worldly life. They disregard and dislike the Buddhist doctrine. They cannot form a good society. Indeed, only healthy social members can establish a peaceful society.

3. Peace-makers should come from righteous and peaceful families. Righteous and peaceful families know their duties and obligations to others. They act according to the Buddhist doctrine. Those who come from righteous and peaceful families are responsible social members. For example, if they are the superiors, they will treat inferiors with compassion; if they are children, they will respect and care for their parents. They can always secure peace in their society.

4. Peace-makers should live according to a *dhammic* economic plan that is moderate in living, in spending and in possessing, being neither too poor nor too rich. If we live moderately, we shall feel content with ourselves. We shall not struggle for anything more than we need to survive. If we are too poor and our morality is not strong enough, we may be trapped into misconduct and be harmful to ourselves and others in order to survive, e.g. stealing or even killing others for some money. On the other hand, if we are too rich, we many be indulgent and careless about others. In Thailand today, rich people are generally extravagant. The word *sresthi* in Thai means the rich. In Pali and Sanskrit, it originally and literally means the *noblest.* At the time of the Buddha, the Buddhist rich people were philanthropic and righteous. They built alms-houses to serve the poor, ascetics and all in need. Peace-makers should adopt the spirit and practices of the rich in the Buddha's time so that all members of society can live happily and peacefully together.

5. Peace-makers should know and practise the *dhamma*, the life duty of all human beings. Such duty demands all human beings to work and live for the sake of all beings and in accordance with the law of nature. In order to fulfil one's duty, one needs to get rid of one's selfishness and cultivate concern and responsibility for

the sake of the world.

6. Peace-makers should be unselfish and altruistic, realizing that all people are companions in the process of birth, old age, sickness, and death. They should try to cooperate with others in order to establish a peaceful and loving society.

7. Peace-makers should be moral in thoughts, words, and actions. Morality keeps the world in balance and equilibrium. Those who think, speak or act morally always keep themselves to this normative balance leading to peace and happiness of others. On the other hand, those who act against this equilibrium create disturbances. Thus, morality is indispensable for the realization of peace on earth.

8. Peace-makers should have the right view (*samma-ditthi*). The right view is the knowledge of morality in the fundamental sense. One cannot conduct oneself morally unless one understands the real meaning and value of morality. The right view is the only means to free oneself from all suffering and is crucial for overcoming one's selfishness. It gives us the true knowledge of the world and thus asserts the necessity of world peace.

9. Peace-makers should have a 'cooled' life. Whenever all defilements are eliminated from our minds, our lives are 'cooled down' (*nibbana*). *Nibbana*, which can be experienced in this life, is generally understood as two stages of a peaceful life, ordinary and ultimate. The ordinary or worldly stage is the peaceful lives of ordinary people. The ultimate stage is absolute freedom from all pains and is exclusively experienced by holy people or the enlightened ones. If all people had 'cooled' lives, the world would certainly be in peace.

Apart from meditation and moral cultivation, peace can be attained through all religious arts, e.g. paintings, sculptures, images, and so on. In Thailand, Buddha images are intentionally made to inspire peace in the hearts of all who see them. The smiling face of a Buddha image and his eyes gazing downward seem to invite all sufferers to come and take merciful guidance from him. Entering the consecrated assembly hall of a Thai Buddhist temple, one finds the Buddha image presiding at the end of the hall. Looking around, one can see murals depicting the history of the Buddha's life showing his moral activities and compassion for all beings. Going to a temple for an appreciation of religious arts is thus a way to create peace in one's heart.

Besides, all Buddhist temples are sanctuaries. They are places of peace and protection of all lives. Formerly, those who had a death sentence and could escape to a temple and be ordained as monks were forgiven and freed. Nowadays, all kinds of people love to free animals, such as dogs, cats, birds and small turtles in a temple or a monastery compound. They know that the animals will be safe there since it is a Buddhist tradition not to harm any being in a temple.

It is important to call for peace education. All institutions should teach people to love peace. A proper educational system should be established to promote humaneness and moral wisdom. Since the word *manussa* (human being) in its original sense means 'one of noble heart', the right educational system should endow students with noble hearts and make them complete human beings. Once people become human beings, peace can be restored to the entire world.

Reference

1. Translated by Pataraporn Sirikanchana in Donald K.Swearer, ed., *Me and Mine*, New York: State University of New York, 1989.

13

Buddhism as a Contribution to Peace in Vietnam

Cao xuan Pho

I. The Concept of Peace

In Vietnam since early times, peace has been largely conceived of as peace in one's mind, peace towards one's fellows, and peace with nature. Those aspects of peace are greatly influenced by Buddhism. Each social stratum has its own approach to the serenity of mind through Buddhism. The intelligentsia practised Zen (*dhyana*) firstly through Zen masters coming from India[1] and later from China[2] to ultimately establish their own Zen sect in the thirteenth century called the *Thien Truc Lam* (Bamboo Forest Zen Sect).[3] They abided by the teachings of Buddha:

> Those who practise meditation steadfastly,
> Always strong in determination and perseverance,
> The wise ones enjoy *nibbana*,
> Safe from any bondage, the highest
>
> *Dhammapada*, 23[4]

or

> . . . He does not cleave to sense-desires,
> Cool he is, and without germs to a new life,
> All clinging are cut down,
> Pains in the heart are overcome,
> Serene and calm, he leads a life of happiness,
> And his mind has attained peace and calmness
>
> *Samyutta Nikaya*, I, 263[5]

Learned Buddhist scholars enjoyed great influence on the daily life of the common people. Through them the commoners could have an understanding of the gist of Buddha's teachings on His attitude towards other religions and antagonistic doctrines, His love and compassion for the world, and on fundamental topics of daily life such as dispute and harmony, anger and gentleness, harmfulness and harmlessness, hatred and friendliness, killing and respect for life, etc. Among many teachings they were most impressed by such words as:

> One should take oneself as one's own refuge,
> Because there is no other refuge,
> By a self well tamed and restrained,
> One obtains a refuge that is very difficult to obtain
>
> *Dhammapada*, 160[6]

or

> By oneself, evil deed is done,
> By oneself, one is defiled,
> By oneself, evil deed is not done,
> By oneself, one becomes purified.
> Purity and impurity are done by oneself,
> No one can purify another
>
> *Dhammapada*, 165[7]

They were fully aware of the value of self-reliance on the way of deliverance to obtain fundamental peace, that in one's mind. They had an insight into the expression of Buddhism, that to be born as human is the most advantageous status for every living being, as it is only he who may realize the Four Holy Truths and practise the Eightfold Holy Path to deliverance. It is the human, rather than any deity or other supra-human force, who determines his own happiness, his own destiny. They understood the statement by Buddha: 'Over is Sky, under is Earth, only the Self is exclusive.'

Peace in one's mind lays the foundations of peace in the community and the world, as was expounded by Buddha:

> Oh Bhikkhu, you should go forth for the welfare of the many, for the happiness of the many, out of compassion for the world, for the advantage, for the welfare, for the happiness of the deities and human beings. . . . Oh Bhikkhu, teach the *Dhamma*, that is good at the beginning, good in the middle, good at the end, with meaning and with form. Reveal the holy life that is completely and entirely pure. *Samyutta*, I, 128[8]

That is the work to be done by the Samgha. As for common people, they try their best to exercise the Four Cardinal Virtues put forth by Buddhism to maintain and expand harmony and peace in their community. These are loving-kindness (*metta*); compassion (*karuna*); happiness (*piti*); sacrifice (*upekkha*) under the disinterested and altruistic spirit. People understand *metta* as bringing happiness and tranquillity to others; *karuna* as relieving suffering and danger to others; *piti* as being happy with the achievements — material and mental — of others; *upekkha* as being ready to give up personal belongings, including body, wealth and happiness for the benefit of others; disinterested as acting fairly, not being influenced by personal advantage; and altruistic as being forgiving towards those who sincerely show repentance after having been led astray.

These virtues have had a strong impact on the minds of the Vietnamese people and together with Confucianism have shaped their behaviour. If Buddhism provided the Vietnamese people with a good-natured *heart*, Confucianism provided them with *wisdom* translated into the sense of order, discipline and responsibility. Two major contributions of Confucianism to traditional Vietnamese society are the materialization and institutionalization of benevolence as advocated by Buddhism into regulations and laws; and defining the responsibility and duty of each individual towards himself and the community in which he is living, including family, village, and the country, out of the concept of the Five Constant Virtues (*Ngu Thuong*). They are humanity (*Nhan*), righteousness (*Nghia*), rites (*Le*), wisdom (*Tri*), and trust (*Tin*); the first three have been set great store by.

Humanity is conceived of as benevolence and charity. Righteousness means that speaking and acting should be in accordance with the conscience, in line with the right way. He who can respond to these two criteria is worthy of being human. It was written in the Book of Changes: 'Yin and Yang are the principle of Sky, Rigid (Hard) and Flexible (Soft) are the principles of Earth, Humanity and Righteousness are the principles of Humanity.' Rites are regulations, discipline, order in society and respect towards these institutions. Rites were set up to ensure the maintenance of Humanity and Righteousness. Obviously, these five Confucian virtues complement the four Buddhist virtues for the peaceful behaviour of the Vietnamese people, especially the sense of tolerance and benevolence towards their fellows. Buddhism and Confucianism constituted the basis of Vietnamese people's individual and social behaviour in every circumstance, especially in peace-making and peace-keeping.

II. Buddhist Experience

The Buddhist contribution to peace in Vietnam could be seen through various aspects prevailing in four major instances:

1. In times when people suffered the atrocities of foreign domination, aggression and wars. At those junctures, Buddhism was closely connected with national independence, which was considered indispensable to a socio-political environment for peace. Without national independence there is neither freedom nor happiness, which are seen as two major factors of the peaceful life. Buddhism then came up as a mental support to the striving for peace of the Vietnamese people. It served as a means for rallying people against the tyranny of oppressors by its basic tenets of democracy, self-reliance and self-deliverance as happened in the sixth century when an insurrection against Chinese domination burst forth under the leadership of a leader who named himself Ly Phat Tu (Ly the son of Buddha) versus Thien Tu (son of Heaven), the appellation of the Emperor of China.

   In and after resistance wars against aggressors, the typical Buddhist sense of humanism and forgiveness has been extended to war prisoners. They were treated with humanity, as was shown during the wars against the French colonialists and the American imperialists in the second half of this century. They were provided with food and means of transport to return home, as were Chinese war prisoners in the fifteenth century.[9] The Vietnamese people considered them victims and dupes of their ruling circles; and such an act was just aiming at maintaining peace between nations.

2. In times when people could live in peace to rebuild their country after disastrous wars, Buddhism served as a means for relieving people's sufferings caused by wars and natural calamities out of its spirit of mutual help, its sense of tolerance and benevolence. This tolerance policy prevailed in eleventh to early thirteenth centuries under the Ly dynasty, and was expressed through edicts of exemption from reducing taxes, declaring amnesty and reduction of sentences. A very compassionate word of Emperor Ly Thanh Tong (eleventh century) has been recorded in the Annals: 'My affection for my daughter [princess] is the same as for the common people to whom I assume the role of parents. They are guilty due to their lack of knowledge. I am full of pity for them. From now on, howsoever serious or light a guilt may be, the sentence should be reduced.'[10]

   It was by practising the benevolence policy that the Tran Dynasty (thirteenth to fifteenth century) could raise the living standards of the people and ensure stability by defeating the Mongolian invaders. Especially in the era of the Democratic Republic, such great events as the Dien Bien Phu victory (1954) or National Reunification (1975) could have not happened if the people could not exercise their freedom, democracy, equality in specific conditions of war under a national spirit imbued with the Buddhist sense of self-reliance and benevolence.

3. Nowadays Vietnam is practising renovation and developing the market economy in the situation of peace and stability inside the country and the boom of the information revolution over the world. Stability is the basic condition for healthy and sustainable development. Social stability requires, first, the stability in each person, or in other words the peace in one's mind. The Vietnamese people always keep cheerfully in mind the philosophy: keeping still to cope with changes. *Still* does not mean motionless, immobile or frozen, but rather a state of equilibrium and harmony. Equilibrium implies inner motion of each element sharing the structure. And the harmony of something is the way in which the parts of it are combined into a suitable and desirable arrangement. Equilibrium and harmony bring about force, just as the practising of Buddha's teachings gives us peace in our minds.

   By the practice of this philosophy the Vietnamese people could overcome many historical vicissitudes. Now, in the market economy, there are many negative aspects, especially the 'superstition' of money and supra-consumerism, and the endangering of Vietnamese ethical values. The question is how to combat them successfully. Administrative measures to tackle this problem are necessary but not radical. That requires rather the enhancement of the spiritual life, or in other words equilibrium between material and spiritual life. At this juncture Buddhism, combined with Confucianism, is playing a significant role in Vietnam. Buddhism in fact does not deny the material life, rather it preaches the ethical and spiritual life by encouraging good deeds and shunning evil actions which are deeply rooted in the selfish cravings of human beings. It is indeed somewhat unrealistic to destroy thoroughly the selfish craving in human behaviour. It would be better to tame and restrain it, first in oneself, and further to behave as such towards others as is taught by Buddha:

   > You should do to yourself
   > What you have instructed others to do.
   > Well tamed yourself, you should tame others.
   > Truly difficult indeed, is self tamed.
   >
   > *Dhammapada*, 159[11]

   or

   > Thinking of his own benefits, he does harm to others.
   > When other do harm to him in return,

Being harmed, he harms others.
Such is what the fool thinks,
When his wicked actions do not mature.

Samyutta Nikaya, 103[12]

Vietnam is a latecomer on the way of industrialization and modernization. However, this could be advantageous as the country could draw experience from the success as well as failure of other more advanced countries in the reducing of negative aspects of the market economy. The most appropriate approach should be relying on traditional culture, in which ethical values of religion are salient features. In the case of Vietnam, these are Buddhistic combined with Confucian ones. Actually, there is a Government Committee for Religious Affairs to regulate the activities of various religions for the benefit of the many; an Institute for Buddhist Study, in the framework of the Vietnam Buddhist Congregation with its various periodicals to deepen Buddhist knowledge and popularize Buddha's teachings, especially on ethical values and peace. Noteworthy are a good many humanitarian societies operating in the Buddhist spirit of benevolence and under the motto 'untorn leaves protect and help torn leaves', aiming at relieving the pain and suffering of the disadvantaged. Many central and local funds initiated by Buddhist monks and named 'funds for eradicating starvation and reducing poverty' were raised and responded to warmly by people from various social strata. Now Buddhist monks and laymen are among the most fervent humanitarian activists.

4. In foreign relations. In the course of history Vietnam has had two aspects of foreign relations: peaceful and conflicting. In these two, Buddhism had made contributions to positive solutions. No great matter is to be commented on the first issue, as Buddhism is a champion of peace — peace in one's mind and peace among humankind. As far as conflict is concerned, some remarks need to be made in this context as it is related to peace.

   Among the commandments of Buddhism, the first deals with non-killing. That is to ensure peace and harmony between humans. Non-killing is the antagonist of killing. As the act of killing, like every act of a human, is generated from the mind, the question is how to generate a good thought rather than an evil one in one's mind. That could be achieved through Right Meditation, one stage in the Eightfold Path. So, an act could be asserted as good or evil only when it is considered from its motivation. There is no room here for the concept of 'the end justifies the means'. An act is good if it is done for the benefit of others or to help others. On the other hand, Buddhism preaches that the origin of evil acts lies in one's selfish craving.

That is the concept of peace and war of the Vietnamese people. They had to face repeated invasions by enemy forces. They had to safeguard their Fatherland by every means available, including killing aggressors, for the sake of peace for their country and their fellows. While practising Buddhism, the Vietnamese leaders and people had to undertake resistance wars to fight against aggressors, wars waged by those people excited by so much selfish craving. And, as always, after such wars, wherein they always came out victorious, the Vietnamese leaders resumed their policy of good relations with those states who were once invaders. Even some of them, such as Emperor Ly Thai Tong (eleventh century), Emperors Tran Thai Tong and Tran Nhan Tong (thirteenth century), had cast off their monastic dress to put on armour and lead the whole people to defeat the Chinese and Mongolian invaders. Especially Emperor Tran Nhan Tong, after his sound victory over the Mongolian troops, re-took his monastic dress and went into the forest to found the national Buddhist Sect of Zen, the Truc Lam (Bamboo Forest) Zen Sect. Deeply imbued with the sense of Buddhist benevolence and tolerance, the vast majority of Vietnamese always support the state policy of good relations with foreign countries. Nobody other than the Viet people, who suffered great hardships caused by wars, eagerly wish for peace and stability of society and peace and good relations with other countries in order to improve their living standards, their quality of life.

Conclusion

Buddhism in Vietnam is becoming a factor in traditional and national culture. It is so combined with Confucianism that it is hard to define it explicitly. Buddhism is so closely connected with national consciousness that one cannot understand it thoroughly unless it is seen in the context of national history. It has made significant contributions to the maintaining and preserving of peace and stability for Vietnamese society during periods of peace as well as war. Now, when Vietnam is practising renovation and the market economy and the open-door policy, Buddhism is proving indispensable, especially for the maintenance and improvement of ethical values of restraint and to reduce socially negative aspects. Its sense of benevolence and tolerance is of great support to peaceful coexistence and friendly relations between various countries.

References

1. The Indian monks Mahajivaka and Kalacharya(?) came to Giao Chau (Vietnam) between 168 and 189 AD. These two monks were quite popular among the local people

for their powers (*abinna*), especially the power of calling rain for peasants to cultivate their rice fields.

Another monk, named K'ang-san-hui (transcripted from Chinese), originated from Sogdiane. His parents came to India, then settled in Giao Chau (third century AD), where the monk was born. He devoted himself to Buddhist studies and was strongly influenced by the Middle Discourse (*Madhyamikà*) of Nagarjuna. Noticeable among many *sutras* he had translated from Sanskrit to Chinese is the *Astasahasrika*, a discourse on the Madhyamika.

In 580, Vinitaruci, an Indian Zen master, came to Giao Chau and founded the first Zen sect in Vietnam, laying emphasis on meditation. This sect existed until the second decade of the thirteenth century. The most prominent representative is Tu Dao Hanh (?—1117).

2. Vo Ngon Thong (Enlightened without Speech), a Chinese Zen master, came to Vietnam in the early ninth century and founded the second Zen sect in Vietnam, influenced strongly by Chinese Zen, laying emphasis on sudden enlightenment. It lasted until the early thirteenth century.
3. Founded by King Tran Nhan Tong in the early thirteenth century, emphasizing *sunyata* and Absolute Truth in Heart. It is a mediator between Sudden Enlightenment and Gradual Enlightenment.
4. Quoted from Bhikkhu Thich Minh Chau, *Some Teachings of Lord Buddha on Peace, Harmony and Human Dignity*, Vietnam Buddhist Congregation, Ho Chi Minh City, 1984, p.154.
5. *Ibid.*, p.125.
6. *Ibid.*, p.166.
7. *Ibid.*, p.142.
8. *Ibid.*, p. 20.
9. *The Complete History of Dai Viet* (*Dai Viet Su Ky Toan Thu*), T.II. Social Sciences Publishing House, Hanoi, 1985, pp. 281-83. Before the ending of the resistance war against the Chinese expeditionary force in 1427, Emperor Le Thai To ordered governors of the provinces of Bac Giang and Lang Giang to repair bridges and roads, afford boats to those Chinese war prisoners and surrenders — about 30,000 persons — returning home. And right after the war, prisoners and surrenders were provided with 500 boats, 20,000 horses and sufficient food for their withdrawal.
10. *Ibid.*, T.I., p.165.
11. B. Thich Minh Chau, *Some Teachings . . .*, p.169.
12. *Ibid.*, p. 68.

14

Buddhism and Peace
A Personal View

Sirima K. Goonesinghe

IT gives me great pleasure to be able to address you as a simple Buddhist Mother, sharing some of my long years of experience. This, in fact, is the path shown to us by Lord Buddha. I am a happy, contended, humble person, unshaken by today's world of chaos, but certainly not unconcerned with it. The duration of my professional duties of 'giving vision' to people has added colour to my happiness and has enhanced it much. What is the secret of this achievement? It is the development of *metta*, loving-kindness to one and all, with great effort and determination. *Metta* is a friendly feeling of loving-kindness to all beings in every situation, regardless of race, creed or caste. It is love without desire to possess, embracing all beings, big or small, far or near.

As we are told in our Buddhist books, the development of the human personality should be based on four moral foundations:

(i) *Metta*, loving kindness; (ii) *Karuna*, compassion for all who suffer; (iii) *Muditha*, sympathetic joy. (To be happy in others' happiness, in their prosperity and success, thereby counteracting feelings of jealousy and unhealthy rivalry between individuals and groups.); and (iv) *Upekkha*, equanimity, the maintenance of a balanced mind when faced with the ups and downs inherent in life.

These moral qualities are known as *brahma-viharas*, the four sublime states. It is by cultivating these noble qualities and practising them that we will be able to maintain a healthy mind and a healthy body.

All these qualities convey a universal message. They give the most satisfactory way of living in harmony with one's fellow men and women, the path to true happiness, to everlasting world peace.

Here I must stress that one has to first practice and experience these moral values and create peace within. Only then can one radiate its effect in all ten directions of space to create the desired effect on others, to build the desired peace around the world.

In my own life this kind of moral cultivation started at home, in my childhood, guided by my parents and elders. I can remember we were trained to practise five precepts. These are to refrain from killing, stealing, lying, sexual misconduct and the use of intoxicants, and it is these precepts that formed the foundation stones for the development of true loving-kindness later in my life.

There is no particular time in life at which one must practise these moral qualities. They must be continually practised at all stages of life as students, as family members and fellow members of the community at large. By regular meditation on loving-kindness one can successfully realize inner peace. This is an energy which can be radiated to the whole world.

I have tried in the recent past to promote the practice of meditation on loving-kindness in the community eye-care programme in villages schools and pre-schools and it has been a very successful effort.

This is my personal experience over the last 50 years, both as student and as a professional. I have experienced the happiness of promoting peace and goodwill among various communities at the grass-roots level. I was able to reach many levels of the community with my health care programmes in various parts of the world. This is where we have to plan to use our energies and abilities to create a peaceful atmosphere. I have worked as a consultant eye surgeon, as a volunteer worker in government and non-government organizations like the Sarvodaya, International Lions Clubs, Dharmavijaya Foundation, Eye Donation Society, women's and students' organizations in Sri Lanka and also in other underdeveloped countries. I was able to convey to the world at large the message of universal peace and universal benevolence.

Today most people are blind to the norms and value systems of their forefathers. In the Buddhist world, the value systems of our forefathers guided us to live a simple, happy and contended life, following the middle path in our day-to-day activities. Extremes are avoided. The ability to live in harmony with ourselves, with nature around us, and with all living beings amidst us is the very objective of that value system.

Let me quote the words of a great son of India, Shri Jawaharlal Nehru.

> If we follow the principles
> enunciated by the Buddha
> We will ultimately win
> peace and tranquillity for the world

If all of us gathered here today make a determined effort to develop *loving-kindness* and radiate it to the world, I am sure we can achieve our target to create a world of peace and harmony.

May all living beings be well and happy.

15

The Sufi Paradigm of Peace-Making

Mohammad Reza Rikhtehgaran

"يا أيّتها النّفس المطمئنّه ارجعی الیٰ ربکِ راضيةً مرضيّه
فَادخلی فی عبادی و ادخلی جنّتی"

"O soul at Peace, Come back unto thy Lord, well — pleased, well-pleasing! Enter thou, then, among My Servants! Yea enter thou My Heaven."

(Holy Quran, Chapter 89, Verses 27-30)

I

THERE are three stations of peace in Sufism and the traveller on the spiritual path enters one of these stations according to his spiritual state. Of course the dweller at a lower stage has no access to the upper stations, and due to differences in rank, a single criterion is not to be applied to the dwellers of each station.

These three stations consist of peace at the stage of *Islam* (submission, abandonment to the Divine will), peace at the stage of *Iman* (the Divine peace that enters the believer's heart), and peace at the stage of *Ihsan* (the Sanctifying Virtue through which the sovereignty of evil comes to an end).

Peace at the stage of *Islam* pertains to the corporeal and social aspects of human beings, whereas at the stage of *Iman* it pertains to the heart and the microcosm, and finally at the stage of *Ihsan* peace pertains to the Spirit and to the macrocosm.

II

The word 'peace' comes from the Latin *pax*, which is derived from *pak*, meaning 'fasten'. 'Fasten' itself goes back ultimately to the Germanic *fastuz*, which denotes 'firm' and from which came the English 'fast', signifying 'standing firm, firmly fixed, not easily moved'. In Latin *stabilis* is used to express 'standing firm'. So, as its root suggests, 'fasten' once meant 'to establish'. The notion of 'fastening' which underlies 'peace' is extended to the notions of 'stable' and 'stability' which are derived from the same Latin root: *stabilis*. Therefore peace means achieving a stable condition in which there are no elements causing instability.

Political peace is related to social stability. When a society reaches stability, it becomes fast and firm, free from violence and disharmony. In the religious context, however, peace signifies firmness in spiritual status and stability in the Right Path (*magham*). In Sufi terminology, *maqham* (spiritual station) denotes the inner permanent realization of a spiritual status.

A wayfarer reaches a certain station only when he is through with his spiritual journey on the path of *talveen* (a stage of capriciousness and constant shifting of states). Stations are innumerable and a wayfarer has to tread further towards higher stations closer to the ultimate goal beyond which there is no path. Such a traveller will not revert to former states in which confusions and disturbances are abundant.

Once fast and firm in a higher spiritual station, the wayfarer attains freedom from the harm and evils of the lower stations. Freedom is the essence of peace. That is why the German word for peace, *friede*, means the free, *das Frye*, and *fry* means preserved from harm and danger, preserved from something, safeguarded. To free really means to spare. The sparing itself consists not only in the fact that we do not harm the one whom we spare. Real sparing is something positive and takes place when we leave something beforehand in its own nature, when we return it specifically to its being, when we free it in the real sense of the word into a preserve of peace. To dwell, to be set at peace, means to remain at peace within the free, the preserve, the free sphere that safeguards each thing in its nature. The fundamental character of dwelling is this sparing and preserving.

The Arabic words for peace are *selm* and *salam*, both of which signify a positive connotation. *Selm* and *salam* are something to be realized inwardly. It is noteworthy that the Arabic word *salam* has been in general use as a greeting or salutation since the time of the Koran. One of its oldest chapters speaks of the descent of the Koran on 'the Night of Power' and concludes that 'it is peace until the rising of the dawn' (97:5). God calls men to the 'abode of peace (*dar-us-salam*), both in this life and in the next, (10:26). In the Holy Koran we read:

> O believers, enter the peace, all of you, and follow not the steps of Satan;
> He is a manifest foe to you (2:208).

This verse clearly indicates that peace is reserved for true believers, precluding ordinary people. Furthermore, we can infer that God's rules and instructions are feasible and practical. In other words, 'on no soul doth God place a burden greater than it can bear' (Holy Koran, 2:286). So peace and concordance, which culminate in physical and spiritual well-being, are accessible and possible to attain. The next implication of the verse is that God's command includes *all* believers, and thus within this category no soul shall be excluded from entering the peace. Another implication, of great importance, is the Koran's interpretation of the path alternative to the peace, i.e., anyone who does not enter the station of peace shall inevitably follow the Satanic path. Therefore, peace is to prevent the onslaught of the army of the Left Dimension of human existence, turning the face of the heart to the Right Dimension, the right path: righteousness.

According to the Sufis, the way to peace, or the path of righteousness, is an approach to the realm of the heart, cordiality, concordance: literally, a coming together of the hearts as one.

On the other hand, the Arabic word for heart is *qalb*. The root from which this word is derived has the sense of turning, revolving and inverting. The heart is called *qalb* because it has two faces, one turning towards spirituality and the other towards materiality. Thus, the human heart is constantly turning or vacillating between the two opposing poles.

Furthermore, heart is the realm of *iman*, achieved when the spiritual tie between the wayfarer and the guide is fastened. This stage is referred to in the Holy Koran as the Divine Peace (*sakeenah*), which dwells in a sanctuary or in the heart. The word *sakeenah* comes from the root *sakana*, comprising both 'immobility' (*sokun*) and 'habitation'. It is analogous to the Hebrew *shakhinah*, The Divine Glory which dwells in the Ark of Alliance. In the Holy Koran we read: '. . . It is He who sendeth down Divine Peace into the hearts of true believers. . . .'

Those whose hearts are enlightened by the Divine Peace are but a single soul. Their physical manifestations may seem diverse but in their origin they are united. This multitude of manifestations may be compared to the innumerable rays that different surfaces receive from a single source, i.e. the sun.

In each of these three stations, peace has its due manifestation: first, in the realm of exterior and social practice; and second, in the realm of interior and spiritual stations in which the wayfarer dwells.

Regarding the exterior and social aspects of peace, we read in the Holy Koarn:

> Obey God and the Apostle; happily so you will find mercy. And vie with one another, hastening to forgiveness from your lord, and to a garden whose breadth is as heavens and earth, prepared for the righteous. . . .

Those who:

> Restrain their anger and
> Forgive the offences of their fellow men; and
> God loves *Muhsieen* (dwellers of the station of *Ihsan*).
> (*Holy Koran*, Chapter 3, Verses 132-34)

According to the above verses the dwellers of the first stage have to 'restrain their anger'. Obviously in this station we are dealing with a social problem the solution of which is clear: if it happens that somebody utters blasphemy, the believer should pass over it peacefully and pay no heed to it. If his anger bursts into flames, he should keep himself away from violence, which is a kind of madness. He should suppress his anger and calm it down with the water of patience.

Anger is a natural psychological reaction in a social situation. One may therefore not object if a person feels insulted, but in spite of his wounded feelings he is expected to restrain his anger and behave peacefully. This is the duty of the dwellers of the first stage, who form the majority, and such rules are within their own power.

Forgiveness is a more dignified state in which the wayfarer resides beyond the realm of anger and hatred. He does not think of revenge and will not become violent, for he understands the ignorance behind all hostile acts. So he forgives passionately.

وفاکنیم و ملامت کشیم و خوش باشیم
که در طریقت ما کافریست رنجیدن

A wayfarer at the stage of *iman* (that is the second stage) cannot and shall not feel hatred. He is dwelling in a higher spiritual position, therefore reacting in the manner of an inferior stage would not be merely a fault but rather a sin. At this stage the wayfarer should try to forgive, as far as he can, for the Beloved loves forgiveness; besides, he himself expects forgiveness from the Beloved. Moreover, the believer should endeavour to attain such a station that he may regard the offences of both his enemy and friend as something coming from God for his own training, and may find that 'there is no power and no strength save in God' within his own being. He should be benevolent even to those who hurt him.

At the highest stage of the Divine Peace, the wayfarer achieves self-annihilation (*fana-fil-lah*). Then if he attains subsistence in God (*bagha-bil-lah*), he will enter the station of *ahsan*. The word *ihsan* is derived from the root *husn*, meaning 'goodness and beauty'. At this stage union with the Beloved and subsistence in God are achieved. This is the Divine Unity in which no duality exists. This is the vibrant peace of the essence, not the relative harmony among diverse substances. On this subject we have the following tradition (Hadith) from the Prophet: 'Thou dost adore God *as if* tradition (Hadith) from the Prophet. Thou dost adore God *as if* thou saw Him; if thou dost not see Him, however, He sees thee.' The qualifier *as if* signifies that the wayfarer at this stage cannot yet behold God, for he is still attached to materiality. Thus, in order to attain the Divine Vision (pertaining to the station of *ihsan*) he shall strive to cast off all selfishness and material attachments. It is advised by the masters that the wayfarer first undergo a phase of intense divine contemplation and meditation, and thence, hopefully, reach the station of Divine Vision unveiled.

One who attains to the stage of subsistence in God, himself becomes a manifestation of divine attributes. Having reached total extinction, he now achieves existence in the Reality of God. From then on it is not he who acts and talks, but God. At this station, the sovereignty of evil terminates—there is no conflict, no violence, no evil: nay, even no peace; for there is no one to be at peace. 'Whose is the Kingdom at this time? God's, the One, the Omnipotent' (Holy Koran, 40:16). It means that in the impeccable and unlimited view of the spiritual master who sees the world as a unified Divine manifestation, all errors and corruptions revealed to limited sights shall disappear. The world is the shade of God, the Perfect, the Beautiful. The shade of the Beautiful must necessarily be beautiful—it cannot be otherwise. When a person reaches the station of *ihsan* in which he sees God with his inner insight or He is illumined and perfectly revealed, he himself is the owner of the virtue and the beauty. He beholds The One, who is the possessor of Absolute Virtue and Beauty. (ان اللّه جميل و يحبّ الجمال) 'God is beautiful and loves beauty'. In fact, it is His virtue and beauty that influences the seer.

The human being by his nature is a seeker of beauty and virtue. But in what do beauty and virtue culminate? They culminate in love. In other words, man is in search of beauty, which leads to love. This love is mutual. The almighty is the Lover and the Beloved. Man falls in love with the Almighty's Beauty, but the Beloved falls in love with His lover, who is his own beautiful and virtuous Self. In different verses of the *Koran*, the divinity declares: 'God loves the virtuous'.

> Through the mouth of the Prophet God says:
> The one who seeks Me, finds Me out,

> The one who finds Me, knows Me,
> The one who knows Me, falls in love with Me,
> The one who is My lover, I would be his,
> When I fall in love with him, I would extinguish his existence
> and I am his fine.

A line of verse by Hafiz reads:

> O Beloved, your beautiful face discloses for me a sphere of subtle beauty.
> That's why what I have to say is nothing but beauty and goodness.

At the stage of *ihsan* the creation of evil is regarded as goodness. As a result, whatever is in the universe is good. One cannot consider anything evil. If there is any, it takes its origin from man's ego. So the whole of creation is submitted to God's order. Satan too is the manifestation of the attributes of His Misguidance, and the prophets are the manifestations of the attributes of His Guidance. Satan spins the veil, and he veils what should be under the veil. So, he serves the very same threshold. The dweller of the station of *ihsan* beholds Satan and the evil-doer as necessary beings. The Absolute Benevolent emanates only blessing.

Peace at this stage culminates in the *solhi-kull* (the Universal Peace). At this stage the Truth manifests itself and this is only possible after one has attained complete self-annihilation. Thus the hardness is melted, the limitations are removed, and the soul is liberated from its constrictions. Now the microcosm becomes the macrocosm, and the interior peace becomes Universal. The Dark Time will end and the morn of Truth will dawn.

According to the Sufis, tyranny, mischief, chaos and disorder are not enduring and come to an end in the long run. So, one should avail of every opportunity to achieve and maintain peace. One should not, due to the overwhelming disorder and injustice in the world, become so hopeless as to refrain from making efforts to achieve peace.

The way to the Universal Peace is from the microcosm to the macrocosm, and not *vice-versa*. Peace is realized first in the microcosm and only then in the macrocosm. Furthermore, the Universal Peace is achievable in the outer world, and it has been promised in the Sacred Scriptures. In the Sacred Scriptures, the Awaited Universal Peace-Maker who will eventually come and establish Universal Peace throughout the world is referred to by different names but possesses the same characteristics. Universal Peace is a station in which the spiritual traveller lives amongst people only bodily, while keeping his heart aloof from them. At this stage, the attachment of one's heart is turned towards the non-material world. Thus, having one's hands busy with work (for example, to keep oneself busy with a profession, trade or craft, occupying oneself with achieving and maintaining peace in its political sense), while having one's heart with the Beloved (to melt the hardness and to liberate the soul from its constriction). That's the only way to the Universal Peace.

III

Political peace is institutional, whereas spiritual peace is existential (pertaining to the existentiality of human beings). The former is something to be established by social institutions; but the latter is founded upon the soul's ability to be, and consequently it is something to be realized inwardly. An institution is 'an interrelated system of social roles and norms organized about the satisfaction of an important social need or function'. Therefore institutional peace pertains only to the social aspects of the human being. It signifies the station in which one associates with people. Spiritual peace, however, indicates the station in which the traveller on the spiritual path, as he associates himself with people, keeps his heart aloof from them. He is just *among* others and not *with* them. Actually, the face of his heart has been turned from the world of materiality to the world of spirituality. Etymologically, 'institution' denotes 'standing *in*', while 'existence' means 'standing *out*'. The way to spiritual peace and salvation, and eventually to Universal Peace, lies in turning away from the *IN* and turning towards the *EX*. Salvation lies in being seized by Divine Ecstasy (to be *out* of one's mind, dwelling in the grip of Divine attraction and mystic trance). To 'stand out' is to be ahead of oneself and to remain open to the openness of Being. 'Man is and is man insofar as he, existing, stands exposed to the openness of Being, an openness which is Being itself. . . . World is the clearing of Being, wherein man stands out from his thrown existence. "Being-in-the-world" describes the essence of existence in relation to the cleared dimension out of which the "ex" of existence essentially arises.'

In Saadi's words:

> As you entered through the door, I stepped out of myself. It was as if I stepped from this world to the next!

Being seized by Divine attraction, the wayfarer is oriented to the station of the heart and becomes receptive to spiritual truths. When the Holy Prophet (P.B.U.H) is asked, 'What is the sign of the openness of the heart?' He replies: 'Returning to the Hereafter, to the abode of immortality, and turning one's back to the abode of deception and to prepare oneself for death before it comes down to him.' On another occasion he said: 'Die before you die.' This statement signifies the dying of the self, the shedding of all reprehensible characteristics and reviving the heart with praiseworthy attributes while maintaining one's worldly life. At this station the wayfarer achieves a new relation with the world, as his previous relation undergoes transformation to realize this spiritual status. The word 'relate' is based on *relatus*, the past participle of the Latin *referee*, meaning 'carry back, refer to', but 'latus' is not the original past participle of the Latin *ferre*, meaning 'carry'; it was drafted in from *tollere*, meaning 'raise', the source of the English 'tolerate'. By the notion of 'carrying', we come to the Indo-European base *bher*, which already contained the two central meaning elements that have remained with its offspring ever since, 'carry' and 'give birth'. This base, ultimately, stands as a root for a large number of English words among which the words 'bear' and 'burden' are the most important for the subject on hand. Having considered these etymological remarks we come to the following conclusion: To tolerate something is to 'bear' it.

At this station, the wayfarer is bestowed a new life. It is as if he's 'born' again and would live a life which is good and pure. His heart would be unveiled and his sight would be sharp. In a nutshell, he would attain the openness of his heart.

Relation in its international context, too, has to deal with 'tolerance'. Now, we may say that if international relations entail tolerating and bearing the burden of the other side, then the basis is correct. However, if the relationship between two nations entails imposing one's burden upon the other, then the basis is malicious. In other words, if the relationship is based on appreciating what the nations have in common, and being in tolerant of their differences, then they enjoy a healthy relationship. Here, the relation itself has changed to toleration.

IV

Tolerance may not be achieved unless the heart is opened and the mind is all-encompassing and in communion with all things. The result is perfect compassion. But the moment one loses this openness, one perceives differences and diversities as opposing forces against oneself and does not tolerate them.

Openness of the heart is the ground upon which all of these are founded. And now, I would like to conclude my talk and bless this gathering with the divine words:

> O people of the Book! Come to common terms as between us and you: that we serve none but God, and that we associate not aught with Him, and do not some of us take others as Lords, apart from God.
>
> (Holy Koran, Chapter 3, Verse 64)

Referenecs

The Koran Interpreted, A.J. Arberry, George Allen and Unwin, 1981.

Nahj-ul-Fasaha, *Sermons and Sayings of Mohammad, the Holy Prophet (P.B.U.H.).*

Nahj-ul-Balagha, *Sermons, Letters and Sayings of Imam Ali (P.B.U.H).*

William P. Scott, *Dictionary of Sociology*, Goyl Saab, 1988.

Mirca Eliad, *The Encyclopedia of Religion*, Vol. II, 'Peace', pp.121-24.

Saadi, *Kulliat.*

Martin Heidegger, *Poetry, Language, Thought*, trans. A. Hofstadter, Harper Colophon Books, New York, 1971.

Hafiz, *Divan*

James L. Perotti, *Heidegger on the Divine*, Ohio University Press, 1974.

John Ayto, *Word Origins*, Goyl Saab, 1992.

Muhyi-d-din Ibn Arabi, *The Wisdom of the Prophets (Fusus-ul- Hikam)*, trans. Angela Culme-Seymour, 1975.

16

The Contribution of Indian Sufis to Peace and Amity

K.A. Nizami

HIGHER spiritual experience in all religions of the world aims at bridging the gulf between humans by imbuing them with high moral ideals. Bergson very rightly observes that 'a great mystic feels the truth flow into him from its source like a force in action. His desire is with God's help to complete the creation of the human species. The mystic's direction is the very direction of the *elan* of life'.

The contribution of the Indian Sufis to society lies in their sincere and dedicated struggle to find a unity for the heterogeneous elements that make up its totality. They appreciated the multi-racial, multi-religious and multilingual pattern of Indian society and, to use Rabindranath Tagore's words, 'set at naught all differences of men, by the overflow of their consciousness of God'. For them God was not a logical abstraction of unity, but a living reality who can be approached through the service of mankind. Their efforts were, therefore, directed towards the creation of a healthy social order free from dissensions, discords and conflicts. It was a herculean task but they undertook it as a divine mission. In love, faith, toleration and sympathy they found the supreme talisman of human happiness. Shaikh Nizam-u'd-din Auliya often cited in his assemblies a remark of Shaikh Abu Sa'id Abul Khair (ob. 1049) that though there were myriads of routes and roads leading to God, none was quicker and more effective than bringing happiness to the hearts of men. Ibn Battuta found in Damascus a trust which existed for providing balm to afflicted hearts.

The Sufi *weltanschauung* was based on three basic postulates which determined their attitude towards God, man and society.

1. All people are the children of God on earth (الخلق عيال الله) . The *Sunnan-i-Abu Da'ud* reports that the Prophet used to pray at night: 'Oh God! I bear witness that all Thy creatures are brothers (أنا شهد أن العباد كلهم اخوة) '. Sa'di said that the reason for human brotherhood was that all human beings were made of the self-same clay and were as interdependent on each other as the limbs in the human body.

Once Dara Shukoh asked Shah Muhibb-ullah of Allahabad, a distinguished saint of the Chishti order, if religion permitted making a distinction between a Hindu and a Muslim. The saint's emphatic reply was 'no'. To strengthen his point further he said the Prophet was sent as a 'Blessing for all Mankind' (رحمت اللعالمين) and therefore no distinction could be made between one individual and another on the basis of religion (*Maktubat-i Shah Muhibbullah*, MS). Shaikh Hamid-u'd-din Nagauri, a distinguished disciple of Khwaja Mu'in-ud-din Chishti of Ajmer, did not permit his disciples to use the categories of *kafir* and *momin* as the basis of any social discrimination. Shaikh Abdul Quddus of Gangoh, a renowned Chishti saint of the sixteenth century, thus admonished his disciples in a letter:

> Why this meaningless talk about the believer,
> the *kafir*, the obedient, the sinner,
> the rightly guided, the misdirected, the Muslim,
> the pious, the infidel, the fire worshipper?
> *All are like beads in a rosary.*
>
> (*Maktubat*, p. 205)

It would be vain and whimsical to think that they did not believe in their religious identity. While firmly adhering to the basic principles of their faith, they did not carry this difference to social relationships. Their toleration was the toleration of a spiritually powerful man who, while jealous of the frontiers of his own faith, admires other forms of thought and behaviour. When Shaikh Nizam-u'd-din Auliya saw Hindus bathing in the Jumna and singing devotional songs, he said,

> ہر قوم راست راہے دینے و قبلہ گاہے
>
> (Every people have their own path, their
> own religion and centre of worship).

A whole world of religious broad-mindedness and tolerance is epitomized in this hemistich which came to be frequently cited inside and outside the *khanqahs* of medieval saints. Iqbal considered the following verse of Amir Khusrau as the best illustration of religious toleration:

اے کہ ز بت طعنہ بہ ہندو بری
ہم زوے آموز پرستش گری

(O you! who sneer at the idolatry of the Hindu,
Learn also from him how worship is done.)

The spirit of toleration, as Gibbon has remarked and Iqbal has approvingly quoted, springs from very different attitudes of the mind of man. There is the toleration of the philosopher, to whom all religions are equally true; of the historian, to whom all are equally false; and of the politician, to whom all are equally useful. There is the toleration of the man who tolerates other modes of thought and behaviour because he has himself grown absolutely indifferent to all modes of thought and behaviour. There is the toleration of the weak man who, on account of sheer weakness, pockets all kinds of insults heaped on things or persons whom he holds dear. It is obvious that these types of tolerances have no ethical value. On the other hand, they unmistakably reveal the spiritual impoverishment of the man who practises them. True toleration is begotten of intellectual breadth and spiritual expansion. (*Islam and Ahmadism*). The Sufis' toleration was an expression of confidence in their faith. For them all people were the children of God on earth and any social discrimination was a negation of the true spirit of faith.

The second foundational principle of the Sufi approach and ideology was their firm faith in تخلقوا باخلاق الله (adopt the ways of God). It meant that the aim of human life is to reflect in one's own thought and activity the attributes of God. Perfection in human life could be reached only by expressing in one's life more and more divine qualities. God's way is that He extends his bounties to all — the pious and the sinner, the believer and the non-believer, the high and the low. When the sun rises, it gives light and warmth to all living beings; when it rains, all benefit from the showers; the earth keeps its bosom open for all. Maulana Abul Kalam Azad calls it the mark of *Rububiyat* and thus explains its spirit: 'The strangest thing about this scheme of Providence, though the most patent, is the uniformity and harmony underlying it. The method and manner of providing means of sustenance for every object of existence are the same everywhere. A single principle is at work in all things. The stone may appear different from the fragrant flower, but the two receive sustenance in the same way, and are granted growth in the same style. . . .' (*Tarjuman ul Quran*, Eng. tr. Vol. I, p. 24)

Khwaja Mu'in-u'd-din Chishti, the founder of the Chishti *silsilah* in India, advised his followers to develop river-like generosity, sun-like affection and earth-like hospitality (*Siyar-ul-Auliya*). As these phenomena of nature make no distinction between any creature of God, likewise man should not discriminate between one human being and another.

Shaikh Nizam-u'd-din Auliya told his audience that once Prophet Abraham was reluctant to ask a non-believer to partake of food with him. Prompt came the admonition from God: 'Oh Abraham! We can give life to this man but you cannot give food to him.' The Sufi *khanqahs* supplied food and shelter to all sorts of people, no matter to what religion they belonged. Shaikh Nizam-u'd-din Auliya used to fast regularly. When food was brought to him at the time of *sahri*, morsels would stick in his throat as his mind went back to persons who had gone to bed without food.

A necessary concomitant of this approach was that man promptly responded to human misery and strained his every nerve to save people from hunger and misery. *Sahih Muslim* contains the following *Hadis-i Qudsi*:

> On the Day of Judgement God will address a particular individual: 'O Son of Adam! I fell ill but you did not attend on me.' Bewildered, this individual will say: 'How is that possible? Thou art the Creator and Sustainer of all the worlds.' God will reply: 'Doesn't thou know that such and such a creature of mine living near thee fell ill, but you did not turn to him in sympathy? If you had but gone near him you would have found Me by his side.' In like manner, God would address another individual: 'O Son of Adam! I had asked of you a piece of bread but you did not give it to me!' The individual would submit: 'How could this happen? Thou doesn't stand in need of anything'. And God will reply: 'Do not you remember that so and so among the hungry creatures of Mine had asked you for food and did you not refuse to give it to him? If you had fed him, you would have found Me by his side.'

The Sufis identified service of God with the service of man. Shaikh Junaid Baghdadi was quoted in the mystic circles of Delhi as saying that he found God among the poor people in the streets of Medina.

Bibi Fatima Sam, a very respected mystic woman of medieval India whose hut in Delhi attracted people from far and near, used to say that the divine reward for giving a piece of bread and a glass of water to the hungry was greater than offering thousands of genuflexions of prayer and keeping thousands of fasts (*Ma'arij-ul-Walayat*, MS).

Shaikh Nizam-u'd-din Auliya classified devotion to God into two categories: *ta'at-i lazmi* and *ta'at-i muta'addi*. *Ta'at-i lazmi* consisted of prayers and penitences that an individual performed; the *ta'at-i muta'addi* consisted in helping the needy and the poor and feeding the hungry. He told his disciples that the reward of *ta'at-i-muta' addi* was greater than that of obligatory prayers. Sa'di, the famous Persian poet, echoed the same sentiments when he said:

طریقت بجز و خدمت خلق نیست

به تسبیح و سجاده و دلق نیست

(Higher spiritual life is nothing but service of humanity,
It is not (chanting) the rosary, (remaining on the)
prayer carpet or (wearing) coarse garments.)

The third foundational principle of Sufi ideology was their faith in the Unity of Divine revelation, which paved the way for contact with people of diverse faiths and denominations. Commenting on this concept in the light of the *Koran*, Maulana Azad remarks:

> The *Koran* points out that the tragedy of man has laid in his effort to make distinction between prophets or in his accepting some and rejecting others. Its attitude is summed up in the following verse:
>
> Say: We make no difference between
> them (prophets of God) and we are
> Muslims resigned to God (3:78).
>
> (*Tarjuman*, Eng. Tr. I, p.78).

This basic approach opened the doors of deeper ideological contact and communication with people of different faiths, and put an end to 'all notions of exclusiveness which had hitherto prevailed among mankind assigning divine blessings and favours to one's own community' (*Tarjuman*, I, p. 8). Amir Khusrau, who had delved deep into the Hindu religious literature, said:

نیست ہنود ارچہ کہ دنیدار چو ما

ہست بسے جائے باقرار چو ما

(Though Hindus do not believe in the
religion in which we do,
In many matters they and we believe in
the same thing.)

(*Nuh Sipihr*, p.163).

Mirza Mazhar Jan-i-Janan believed in the divine character of the Vedas. Works like *Bahr-ul-Hayat*, *Jawahir-i Khamsa* and *Marj-us-Bahrain* could never have come into existence without being inspired by this basic ideological position. The Upanisads, which contain the earliest exposition of pantheistic philosophy, inspired Muslim mystic thought in many ways.

Toynbee has very correctly observed that the missions of the higher religions are not competitive but complementary. If the unity of Divine Revelation is accepted, it would automatically lead to this attitude of mind and soul. The Sufis not only preached it but practised it and helped in pulling down the barriers between various religious groups. Shah Niaz Ahmad of Bareilly thus declared the essential unity of all religions:

یہ سب ادیان و ملّل ہیں شاخ ہائے یک درخت
اک جڑ سے ہیں نکلی ڈالیاں سب پھوٹ پھوٹ

(All these religions and faiths are
branches of the same tree,
They have sprouted from one and the
same root.)

The difference in the religious accents of different faiths was thus explained by him:

طوطی جو ہود ستاں سرا سو سو طرح سے دے نوا
ہر دم نئی بولے صدا اور ہے وہاں منقار اک

(When the bird-nightingale starts its
melodious songs, it raises hundreds of notes,
It splashes a new tune every moment
but it comes from the same throat,
the same beak.)

The songs of the *bhakti* saints reverberate with such ideas. A south Indian folk song thus echoes feelings of universal peace and brotherhood:

Into the bosom of the one great sea
Flow streams that come from hills on every side.
Their names are various as their springs,
And thus in every land do men bow down
To one great God, though known by many names.

(Gover, *The Folksongs of Southern India*, p.165).

Chaitanya, Kabir, Guru Nanak, Namadev, Pipa, Sen and others familiarized themselves with the cosmopolitan ideas of the Sufi cult and broadcast them in their respective regions.

All religions have three essential elements — metaphysical, institutional and social, i.e. a conception of a Supreme Being, rituals and a code of ethics. The code of ethics assumes two forms: personal morality and social ideal. Richard Gregory in his *Religion in*

Science and Society and Salter in his *Ethical Religion* have considered these as the central themes of any religious enquiry. After having surveyed the march of humanity in space and time, Toynbee has come to the conclusion that the practical test of a religion, always and everywhere, is its success or failure in helping human souls to respond to the challenges of suffering and sin.

The Sufis in India have played the same role. They lived in the midst of the lower strata of society and identified themselves with the problems and perplexities of the people. Shaikh Hamid-u'd-din Sufi lived in Suwal, a small village of Nagaur, like Rajasthani peasants, mixed with people of all castes and creeds and adopted vegetarian habits. Shah Waliullah, in a very illuminating chapter on urban life and organization in his *Hujjat Allah al-Baligha*, advocates the peaceful integration of all the components of society and their harmonious functioning to achieve human well-being. In fact, peace and goodwill between human beings was the end all and be all of Sufi endeavours. A visitor presented a pair of scissors to Shaikh Farid Ganj-i Shakar but he refused to accept them, saying: 'Give me a needle: I sew, I do not cut.'

The Sufi saints were anxious to create in society the harmony of a perfect orchestra. Their principle was to return hatred with love, violence with affection. Shaikh Nizam-u'd-din Auliya used to recite the following verse of Shaikh Abu Sa'id Abul Khair as his motto in life:

هر که ما را رنجه دارد راحتش بسیار باد

(Whoever causes grief to us,
May his life get more and more happiness.)

A non-violent approach, sympathy with the weak and the downtrodden and consciousness of a divine mission to bring happiness to the hearts of men characterized the efforts of the Sufi saints of India. They did not indulge in criticism of other customs or practices. They disliked linguistic chauvinism and regarded all languages as different vehicles for the communication of feelings. They helped in the development of regional languages — Bengali, Punjabi, Marathi, and so on. They were instrumental in the rise of a common lingua franca. The earliest sentences of Hindi were spoken in the *khanqahs*. In the matter of language, their approach was:

سخن کز بهر دیں گوئی چه عبرانی چه سریانی

(When you are talking about faith
what does it matters it whether the words you
utter in prayer are Hebrew or Syriac?)

Their approach towards human relationships is neatly expressed in the imagery of eyes:

یگانہ بودن و یکتا شدن ز چشم آموز
کہ ہر دو چشم جدا و جدا نمی نگرند

(Learn from the eyes the way to develop
unity and oneness.
The two eyes appear different
but their vision is one.)

17

The Call of the Forest

Som Raj Gupta

THE Greeks placed man between god and beast and the *polis*, his ontological place, between heaven, the place of the gods, and the desert, the place of beasts. Strange creature appeared this *deinon*, this wonder, to them, this creature of fierce contradictions, with the radiance of heaven shining in his head and the fury of a beast raging in his breast, heaven unattainable for him and the beast inescapable. So sinister was the real *polis* for Plato, so rotten, that he was forced to weave an unrealizable dream, an ideal state, where man could live meaningfully and with purpose. The first philosophical treatise on the *polis* is already a cry of despair, implicitly as little hopeful about man as was Homer. The latter had visualised, in the *Iliad*, man as a being not merely human but one with cosmotheandric dimensions. Yet even this being, with his identity fashioned by Hesphaestus, the divine smith, could be saved neither from bestiality nor from tragedy. What redeemed man from his sordidness and his meanness was his mortality, the realization and acceptance of that *moira*.

That man's being as a mere human communality, as a *zoon politikon* was a distortion, a *vikara*, of his true being, the result of a false vision, is the central insight of Vedic wisdom. To live as a part of a human civilization cut off and isolated from the sky and the earth, from birds, beasts and gods and, most importantly, from *Brahman* the Absolute, was to live in sin and in pain. There could be no peace for such a being because there was no place of rest, no ontological mooring, for such a deviation. Accordingly, the Vedas never pray for the peace of man alone, as we in our blind narcissism dare to do. When the Vedas pray for peace they pray, first, for the peace of heaven, of the sky, of the earth, of all that lives on earth and all that grows on it and then for the peace of man. Even the peace of gods and of *Brahman* the Absolute has precedence in this prayer over the peace of man. They make this prayer because the self of man, his *atman*, is not merely a human self; it is the *atman* of all, the *atman* of all in each. Unless and until his self becomes expansive enough to become all and small enough to become each he cannot know what peace is, what *santi* is. For those who live alienated from themselves, their own native beings, can only be creatures of fear and of violence, not creatures of peace and bliss.

It was, I think, for this reason that the Upanisadic seers found the creative centre of a peaceful civilization in the forest and not in the *grama*, the village, or the *nagara*, the town. For man could, they believed, live in genuine peace only if he loved all that he beheld from the sky to the earth, from the birds of the air to the beasts of the jungle. Man could not have care and concern for his fellow beings unless he cared for all these, for all that moves and does not move. The forest was his purgatory, his *tapovana*, which redeemed his *nagara*, from a place of conflict to a place of harmony. The *nagara* that distanced itself from this purgatory would degenerate into a lustful hell as Valmiki was among the first to perceive, which precisely was what has happened to Ravana's Lanka. Every *nagarika* must realize that it is in the forest alone that man truly opens out to earth and sky and lets the peace of the mute and insensate come to dwell in him. It is there alone that he truly comes to own up and accept all that the civilized man hates and would avoid: his death and mortality. The authentic life that thinkers like Heidegger get so eloquent about, the life that owns up our mortality, comes to be possible only in the forest, not in the halls of legislature or justice. It is there alone that man can realize, in concrete and immediate terms, that our only true *moira* is the *moira* to die.

What kind of being is the being of this man, what is his disposition, his self, his discourse, of him who lives owning up his mortal lot? What is there that sets him apart, differentiates him from the man of civilization? Civilizations, with all their differences, have one thing common about them: they are informed, each one of them, with a common pursuit *vis-a-vis* inanimate nature. Civilizations come to be civilizations to the extent they can control and tame the wild forces of nature, to the extent they come to evolve a common action in relation to nature, an action more or less systematic, communicative, criticizable and revisable. Most civilizations will count themselves successful if they are able to carry out this kind of action more or less successfully. This is as true of our modern civilization as of any other. Indeed, modernity is, in every truth, another name for communicative and criticizable action. There have been civilizations that, despite the fact that common action was their basis, never equated man's being with that action. They recognized his being apart from social relationships too, in his spiritual depths, at least in his mortality that set him apart from others. Our civilization is probably unique in equating man with a *zoon politikon*, with *Mitsein*, a being with others. In this respect, we follow the Greeks only half-way, for we tend to sleep over our *moira* of mortality, which the Greeks never did, never dreamed of doing. For them, the *polis* was indeed the ontological place of man but of man the *zoon politikon*, not of man the mortal, that tragic being placed precariously between god and beast. For us modern man is only a man, related to nature through the bonds of exploitation, to fellow beings partly through ties of kinship but mostly through contracts and a cold system of give and take. A chilling account of our civilization do we find among artists and writers, even among some social writers. The Freudian account of civilization remains as true of our civilization as of any other. History, it appears, was created in vain and will be created in vain.

A bleak and unhealthy darkness seems to hover over this civilization. For men and women do not live here as men and women nor die as men and women. They do not live and do not die as men and women would do because they do not live as mortals but as concepts and categories, as functions and roles. These concepts and functions can speak and communicate through what may be called ready-made terms, terms that they pick up as they would a tool. They do not, cannot, speak words that are truly and genuinely their own because they never lie truly and genuinely as themselves. Public labels themselves, they speak and understand only public labels, not the words native to their soul, their self, their *atman*. And state things do they perceive, things that a concept can sum up and a common name can communicate. They cannot speak a name truly proper to a thing because they notice not its life and being, its self and its *atman*, only what is commonplace to it, something which it shares with other objects belonging to its class, not something which makes it alive and unique. They speak in terms of classes, perceive classes and live as classes. It is these that are relevant for functions in a common action, not the name proper to a thing, truly native to it, a name without which the thing in question will never become that thing, that unique thing, the name without which it simply cannot be a thing with an *atman*, with a self. The proper names which we ordinarily give ourselves and to things around us are more arbitrary, more of the nature of labels than even the common names, which can only classify things but not reveal their being. Our entire discourse is thus a violence against the *atman*, the self of things and persons, our knowledge a violation of their being and life. We think that our cognitive pursuit ends with classification; we do not realize what a sacrilege it is against the self of a person and the being of a thing, *this* thing before us.

Classification is relevant for communicative action, but not for the perception of a thing. When I perceive a thing it so deeply and intimately suffuses me with its presence that the concept in terms of which I classify and differentiate it, in terms of which, that is to say, I discourse about it, comes to be forgotten. Everything, every object that we behold is thus ineffable and incommunicable; it can only be classified and differentiated but not revealed by concepts and common names that we use in our cognitive discourses. The truth, the being, the self of a thing reveals itself to us only when we do not talk about it but pay heed to it, when we do not remember the name with which we identify it and communicate about it to others, when, that is to say, we are so intimately filled with its presence that we cannot but become it, become the thing we perceive. Only this sensuous participation in a thing, this dwelling in it, this becoming one with it will reveal the being, the *atman* of the thing before us, not the discourse that we carry on with our abstractions, our universals, our common names. When we have actually lived these moments of revelatory participation, the moments that reveal to us the life and being of a thing, then we truly come to realize how adventitious are the common names through which we carry on our discourse about them in our social or conceptual discourses. Neither commonsense can gauge the depth of this innocent participation nor can science, which too carries out its discourse in abstract terms and concepts.

When we perceive a thing, a redeeming invitation is extended to us, to each one of us, to dwell in it and as it, to participate in its life and in the harmony and peace that constitute that participation. This invitation we disregard because we in our blindness and confusion are more anxious to make of it a thing of use or of consumption than to see into its life and live that life. Such is the power of our theoretico-practical concerns that we would not hesitate to turn that living thing into an example of a category or a concept, the child of our theoretico-practical passion. A primordial blemish informs our being as *zoon politikons*, an original violence. This violence, this blemish does not allow us ever to live at peace with ourselves or with the world. We do not have the patience and the meekness to let the thing come to us, we do not have the required generosity, the openness to welcome it and to do what the ancients in our land called the *upasana* of it. *Upasana* in Sanskrit means to sit near an object, to be intimate with it, to contemplate it with passive and open disposition. This was the way to know the thing in question, this sitting near it, speaking to it and not about it, to dwell in it and as it. The word that revealed an object was this word of communion, the word with which you spoke to it, not the word with which you spoke about it.

All this we have all but forgotten, this *upasana* of things. Knowledge for us has come to mean relating a thing to a concept, a concept that we in our narcissistic passion have forged, and not paying heed to it. So obsessed are we with our concepts that we have all but forgotten the violence we do to things and ourselves through what we choose to call our knowledge. For it is not merely our percepts that become victims of our reductionist formulas but also the thoughts that occur to us, the words we spontaneously speak, even the air that we breathe. How many of us can really flow with the current of our breath, move out with it and die with it and move in with it and again die with it at the navel? Yet how many are there, how many *yogins* and how many poets, who tell us what it means to die with our breath, how when its motion is suspended, we are, in Wordsworth's words, become a living soul and see into the life of things. Despite such revelations, there is nothing in the world that we insult more and ignore more than this our breath, this our very life and being. Such is the depth of our impoverishment that to flow with the current of breath is practically death for us; there is nothing more chilling for us than the prospect of being reduced to the act of 'mere breathing', the lifetime goal of a *yogin*. If to 'breathe merely' is death for us, to be an abstract category is life for us. Yet we have the presumptuousness to talk about peace, we who ever do violence to all that we are and all that we behold. We must remember that hollow men, bare abstractions, are not to talk about peace or *shanti*, it is only living men, those who live their breath, their thoughts, their words, who can legitimately talk about it and bring it about.

The same fate awaits our thoughts and words. As we pay no heed to a moment in the being of a thing, its passing appearance or the play of an ephemeral gleam upon it, so we do not pay attention to passing thoughts in us or the words we may chance to hear or speak. Thoughts are important for us, for those engaged in communicative action or discourse, only to the extent that they can help accomplish that action or carry on that discourse. An individual thought in and for itself is a distraction for us, a sign of our weakness, of our lack of character or personality. We must relate it to the system of thought we seek to fashion or the scheme of action we would turn into reality. The treatment we mete out to thoughts, we mete out to individual words too.

A man living in solitude has a different attitude towards objects around him, towards their passing miens and expressions, towards the words he may chance to hear and speak, even the syllables that may constitute those words. With no theoretico-practical axe to grind, he does not find himself a function or an example and illustration of a concept, nor the things around him. He lives a participant in the life of the earth as her true inmate. The same innocent disposition he has for what occurs within him, his thoughts, his feelings, the movement of his breath, the feel of his sensations. We must, of course, remember that only that man can live in this innocent way, free from desire and narcissism, who has passed through a hard period of probation in society. According to the ancient Indian tradition, only a man who can distinguish between the eternal and the non-eternal, who acts without any desire for the fruit of his actions, holy or secular, who is calm of mind and restrained in senses, who is kind to all and patient in suffering, and who, moreover, loves the creatures of the earth and is grateful even to water, air and fire, to earth and sky, only such a man can live as a genuine participant in the *rita*, in the harmonic law — he alone can become what he sees and perceives, only he can know what peace is, the peace that dwells alike in man and in the world, dwells in them as their inbeing, as their inmost self, as also their life and sustenance.

There have been artists who have had a remarkable gift of openness towards the things they perceive, with almost total allegiance to perception. A percept, an image, an impression win their fealty more than any theory or plan of action. There have also been some poets whose love for words is overwhelming, who would listen to them more intently than they would listen to a person, linger on them more fondly than they would on a beautiful image or a sight. They write not to express ideas but to sign the words they have heard in moods of intent stillness. The meaning that the contemplative artist finds in a gesture or an expression, or the poet in the rhythm and movement of a phrase or a line, is a useless thing for a technocrat or a social planner but it is profoundly significant for many a man and woman in every age and every civilization. The present occasion is not the right one to dwell on the wealth of meaning that a single gesture of a hand can convey to an artist or the appeal of a word to the poet. What I wish to emphasize is the element of withdrawal from our ordinary social concerns and personal ambitions involved in the portrayal of that gesture or the saying of that word. To contemplate the gesture that the artist has portrayed for us or to listen to the word he has heard also leads us, their contemplators and listeners, away from our daily concerns and interests, rendering us, for sometime at least, unfit for them. We value these moments of profound idleness because they enable us to cease to be mere functions or abstractions and to come, to an extent, to be ourselves. In such moments of emancipation we come to know what it is to breathe freely and live freely, what it is to feel our own sensations, to *live* our own thoughts and speak our own words.

In our ordinary social life, we coordinate our actions and thoughts when we study and control nature. When we come to enjoy the fruits of these acts and thoughts we become brutally narcissistic and self-oriented. Most of the conflicts that afflict societies spring from this contradiction between intersubjective action and subjective consumption. In the appreciation of art and literature this contradiction between the active intersubjectivity and the consuming subjectivity comes to be reconciled. When I appreciate a gesture or an expression depicted by an artist, I do contemplate it all alone, but this contemplation and the joy it gives rise to do not make me possessive or narcissistic. Other contemplators and other appreciators can participate in the given gesture without being competitors. The appreciative self in me can freely share the object of art with others but will enjoy the appreciation all alone. Redemptively sharing is this *alone*, this contemplatively appreciative self. This self never comes to be in conflict with others because its joy is its alone, uniquely and immediately its own. All peaceful can this self sit with others, with co-sharers of the wealth that an object or art is.

Art and literature thus reveal to us what co-sharing is and what solitude, joyous solitude is. The rift between the subjective and the intersubjective that we find in our ordinary civilized life is remarkably healed here. Yet the freedom they give us from our fretful life and conflicts is not a lasting freedom. We get only relief from our fever not a cure for it. For the vast schism that divides the enjoyer of fame and honour in an artist from the innocent creator in him is not easily bridged. The malady of the divide between the worker and the consumer afflicts the artist too. He too enjoys his fame like a Narcissus, giving rise to all the tensions that an ordinary consumer would generate. Artists can give us a taste of peace but only when we are in contemplative moods. They also in a way contribute to a culture of peace by making us live, for some moments at least, in the deep solitudes that lie hidden within us. But what the artist creates, the man in him often takes away. The latter contributes a lot to the decadence of art because of his temptations and weaknesses. The vanities he shares with common people are plentiful enough to render him, generally speaking, incapable of creating an endurable culture of peace.

If knowledge at the level of commonsense and science is divisive, knowledge at the level of art is fragile and, ultimately speaking, unredemptive. Does this mean, then, that all knowledge is a curse as the myth of Adam and Eve would assure us it is? Not really, for there is a knowledge which is not an antagonist of innocence but one with it. This knowledge they give the name *shruti*, a knowledge which is a gift but not an acquisition, a revelation that man can hear but not speak. It is not the privilege of man the *Mitsein*, of one whose being is constituted by others, to receive this knowledge. Man the *Mitsein* is too much of a speaker, too much of a communicator to have enough stillness in him to allow the *shruti* to resonate in that stillness. This knowledge is revealed to one who has no already forged terms ready at hand for communication, who has to find the word, the word that is his own word, the word that is native to his self and to the moment of its utterance and to the world where it is uttered. The speaker cannot precede this word nor the moment nor the world because they come into being with the coming into being of this word, cannot be without it. The speaker utters the word as the word, the world hears it as the word. There is nothing apart from this word, neither the speaker nor the hearer nor the world. The word is all, the word is each, it dwells in each as the all and in the all as each.

Not many can hear the *shruti* this way, those words of redemption. But many can self-submit to those words, submit to them with a passive disposition. Now, it is not a big problem to distinguish the word of revelation from the word of discourse. Discourse can and does replace one interpretation of reality with another interpretation but it does not give up interpretation as such, for reality is always an interpreted reality for it. *Shruti* is an interpretation that is oriented towards its own disownment, it is a knowledge that ends in innocence. When the hearer of *shruti* is purified of all interpretations, he, all innocent, self-submits to its word, gives himself up to its contemplation to become that word. When this happens, when man becomes the word, the syllable, there remains no other words for him to relate to. All language comes to reside in that single syllable, all the words and whatever they may refer to or interpret. The word becomes his self, and so does their interpretation, the world. This is what the contemplation of a single syllable brings about, the syllable called *aum*, which reveals itself, when so contemplated, as the dwelling place of all that is, has been and will be, as all that is immanent as well as transcendental.

When this knowledge dawns upon man, when he becomes the word to become all and more than all, only then does he come to have peace that no event can undo, no upheaval can destroy, no catastrophe can uproot. Men of the world, those inhabitants of the *polis*, find it hard to believe that a single syllable, with no propositional value, can become the all. A short paper is not the place wherein to dwell on this extremely complex theme. I have tried to explain the matter in details elsewhere. I would, however, emphasize the point that a very rigorous defence of the 'position' of the *shruti* in this regard can be made and has indeed been made in the philosophical tradition of India. If man, the *shruti* says, contemplates, with passive openness, the word *aum*, he, becoming one with it, will become the self, the *atman*, of all. The altar, the Vedas say, is the utmost bound of the earth and sacrifice, *yajna*, its centre and word of the Vedas, the *akshara*, the dwelling place of all the gods. Only that man, they continue, can sit in peaceful assemblies who knows the word as the home of all that is.

Men of the world, men who live as social beings, men who would claim for themselves only a human self, cannot live in peace with one another. They cannot live in peace because they 'live' as constituted by divisive categories, by linguistic and conceptual distinctions: in one word, by otherness. This divisive language we have to give up, this language of categories, of concepts, of distinctions. This we cannot do unless and until we cease to be conceptually interpreted beings. Instead of being determined in terms of distinctions and concepts, we have to find ourselves in harmony with all and all in harmony with us. We have to find the word that is one with all, the word that is our being, our self. If we wish to live in peace with one another, we should learn to contemplate words, meditate on them, give ourselves up to them. The moment we reify *vak*, speech, into a tool, we turn our life into an irredeemable tragedy. Modernity committed its greatest sin when it forgot the sacredness of *vak*, of the word. For men and women who find words only as interpretative or communicative tools live as creatures of love-hate relationships, more of hate than of love. That civilization, every civilization, should turn out to be a virtual hell for Freud and his followers should not come as a surprise to anyone who realizes the immensity of the fall of one who lives as a mere example of a concept.

The Freudian vision is perhaps the most damning indictment of humanism by a thought which itself is humanistic. Recent attempts to mellow down its sting have failed to be convincing. The theories woven by, for example, the followers of Merleau-Ponty about man as an opening out, as an orientation towards others sound, to say the least, is romantic in the bad sense of the term. The truth is that *human* self of man is a self-centred self, egoistic and violent, and human society is an unhappy and violent society. Our history, the history of civilization, provides enough evidence to bear out the truth of this statement. If earlier civilizations failed to be peaceful civilizations, our own civilization will be no exception. Indeed, if the truth be told, this civilization has a much more bleak future in store for it than earlier civilizations. Witness the systematic way it has reified living beings into things and tools, witness the appalling way it is turning itself into a consumeristic civilization. To be hopeful about the future of this through and through humanistic civilization is to indulge in schizophrenic reveries.

Peace can descend on man only when, to recall the Vedic vision, man realizes that there are more than human dimensions of his self, when he lives that self and as that self. And his civilization can become peaceful civilization only when he lives in harmony with all that is, from the sky to the earth, from the bird to the beast. That is the call a forest-dweller makes to civilization from his solitude; that it live in harmony with all creatures, be they moving or non-moving, be they two-footed or four-footed; let it not flourish in isolation from and with hostility towards them. For men and women must realize that if they cannot respond to the call that these beings make to them, they will fail to respond to the call they make to one another. Bereft of a sense of harmony with the life of things, with the vast expanse of the earth and the sky, they will live as mere acquisitive and possessive things, not beings that are open and sensitive to one another. Man has to be simple and self-restrained to be sensitive to the life of things, and he has to be sensitive to that life in order to be sensitive to the life of his fellow beings. Let us, therefore, try to live in harmony with all that is, let the Vedic prayer for the peace of all be our guide and let the forest-dwellers be our guardians. It is not the privilege of philosopher-kings to make the *polis* peaceful, only a humble *rishi*, a solitary seer, can show us the path. It is only he who can provide the transforming look, so indispensable for our safety from decadence. There are no institutions, no laws, no ethos and no mores that can escape decline and decadence, no human virtue that can withstand the might of vice. Every institution, every civilization sows the seeds of its own destruction. There is something suicidal about every human endeavour which no self-criticism can stall. Human self-criticism is itself too much influenced by suicidal narcissistic tendencies to save human institutions from these maladies. Only the other civilization, the life of solitude, the life that is harmony itself, the life that a serene forest-dweller embodies, can provide the cure, can provide the gaze that will redeem us from our meanness, from our acquisitiveness, from our smallness. It alone can open out the vast dimensions of our beings, dimensions deep and peaceful, which our cleverness cannot imagine, our thinking cannot conceive but which our simplicity, simplicity in our life and in our thought, can enable us to perceive, realize and be.

18

The Culture of Peace
Experiment and Expectation

Biswanarayan Shastri

THE hymn from the *Atharvaveda* quoted in the preamble of the keynote paper of this seminar conveys the earnest desire of the human heart for peace of body and mind, peace in the environment, and beyond, in the space above. Here the desire for peace of body and mind has been taken as undivided. This may be achieved through *yoga*, and *yoga* literally means the combination of the two. In the search for peace for the individual in society and community this point should always be kept in mind. The want of peace of mind is called *adhi*, and a lack of ease in the body is known as disease, *vyadhi*. When an individual is free from *adhi* and *vyadhi* he may enjoy peace and beauty and can share his feeling with others. The culture of peace begins here, and a peaceful atmosphere should be all-pervading.

The hymn further states that thoughts, speech and activity generate violence, and it is absolutely necessary to turn these instruments to work for peace. Hence the desire expressed is: 'May the mind which conceives violence be peaceful, may the speech which incites violence be peaceful, may the limbs of the body which are used for committing violence be peaceful'. It is evident that after experiencing violence, people in the remote past expressed their earnest desire for peace and believed that the instruments or agencies which create or are used to cause violence could be used for ushering in the cult of peace and for creating the conditions for enjoying beauty in nature and man.

yayaiva sasrje ghoram tayaiva santirastu nah.

May the sensory and gross organs which cause violence bring peace to us. Here the saints and poets played their role in the past and that role is expected to continue for ever. They not only expressed the fond hope for peace but wanted it as the dominating trend in life. This is evident from the fact that the dialogue for peace, the *Gita*, was carried on in the battlefield of Kurukshetra and the two interlocutors were face to face with enemies with raised weapons. The essence of this myth is that the desire for peace dominated the trend of violence. The warriors in the battlefield also wanted peace, and the ways and means for achieving it were discussed.

A critique of the *Gita* terms the work an incitement to violence and provocation for war. Krishna encouraged Arjuna to fight by marshalling arguments and citing reasons ranging from prestige to immortality of the soul, and finally succeeded in convincing him to fight. The critique terms those who advocate peace on the preaching of the *Gita*, frauds and hypocrites. This view is mentioned to illustrate the confusion and contradiction that prevails. The *Bhagavad Gita* states that when one withdraws one's sense-organs from their objects one's *chitta* (super intelligence) becomes *prasanna* (in pure state of equilibrium) and all one's sufferings disappear. With the disappearance of suffering one enjoys peace. The *Bhagavad Gita*, however, cautions that such *prasannata* (purity of mind) cannot be achieved by mere forcible detachment of the sense-organs from their objects. It denounces the person who, while restraining his sense-organs from their objects, constantly longs for them as a hypocrite (*mithyachara*).

In common parlance also, a person who has something else in his mind from what he speaks, and who acts contrary to what he preaches, is a fraud and a wicked person. He who thinks what he speaks and acts accordingly is called a *mahatma*. Gautama Buddha, Mohandas Karamchand Gandhi and other great persons were *mahatmas*, because they preached what they believed in, and followed it in action. Buddha wanted to have peace for all by removing suffering, while Mahatma Gandhi wanted it by adhering to non-violence.

Is it a possible or probable proposition to strive for peace in a situation which is dominated by hypocrisy and hypocrites? Perhaps a very difficult proposition. The question posed in the preamble is, 'Can we perceive an ideology of peace derived from practice?' To answer this one may ask, is it not futile to work for peace without a set ideology? In other words, the riddle is: should we try to derive an ideology from practice vitiated by hypocrisy, or should we try to implement the set ideology of peace in the individual as well as the social sphere?

The hope for deriving ideology from practice is bound to be wishful thinking because ideology is regarded as *dhruva* (fixed) and practices vary. On the other hand, the ideology of peace remains idle without practice. In short, an ideology of peace not followed by practical action remains lame, and action without an ideology is blind. The lame ideology cannot move and the blind practice does not know the direction in which to proceed.

The question arises: Can there be a world without wars? The question of a warless world agitated the minds of the allied nations after the First World War and their efforts took shape in the form of the League of Nations, which, however, was a non-starter owing to insincerity on the part of some nations. Some powers had the apprehension of being overshadowed by others, and others wanted to be supreme. The second attempt was made after the Second World War and the United Nations Organization came into being. It is now a world organization of 185 nations, entrusted with the task of peace-keeping in the world.

Can anyone say that the lurking fear of war has disappeared? More than half a dozen wars have broken out after the UNO was established, though they did not assume the dimensions of a world war. In the present arms race who can say there will be no third world war? Jawaharlal Nehru conceived of *panchasheela*, which was accepted by India and China. In practice it was a still-born child and nobody now remembers it. The policy of non-alignment formulated and followed by a few developing countries has in the present context become irrelevant, and there is mutual suspicion among the non-aligned countries. M.K. Gandhi made an experiment with truth, which he called the other side of the coin, non-violence. His personal experiment with truth had become an extension programme when it was accepted both as an end and a means for attaining independence for India. This proved successful for a limited purpose, and the people at large did not follow it sincerely, though there is no dearth of people who speak eloquently on non-violence, in which they do not believe. This is another instance of hypocrisy. What is more, the apostle of non-violence himself fell victim to violence, which means that violence had overtaken non-violence.

Historically speaking, even centuries earlier the preachers of *bhakti* in medieval India went a step ahead of non-violence by preaching love for all living beings. Love is dynamic, non-violence is passive, it is said. Namdev, Guru Nanak, Kabir, Kanakdas, Raidas, Shri Chaitanya, Shankardeva and many others, though they exercised great influence over their followers, were only partially successful in changing the hearts of people. The concept of non-violence was carried to the supreme level by the Jains, who preached *anekanta vada*, that is, anyone who says, 'Only this is right' commits mental violence towards those who do not accept that as correct. This, in the modern world, may compare well with anti-fascist views.

We are now living in a global village, a gift of science and technology. Do we live like the inhabitants of a *grama* of the past? The seers in the remote past conceived of the world as one family, *vasudhaiva kutumbakam*, and of the entire world as a nest (*yatra visvam bhavatyeka nidam*). The conception never developed for obvious reasons.

Now we have the commanding heights of technology at our disposal and the world has been reduced to a small village. It is true that distances have almost vanished, but not mental differences. Why? The causes are to be investigated. There is a rise in suspicion, hatred, and conspiracy. The fear psyche of the people causes anxiety, leading them to take up weapons. This fear psyche is responsible for tribal uprisings and terrorism in the global village.

On the other hand, people have lost faith in values which they followed generation after generation. The unchecked greed for wealth and its acquisition by corrupt means tempted many. There is a race for it among individuals and nations. Again, people living in mental and social isolation, when suddenly exposed to the modern world dominated by people who have advanced technology and money power, become apprehensive of losing their identity and resort to violence. The lengthening shadow of the giant with command over purchasing power and attacking power frightens the poor and defenceless. Poverty, unemployment and underdeveloped conditions add fuel to the fire.

Violence and the consequential suffering are not confined to the people of developing and underdeveloped countries: the developed countries also have their share. However, the cause or causes are different and the effect is also not felt as in the poor countries. The main cause is excessive greed. This was succinctly stated by Mahatma Gandhi: the world has enough to meet the needs of all but not enough to satisfy their greed. For acquiring more one has to deprive others, and thus a country expands its sphere of dominance over others. It is interesting to note that all such nations declare a noble desire to protect the poor and develop the underdeveloped countries. This is one more instance of hypocrisy.

Another instance of greed is the race for capturing the money market. In the process confrontation becomes inevitable. Rabindranath Tagore has presented the situation in a poetic way. He says, '*jekhane manus nijake barai, sekhane se anyake tarai ebam sekhane larai*' (when one expands his power, position, influence, etc., one drives away others, and war takes place). He puts his finger on the weakest point of human being and sums up the situation in the three words, *barai, tarai* and *larai* (expansion, eviction and fighting), the cause of hostility and war.

In this context one may remember the graphic description in the *Mahabharata*: 'Without injuring others to the core, without taking recourse to terrible violence, and without killing people the way a fisherman kills fish, no one can amass huge wealth'.

sarve bhavantu sukhinah, the Indian ideology of peace and happiness, 'may all be happy', was modified to 'may the great majority of people be benefited and happy' (*bahujana hitaya, bahujana sukhaya*). This compares well with the Western notion of the greatest good of the greatest number. Even in medieval India the *Kalika Purana* states, 'the killing of one person for the welfare of many should not be called a murder'.

It may be summed up that the fear psyche of losing identity on the one hand, and excessive greed, crisis of faith and sky-high consumerism on the other, have created conditions for violence. This is to be contained by creating an atmosphere of peace. The road towards this is the sharing of the experience of peace and beauty, which may begin as sensual and be raised to intellectual and finally to the spiritual level.

The arts and literature teach us to love beauty in nature, and people appreciate this. The desire to live in peace, in an atmosphere of all-pervading peace, is the key to entering into the domain of the culture of peace.

One cannot expect to live in a culture of peace by shutting one's eyes to the present stark reality. The reality of operation of democracy is not only a system of administration but a way of life. Experience tells us that it fails to deliver the goods. Despite its failure, and taking the form of plutocracy, we shall have to live with it because there is no better system. The remedy lies in the approach towards individual and collective perfection. Then only may one expect to share beauty in artistic creativity. The promotion of the culture of peace through a spiritual vision of shared human responsibility hints at discharging responsibility on a higher plane.

Shared responsibility ensures meeting the needs of every human being by society. Society may provide for the biological and economic needs of a person in consideration of his service to it and according to his capacity to produce wealth. This has been experimented with in socialist countries. It satisfies one's day-to-day needs but does not and cannot give pleasure, satisfaction and peace, because in the system the mind and ego have been totally ignored. It has also an element of imposition and compulsion. This is resented by the subconscious mind. In view of this the sharing of human responsibility should be spontaneous, based on ideology — the ideology of accepting every human being as having the potential to become free, exercising his conscience without compulsion.

Lastly, how may the culture of peace continue? It may be under a totalitarian system, which seems to be an easy solution. Apparently this solution invites the most dangerous consequences of suppressing human beings, individuality and ego. Hence it should be in a climate of self-disciplined freedom.

A novel interpretation of the mythology of ancient India may throw light on this.

Vishvamitra wanted to usher in universal peace by controlling intelligence with physical force. He failed, and tried to acquire intellectual power. Vashistha, the leader of the intellectuals, wanted to keep the world under control by intellectual power and failed. Rantakara, who felt the agony of the female bird when its mate was killed, appeared on the scene as the poet Valmiki and appealed to the heart of mankind to abjure violence and appreciate the beauty of mutual love. His message was received well by warriors, intellectuals and commoners alike. What I am trying to convey is that the appeal to the heart and its response with warmth of heart, may create not only peace but a sense of beauty. This is the poetic concept of the communion of hearts through a poetic message.

I conclude by quoting the *Ramayana*: 'We desire friendship with all those who are for peace' (*sarvesam santikamanam sakhyamicchamahe vayam*).

19

Creativity, *Pax Mundi* and Gandhi

Ramjee Singh

Crisis of Knowledge and Loss of Creativity

ONE of the important causes of crisis in Western civilization is the loss of creativity. Nobody can deny that the West has achieved a high water-mark in the development of scientific knowledge and material advancement, but in spite of all these achievements the decline of the West has deeply shaken its innate sense of superiority as the natural leader of the world and the source of all intellect and progress. In Spengler's characteristics of the last phase of civilization, the disappearance of creativity is an important feature. No new great creations appear, neither in art or religion, nor in politics. Life becomes intellectualized and commercialized. Though many changes, variations and mixtures of forms may still appear, no fundamentally new forms appear any more. 'All that remains is the struggle for mere power, for animal advantage *per se*.'[1] This lack of creativeness is the characteristic of our time. 'What is practised as art today is impotence and falsehood. . . . We go through all the exhibitions, the concerts, the theatres and find only industrious cobblers and noisy fools, who delight to produce something for the market.'[2] According to Toynbee, the core of the breakdown of civilizations is that the creative minority can no longer bring up sufficient creative force to meet the challenge of the moment. The source of action in each society rests with the creative minority since the mass is incapable of mentally and spiritually living through the same creative experience, hence there is general acceptance of imitation, which Toynbee calls *mimesis*.

We can trace creative forces in European politics to the idea of some form of unification — the Benelux economic union, the Western Union concluded between France, Great Britain and the Benelux countries in 1948, the creation of the Council of Europe, the plan for a European Defence Community (NATO); but the idea of a united Europe would be of little value if it were brought about merely by pressure from the U.S.A. However, the constant activity toward unification is clear proof of the urge of Europe for greater unity. In the field of the economy, we find creative forces in the European economy with the formation of a common European Market, European Recovery Plan, European Payment Union and the Schuman Plan. All these have achieved integration and the mass production needed. In the field of architecture, an entirely new style has sprung up from a maze of hitherto uncoordinated lines and imitative themes: the straight line and the principle of functionalism have emerged as the representative style of our time. In the film of cinematography and music we have achieved great success.

Similarly, we can find some creative force in American technology. That a nation with hardly 7 per cent of the world's population produces about a third of all goods and services is an achievement of human creative power. In politics, both domestic (the federal system and the switch from bourgeois to mass democracy) and foreign (resisting aggression in Korea, Vietnam, Kuwait, etc.), America has given ample proof of that capacity to discern great issues and the audacity to deal with them which have always characterized great nations and great civilizations at the peak of their vitality. Except in the fields of film and architecture, America has not made significant contributions in music, drama or literature. Of course, it has shown startling progress in science and medicine, in chemical science, in biology, psychology and in social sciences.

Both Europe and America have amply proven our century to be one of the most prolific in scientific achievements, but since they are rooted in materialistic values, there is growing moroseness, cynicism and lack of faith. The West has shown creative genius but without direction, it has resulted in exploitation of the worst kind, political and cultural imperialism and arrogance and perfection in the business of arms and ammunition including the clandestine sale of dangerous components of nuclear bombs. They have no doubt shown a great concern for federation, democracy and human rights, but again, it has resulted in perpetuating their hegemony and exploitation. This is because democracy and the problem of human rights are instruments to consolidate their roots and browbeat the Third World countries. The U.S.A. has assumed the role of policeman of the world and also custodian of economic empires through the outfits of the IMF, the World Bank and the WTO. The U.S.A. has stolen the signboard of U.N. and it has made the world body unrepresentative through the permanency of five seats. It is rank hypocrisy to keep the treasure of the atomic stockpile and ask the atomic have-nots to observe atomic fasts. Hence, the West is incapable of seizing the moral and spiritual leadership either for world peace or for a united world. The world has too strongly the impression that the Western leadership limits itself to grants of material aid, and that too for improving its own economies. It is neither charity nor assistance but pure business if not sophisticated exploitation.

Nothing is as killing to initiative as the habit of turning to others for economic or financial assistance. It was the political genius of Alexander the Great to establish his imperial super-system and the autonomy of the Greek *polis*. It will be the almost superhuman task of Western statesmanship in the modern world to strike the right balance between world guidance and respect for the independence of others. If the West reinvigorates its fundamental moral and spiritual values embedded in the Greek and Judaeo-Christian cultures, it can meet the challenges of the present crisis. We need a civilization-wide peace and a civilization-wide world. If the West has to survive as the leader of the world, instead of raising its military might and its economic imperialism, it has to raise the standards of the millions who still exist in the basest poverty and squalor by practising austerity and self-control. This will kindle the creative spirit of the West, which had earlier been found in Beethoven's symphonies, motivated Washington, Jefferson and Lincoln to create respect for individual freedom, erected the Notre Dam and the Rockefeller Center for philanthropy and so on.

The West, in the glamour of achievement, forgot to explore the secrets of the inner world: contemporary Western civilization is still rooted in Cartesian dualistic metaphysics of subject-object dualism. In the pride of science, they have come to despise and reject intuitive and instinctual perceptions that earlier animated and gave perspective and hope and meaning to human existence. For creativity, we need a new instrument of thought and a perception of the 'unbroken wholeness' in a non-dual frame which can understand life directly and in a concrete manner rather than in abstract, linear terms. The subject-object dualistic mode of intellectual knowledge has its own limitations. It cannot understand the deeper level of mind-brain interaction. Max Born also thinks that 'clever, rational ways of thinking are not enough'.[3] It has no cure for psychological imbalances and loss of creativity. 'The world-view implied by modern physicists', as Fritz of Capra says, 'is inconsistent with our society, which does not reflect the harmonious interrelatedness we observe in nature.'[4] The present dualistic knowledge mechanism to bifurcate the 'seer' and the 'seen' is mutilation of knowledge.[5] This is only one-sided and partial knowledge which leads to an 'argument between nature and man'.[6] Dualistic epistemology provides a divided world of subject and object. But as Schrodinger says, 'Subject and object are only one. The barrier between them cannot be said to have broken down as a result of recent experience in physical sciences, for this barrier does not exist.'[7] We need an understanding which is immediate, non-dual, and holistic. This is intuition, which is not against reason but beyond reason and is the fulfilment of all scientific and intellectual knowledge or the logic of creativity.

Logic of Non-absolutism

Aristotelian logic is formal, dualistic and absolutist, hence it is most inadequate to grasp the true nature of reality. Since it is based on the principles of identity and non-contradiction, it is either *true* or *false*. According to this logic, 'there are no two ways about it', 'you must be either one thing or the other'. This leads to the typical disjunctive attitude. Disjunction must disjoin completely because alternatives are alternatives only with reference to one subject and hence both the alternatives can be accepted at the same time. Mechanism says that the fallacy of the false alternative is due to our 'slovenly habits'.[8] The Pragmatists complain that 'any purely formalistic "either . . . or" formulation of contrast eliminates reference to any universe of discourse. The form either-one-or-the-other-but-not both, based on the principle of the Excluded Middle, is meaningless in view of its incompatibility with existence in transition. So the mathematical logicians think that it is a 'mistake to interpret the "either . . . or" as exclusive. In other words, "or" does not exclude both.'[9]

The World is sharply divided into multiple opposed camps. There is an 'either . . . or' in world politics. 'If a person does not agree with you, it is wicked; if a country does not agree with your country, it is wicked; there is no half-way'.[10] Thus neutrality has become a crime and tolerance, a vice. Today one man or one group or one country fights with others because their views differ. But views are bound to differ, because we are guided by different conditions. Hence, it is wrong to think oneself absolutely right and all others absolutely wrong. Such an attitude or outlook is imperialism in thought. Peace, therefore, demands a new logic, a new outlook, a new asceticism and a new civilization. This is the philosophy of 'neither . . . nor', which is simply an extension of the Gandhian principle of non-violence into the intellectual field. This non-absolutist approach is 'an endeavour to frame a coherent, logical, necessary system of general ideas in terms of which every element of our experience can be interpreted'.[11] Even C.E.M. Joad opines that we must have a synoptic view of the universe.[12] In an absolute sense, a thing is neither real nor unreal, neither permanent nor evanescent, but both. Hence formal two-valued logic is inadequate. On the other hand, non-absolutist epistemology avoids vicious intellectualism and the fallacy of exclusive particularity. Such a dynamics of thinking is based on catholicism and regard for truth seen from different angles. Intellectualistic abstractionism has to be given up and we should try to dehumanize the ideal and realize the real. The reality is not a rounded ready-made whole or an abstract unity of many definite or determinate aspects. The multivalued logic shows all possible sides of a thing and thus does not postulate about it in any fixed way. A thing is neither real nor unreal, neither eternal nor non-eternal, neither static nor mobile, neither small nor big in the absolute sense, but has dual nature. Two-valued logic seems to be unreal if there is loyalty to experience.

Non-absolutism is the ideology of a new civilization of peace and non-violence. It is not only an intellectual utopia but a concrete moral guide and a social stabilizer. The 'all or none' approach has brought us to the brink of total annihilation, hence the non-absolutist approach in thought, word and deed is the only way before us.

The Gandhian Approach to World Peace

Peace, as Gandhi envisaged it, is far more than the absence of war and violence.[13] It is a state of positive and constructive world-view and world-order, where individuals, groups and nations eschew to dominate or exploit one another and live in cooperation and mutual aid. This means that peace needs a new life-style and a new culture. However, such a philosophy of civilization of peace does not work in a vacuum. Therefore Gandhi enunciates both an epistemology of peace and non-violence and also formulates a sociology of peace. Unlike others, he starts with *technology*, because technology and ideology largely go together. The mode of technology determines *development*, defence and democracy — in short, our whole theory of life. E.F. Schumacher's *Small Is Beautiful* is already a protest against the present development model and blind worship of bigness. The Club of Rome thesis — *The Limits of Growth*[14] — is a warning against the depletion of non-renewable resources,[15] so is the danger signal given by *Blueprint for Survival.* Fritzof Capra warns us of the dangers of 'environmental pollution, continuing proliferation, and the likelihood of global extinction'.[16] But the root problem lies in our infinite greed and consumerism. An ever-growing material standard of life can only be achieved through the multiplication of machinery and the cruel exploitation of natural resources. Besides, concentration of production in a few hands creates pockets of prosperity leading to a hierarchical mode of social organization and alienation of the population from its own labour. Community life breaks down and quality of life deteriorates. Inequality grows so much that U.S.A., with 6 per cent of the world's population, consumes 30 to 50 per cent of the world's resources. Technological civilization creates confrontation, not only between employers and employees but also between capitalist countries for markets. Even socialization of industries is no cure for industrialization, as exploitation was rooted in machine technology itself. Then technology determines the model of *development* as well as the paradigm of *defence.* Thanks to technology we have perfected the weapons of man-annihilation. If malignant hands manipulate the gifts of science, the Frankenstein's monster of super-technology will swallow up *Homo Sapiens* and burn up civilization. Hence technology has 'become a value-choice between Dawn and Doom, when nuclear power is in issue'.[17] The world spends 600 billion dollars every year on military budgets while millions of humans continue to starve and suffer. The world military machine usurps research and development money (about 135 billion dollars) and engages 50 million people in military support and production. More than 60,000 atomic missiles and bombs have by now been piled up in the bunkers of the industrialized societies, amounting to an average of three tons of conventional explosive per world citizen.[18] Even if nuclear war does not take place, the stockpile will cause havoc: 'By. . . 2000 A.D., there will be less water available, less fertile land, less clean air, less wilderness. One fifth of the *sapiens* will probably be extinct. . . . The gap between the affluent and the hungry is expected to widen.'[19] Hence Professor Toynbee rightly said: 'If we do not abolish war, war is going to abolish us.' Einstein's warning is dreadfully suggestive: 'I do not [know] about the Third World War but in the Fourth World War they will fight with sticks and stones.' In fact, war has lost its dynamics. Today, there is only one alternative to the atom, and that is *ahimsa* (non-violence). Gorbachev had made a declaration of unilateral measures to prevent the militarization of space. Only unilateralism can remove the obstacles in the path of disarmament. The concept of national security is outdated. It is now related to the global context. Gandhi had declared about unilateralism with the greatest emphasis at his command: 'Whether one or many, I must declare my faith that it is better for India to discard violence altogether, even for defending her borders. For India to enter into the race of armament is to court suicide. With the loss of India to non-violence, the last hope of the world will be gone.'[19] Economically, the armaments race is disastrous, strategically it is futile, politically it is like a blind alley. Legally or morally, it is a crime against humanity. Unilateralism, if it fails, might risk the lives of an entire nation, but the present policy of nuclear proliferation risks the lives of all humanity and dooms future generations. If unilateral steps are taken, the moral, social and economic strength of a nation will protect it from its adversaries better than nuclear weapons or nuclear alliances.[20] Gandhi had made many references to unilateral non-violent national defence in his writing: 'If I Were a Czech',[21] 'How to Combat Hitlerism?',[22] 'Appeal to Every Japanese'[23] and so on.

Like the structure of defence, technology has also affected our politics and its democratic fabric. Political leaders 'recognize violence as the foundation of realistic politics'.[24] Modern technology necessarily brings in centralization, which implies concentration of power. Power corrupts and absolute power corrupts absolutely. Centralization adds to the complexity of life, which is a destruction of all creative moral endeavour. It damages initiative, resourcefulness, courage and creativeness and diminishes opportunities of self-government. So the more centralization, the less democracy.[25]

Centralization cannot be sustained and defended without adequate force.[26] So to root out violence in the structure of politics, Gandhi had a vision of self-sufficient and self-managed village republics serving as the grassroots democracy as an alternative to a centralized party system and parliamentary democracy.

The Gandhian concept of *Pax Mundi* is neither Utopian nor simply ethico-spiritual but also structural and holistic. Unesco's declaration of peace-making, that 'since wars begin in the minds of men, it is in the *minds* of men that the defence of peace must be constructed', is significant and fundamental, but structural aspects needs to be highlighted. The minds of men do not work in a vacuum. They are conditioned by structures of society. Unless our socio-economic and political system is re-oriented towards peace, our minds cannot grasp it properly. Even our societal framework is determined by our technological model. These days we talk about dependence theory without realizing that Gandhi had described the international dialectics of industrial development long before the model of centre *versus* periphery was introduced. The foresight of Gandhi can be assessed in his warning against the mad rush to industrialism: 'God forbid that India should ever take [to] industrialism after the manner of the West. The economic imperialism of a single island (U.K.) is today keeping the world in chains. If the entire nation of 300 [now 900] millions took to similar economic exploitation, it would strip the world bare like locusts.'[27] Max Weber reminds us that we must develop a universal development concept. He says: 'Good fortune thus wants to be legitimate fortune.'[28] Gandhi therefore said: 'You cannot build non-violence on factory civilization.'[29] The rural economy eschews exploitation. Centralization as a system is inconsistent with a non-violent structure of society.[30] Gandhi was convinced that the 'mania for mass-production is responsible for the world crisis'[31]. No scheme of global peace can prove lasting unless it is linked to the creation of an equitable world economic order. Similarly, one of the great impediments in the creation of international understanding and peace is our sacrosanct faith in the doctrine of 'national sovereignty'. Gandhi's dialectical approach to sovereignty is useful, by which the role of sovereignty can be reduced but which does not violate principles of equality and justice. In fact, the ideal of 'one world' is the natural Gandhian ideal, but so far as it is not achieved, Gandhi advocated, 'think globally and act locally'. The ideal of a global village is a legitimate step towards overcoming aggressive nationalism. We have also to develop education for peace. In the total crisis of the world, education has its full share. Unfortunately, we have inherited a philosophy of struggle for existence, which is often portrayed as a battle between *creature* and *nature*, neglecting man and his tendency to learn the laws of harmony between himself and the universe. Because of increasing world tensions threatening the very survival of man, peace education has become important.

Conclusion

True, violence has lost its dynamics in this thermonuclear age but 'the hold of violence is so great that even though violence has failed a thousand times, we still put faith in its capacity to succeed'.[32] Perhaps it is rooted in our mental dispositions. It might be that man has inherited from the animals the instincts of aggression, hate and jealousy.[33] He still retains many things that he possessed before he became man. We need a mind which is free from its own conditioning. Hence during very ancient times, there had been provision for the study of military science but so far as the science of peace was concerned, it was left only to religious saints and seers. Today, we badly need a science of peace and non-violence in all our educational curricula and research. We have spent tremendous amount of time and resources to explore the science of violence now it is high time to turn our attention towards the power of non-violence. The only alternative to non-violence is non-existence. What is needed is an intellectual revolution. If we can discard the absolutist style of our thinking, there is hardly any scope for religious fundamentalism, national chauvinism, or even ideological fanaticism. But the ideology of *Pax Mundi* presupposes a *Pax Mundi* in our societal structure also. If bloodshed and murder are violence, exploitation is also violence. A society free from inequality and exploitation can pave the way for *Pax Mundi.*

References

1. Spengler, Oswald, *The Decline of the West*, Eng. trans., New York, 1926-28, Vol.II, Ch.II., VI, p. 49.
2. *Ibid.*, Vol. I, Ch.VIII, IX, p. 293.
3. Max Born, quoted in Hindeki Yukawa, *Creativity and Intuition*, Tokyo: Kodansha International, 1973, pp.189-90.
4. Fritzof Capra, *The Tao of Physics*, New York: Bantam, 1988, 2nd edn., p. 298.
5. Brown, G. Spencer, *Laws of Nature*, New York: Julian Press, 1972, pp.104-05.
6. Hisenberg, A., in Ken Wilber, ed., *The Spectrum of Consciousness*, New York: Julian Press, 1972, pp.104-05.
7. Schrodinger, Erwin., *What Is Life?*, Cambridge: Cambridge University Press, 1967, p.137.
8. Mechanism, F.H., *The Principles of Logic*, Vol. I., p.131.
9. Stebbing, L.S., *Logic For Practice*, p. 57.
10. Seminar on the Contributions of the Gandhian Outlook and Techniques to the Solution of Tensions Between and Within Nations, inaugural address by Jawaharlal Nehru.

11. Whitehead, A.N., *Process and Reality*, 1929, p. 4.

12. Joad, C.E.M., *Logical Positivism*, 1950, p. 29.

13. Hart, Robert., "A Gandhian Approach to the Fourth World", *Gandhi Marg*, Delhi, Vol. III. No. 9, December 1981, p. 515.

14. Gowan, Susan, *Moving Towards a New Society*, Philadelphia, 1976.

15. Statement by 33 Great Britain Distinguished Scientists, *The Texas Quarterly*, 1967, Note 69, p. 89.

16. Fritzof Capra, *The Turning Point, Science, Society and Rising Culture*, London, 1983, p. 3.

17. Iyer, T.R. Krishna, 'Nuclear Nationalism and the Law', *Philosophy and Social Action*, Vol. XI, No. 2, April-June 1985, p. 9.

18. *New Zurchar Zietung*, 6.3.1981, quoted by Detlef Kantousky in *Gandhi Marg*, June 1983, p.134.

19. Thapar, Romesh, 'Unilateral Disarmament', *Gandhi Marg*.

20. Jack, Honur A., 'Gandhian Unilateralism Revisited', *Gandhi Marg*, Vol. IV., Nos. 2-3, May-June 1982, p. 334.

21. *Ibid.*, 15.10.1938.

22. *Ibid.*, 22.6.1940.

23. *Ibid.*, 26.7.1942.

24. Sharp, Gene, *Social Power and Political Freedom*, Boston: Porter, Sargent, 1980, p. 29.

25. Dhawan, G.N., *The Political Philosophy of Mahatma Gandhi*, Ahmedabad: Navajeevan Press, Third Rev. edn., 1987, p. 284.

26. *Harijan*, 13.1.1942.

27. Gandhi, M.K., *My Picture of Free India*, Bombay: Pearl Publications, 1965, p. 52.

28. Weber, Max., *Essays in Sociology*, London: Routledge and Kegan Paul, 1948, p. 271.

29. *Harijan*, 18.1.1942.

30. *Ibid.*, 2.11.1934.

31. *Ibid.*, 2.11.1934.

32. Bhave, V., *Swaraj Shastra* (Principles of Non-violent Political Order) Trans. B. Kumarappa, A.B.S.S. Prakashan, 1955, p. 82.

33. Krishnamurti, J., *Krishnamurti To Himself*, London: Victor Gollancz, 1987, p. 27.

20

The Culture of Peace versus Materialism and Consumerism

N. Radhakrishnan

As humanity cruises towards the twenty-first century with confused visions of a world without war and boundaries, and statesmen, scientists, social activists, religious leaders and others reiterate from different world forums their commitment to the ushering in of a just and peaceful world order, the one thought that troubles the minds of sensitive souls who have no stake in any of these high-profile declamations is: What is happening to the average man, the man who is caught in the web of a soulless consumerist and materialistic culture with all the temptations it offers him? The general scenario is one of utter helplessness and nobody seems to have any control over his future. Added to this is the acquisitive tendency of those who are tempted to go for all kinds of things the market offers. A kind of insatiable greed seems to have taken control of all of us and no effort is being made anywhere to limit one's wants. And this has become a global phenomenon and no country seems to be free from it. Thus the average man finds himself to be truly at a crossroads of utter despair and helplessness. He is swept away by the mighty waves of an all-pervading materialism and consumerism. Economic well-being appears to be the sole purpose of life and the manner in which value systems are being trampled upon raises the big question: Where are we headed?

Mahatma Gandhi wrote:

> I suggest we are thieves in a way. If I take anything I do not need for my own immediate use and keep it I thieve it from somebody else. . . . It is the

> fundamental law of Nature, without exception, that Nature produces enough for our want from day to day and if only everybody realizes this and takes nothing more, there would be no pauperism in this world, there would be no man dying of starvation in this world.

But who listens?

From the world of philosophy, ethics, morality, religion, arts and literature which, in the not too distant past, acted like principal sources and supports to the evolution of the primitive man of yesterday to the computer genius of today, man finds himself caught in the dust and din of production, profit, distribution, interest rate, GNP and forex. While materialism in its original sense cannot be described as something evil by itself, it is the vulgar side of it which is believed to have pushed humanity to the cut-throat world of consumerism with utter disregard for human and ecological concerns. And we justify all this in the name of 'enlightened self-interest'.

One is reminded of the famous story of the rich man and the poor man who happened to pray at the same time in church. The rich man was pleading: 'O God, I need a million dollars to get out of my present financial difficulties.' The poor man's demand wad simple: 'O God, please grant me a loaf of bread or I will die of starvation today.' The rich man heard this, opened his wallet, took out a hundred dollars, and thrusting them into the poor man's hand, said: 'Now take this money and buy whatever you want. For heaven's sake please go away from here for I need God's individual attention. And let me pray.'

It appears that many conveniently forget the simple truth that the threats confronting humanity at this juncture arise mostly out of present-day man's psychological inability to comprehend the gravity of the highly explosive situation towards which humanity is moving. What impels the modern man in his so-called onward march? An insatiable greed for wealth, power and influence seem to have taken him over. And in this, economic clout, in short the purchasing power of an individual or a nation, is all that matters. Man's worth is now measured on the basis of his purchasing power and all spheres of human endeavour are being shaped by economic variables. It appears that economics has emerged as the single determining factor of human achievement and survival, and by 'growth' what is meant today is economic growth and man has all of a sudden been reduced to the level of a commodity whose worth is determined by factors other than what distinguishes man from beast.

> Does 'progress' clash with real progress? . . . I take it, we mean material advancement without limit and by real progress we mean moral progress which again is the same thing as progress of the permanent element in us.

> . . . If therefore material progress does not clash with moral progress, it must necessarily advance the latter. . . .

Gandhi pointed this out six decades ago. The law of growth presupposes that any growth will be subject to the innumerable constant factors which govern human life. Modern planners seem to have forgotten the simple truth that while some thing ought to be growing, others ought to be diminishing. Unlimited material consumption in a finite world is an impossibility, as Schumacher points out.

Man always lived in harmony with Nature, and what sustained him in all the crises he faced in his profound, courageous and determined march towards unravelling mysteries of various kinds is his respect for all forms of life around him. What has guided him in this long, very often distressing and disappointing but at the same time lively search for identity, is the realization of how all things in nature are dependent on one another. This is the core of ancient wisdom. The votaries of modernism, while they scoff at the ancient way of living, describing it as barbaric or jungle life, seem to have forgotten that it is this very system that gave them all the tools that they are using now to decry the worth of the foundation on which they stand. The problem with modern man is that he has proprietary rights over whatever he has conquered and this attitude appears to be guiding him in most of his endeavours.

The self-centred philosophy, and the systems he has developed on the basis of this outlook — the hallmark of which is the belief that nature had unlimited resources for all time to come — govern modern man's style of functioning. All of us who were lulled into the newly acquired instruments of 'liberation' which science and technology put in our hands have been rudely awakened by the alarm bells ringing all around now. From the Himalayan heights of materialistic comforts and belief we are being led to the abyss of all-round environmental pollution, ecological devastation, ozone depletion, the greenhouse effect, and so on, creating waves of shock in all thinking men. When Gandhi at the turn of the present century drew humanity's attention to this eventual scenario many scoffed at him and he was labelled orthodox and anti-progressive.

Eminent Western thinkers and economists like Schumacher, Handerson and Capra were among the earliest to appreciate Gandhi's views on a new economic system which they strongly believed would ensure the emergence of a new world order, and this was reflected in their advocacy of the now famous *Intermediate Technology, Soft Technology, and Technology with a Human Face*. Though one can see a slight divergence in their approach, there is an amazing confluence in their basic ideas. Gandhi with his advocacy of the development of self-sufficient village communities, trusteeship, disapproval of desires beyond the minimum, manual labour, the community-based *Nai Talim* (Basic Education) was aiming at developing a social order where nobody could be an exploiter or exploited and which would ensure the equitable distribution of wealth and justice.

To Gandhi economics and ethics were not unrelated areas of human endeavour: 'I must confess that I do not draw any distinction between economics and ethics. Economics that hurt the moral well-being of an individual or a nation are immoral and therefore sinful. Thus the economics that permit one country to prey upon another are immoral.' There are several issues involved in this assertion and to many of the votaries of unlimited growth words like morality or ethics do not mean anything. And even if they matter it might be just as inconvenient irritants. The Gandhi who strove for the spiritualization of politics so that politics would free itself from the stranglehold of power brokers, was a strange and odd man out, or at least it appeared so when he insisted on the adoption of pure means to achieve lasting and fair ends. Many considered and still consider this proposition of Gandhi's outlandish. And to their faithful followers morality and economics were different domains and only a mad man would think that they are related areas. 'The economics that disregard moral and sentimental considerations are like the wax works, that being life, still lack the life of the living flesh', Gandhi reminded us.

At the base of Gandhi's vision of life lies contentment and simplicity. Under that outlook he was propagating that multiplicity of material wants should not be the aim of life: the aim should be rather their restriction consistent with comfort.

It appears many have not read the remarkable essay, 'Gandhian Economy and the Way to Realise It', by J.C. Kumarappa. He summarized the salient difference between the 'artificial adjustment of demand to supply and the "natural economy" geared to the satisfaction of the primary needs of the largest number'. Kumarappa succinctly pointed out:

> Our life is something higher than material possessions and our life is also to be looked at from the possibilities of development of personality. The personality of an individual does not require for its development the satisfaction of a multiplicity of wants. In fact the simple[r the] life the more conducive it is [to] exercising the higher faculties.

To Gandhi 'life is more than money'. He said, 'It is cheaper to kill our aged parents who can do no work and who are a drag on our slender resources. It is also cheaper to kill our children whom we have to maintain, no matter what their maintenance costs us'.

What J.D. Sethi pointed out in this connection deserves attention:

> What Gandhi did was to lay down principles and methods of practice by which the individual and social utility functions were jointly determined. A non-violent economic society and the replacement of demand-oriented production by need-oriented production are two principles out of the many he put forward. The introduction of such principles makes an entirely new approach to the subject necessary and the methodology a social scientist must follow consequently becomes entirely different from that of modern social sciences.

To Gandhi true economics is the economics of justice. People will be happy insofar as they learn to do justice and be righteous. All else is not only vain but leads to destruction. To teach people to get rich by hook or by crook is to do them immense harm. Gandhi said that 'the art of accumulating much money for ourselves but also of contributing that our neighbours still have less. In accurate terms it is the art of establishing the maximum inequality in our favour'.

The emphasis Gandhi laid on developing alternative sources of energy show how far-sighted he was in his analysis of our duty to preserve the ecological balance. This also shows how Gandhi believed in the fundamental and hierarchical levels of natural phenomena. He was able to cut through academic jargon, expose the basic fallacies of current economic thinking through specific experiments which were there for everybody to see, draw lessons from them and offer alternatives based on sound ecological principles. Schumacher said with prophetic accuracy: 'Instead of listening to Gandhi, are we not more inclined to listen to one of the most influential economists of our century, the great Lord Keynes? Is there enough to go round? Immediately we encounter a serious difficulty: What is enough? Who can tell us? Certainly not the economists who pursue economic growth as the highest of all values and therefore have no concept of which have too little, but where is the rich society that says, "Half, we have enough?" There is none.' Gandhi had worked for such an order with his trusteeship idea.

It can be seen that Gandhi's thoughts were largely shaped by India's spiritual tradition and his own practical experience. He firmly believed that economics, like all other fields of human activity, could not be divorced from ethics and religion. *Moksha* (salvation) the summum bonum, the ultimate goal of the human endeavour, could be attained only through the fair practice of *dharma* (religion), *artha* (economy) and *kama* (desire).

The epoch-making changes humanity has been witnessing in almost all spheres in recent times make one wonder as to where to go from here. The various political developments taking place globally also have raised new doubts. An agonizing reappraisal and a desperate search for alternative strategies are seen everywhere. The international community in this search for a viable, alternative political and economic system is increasingly turning to Gandhi. There is greater awareness of the Gandhian model of development and political pundits, economic experts and even religious leaders seem to be examining Gandhi's views with considerable interest. There are more research foundations, groups and centres devoted to the study and examination of Gandhian thought in countries abroad than in India. Nelson Mandela's words, that humanity cannot afford to ignore the relevance of the path shown by Mahatma Gandhi, perhaps indicate the growing interest in Gandhi, particularly among those who fight for justice.

There has been a change in our outlook. This outlook emphasizes growth and development at any cost. And in this mad rush for material progress man has developed the attitude that he is the master of this universe and Nature and its resources are there for him to be exploited for his insatiable greed. This reminds us of the story of Leo Tolstoy where the greedy man who wants land and when given the option to go round and mark out the area he wants, finds himself driven by an endless desire to acquire as much area before the sun sets and ultimately finds himself lost in his incapacity to control his greed.

The general scenario is frightening. Many do not have even an iota of concern for the future. One cannot forget the caustic remark of that sprightly spirit Puck, in Shakespeare's *Midsummer Night's Dream*, 'Lord, what fools these mortals be'.

Science and technology have been able to provide man with wonderful things which were unimaginable a few decades ago, and the galloping horses of science and technology are largely responsible for altering the rhythm of human life in modern times. The tragedy is that instead of becoming more human and considerate man still acts under deadly passion, and reason and moral principles have become unwelcome aspects fit only for the caveman.

Greed and acquisitive tendencies which cannot be described as anything new to man have also grown along with all our development, but what accelerates their pace now is the unhealthy influence of the monster of consumerism. The widening tentacles of this growing Hydra seem to have cast a spell on almost all those who can afford or cannot. The techniques and strategy the promoters of this 'culture' adopt are temptation and allurement of all kinds, which very few can resist. The latest strategy adopted by them indicates the mindset of these people who exhort us, 'When the going is tough, the tough get going.' Realizing that unless children are attracted to their fold they will not by able to sustain their markets, an all-out attempt is discernible to conquer the imagination of children first and gradually condition their minds and tastes by flooding the markets with all sorts of consumer goods. This is a dangerous trend. Besides enslaving children it acts on life as a kind of opium.

Those who cannot afford to purchase all that the market offers and those whose purchasing power is negligible resort to dubious means to acquire at least some of the most attractive things. This brings in inevitably the unhealthy tendency to acquire money though any means, very often through corrupt practices. The desire to acquire money is not confined to any particular class. The temptation of the market and the lurking desire of people to acquire the latest from the bazaar thus lead to a very unhealthy situation. The developing social system and the resultant pressure on time and convenience in average middle-class families will justify the purchase of anything the market offers and every item in some way or other reduces drudgery, enhances efficiency, is a time saver, money saver and what not. Several juvenile crimes in many parts of the world have their inspiration mostly from the desire to acquire enough money to procure consumer goods. Similarly girls, particularly from low income or middle income groups, fall into the evil practice of prostitution to earn some quick bucks to maintain their social status within their peer groups.

The kind of aggressive, unprincipled rat-race of advertisement techniques the manufacturers adopt not only corrupt minds but also, as several studies have pointed out, a large number of murders, thefts and bank robberies owe their inspiration to the kinds of things that are to be seen in the print and electronic media. TV has become a very important source of generating violent and unhealthy tendencies among people.

It has been found in many developing countries that whenever there is street fighting or mob fury there is looting, and the items the looters take away are mostly consumer items from shops.

Several sensitive souls and visionaries who have been worried about these disturbing trends have been warning humanity of the impending dangers arising out of the obsession with materialistic advancement. Income generation, market, profit, turnover, import — these are some of the important concerns that regulate our lives now. To man now, Nature is just a commodity which can be marketed. Trees are grown mostly for the value of their timber and the value of rivers is based on the megawatts of electricity they can generate or the hectares of land they can irrigate.

> We notice that the mind is a restless bird, the more it gets the more it wants, and still remains unsatisfied. The more we indulge our passions the more unbridled they become. Our ancestors, therefore, set a limit to

> our indulgence. They saw that happiness was largely a mental condition. A man is not necessarily happy because he is rich, or unhappy because he is poor.

Gandhi had written this in his little classic *Hind Swaraj*, which was published when the twentieth century was just being ushered in. Now, these thoughts of Gandhi assume great significance as we are getting ready to welcome the next century.

Part - IV

Forming the Network of Actors in Peace

21

Experiencing Peace while Engaging in Experiments Based on Moral Principles

A.T. Ariyaratne

I

In the mid-1950s when we began the *Sarvodaya Shramadana Movement* the Government of Sri Lanka identified about 150 village communities who were subjected to all kinds of social, economic and political discrimination. It also established a special branch in the Rural Development Department to help these communities. This branch was called the Backward Communities Development Branch and was manned by an excellent head and several highly motivated and committed rural development officers. What was later called the *Sarvodaya Shramadana Movement* was started in one of these so-called backward communities by us who, at that time, were students and teachers mostly from leading high schools in the capital city.

As young people we recognized a serious flaw in our use of language when referring to these people, which in turn was giving rise to a superiority complex in our minds. I am sure that in spite of the good things we were doing, such as constructing roads to their villages, digging drinking water wells, making repairs to their small cottages, putting up a village school building, and so on, we were doing serious damage to their psyche as well as ours by calling them '*backward*'. Worse still, we referred to these villages in our printed programmes by the names of their castes. Even unintentionally we were creating an inferiority complex in the minds of these people while we, who were from well-to-do families from outside, were bloating our small egos.

Immediately after this realization came to us, maybe after two years of working in these villages, we dropped the word 'backward' and the names of castes from our spoken words as well as writing and printed programmes. No human being or community of people should be labelled 'backward' or outcaste for the reason that they are poor or powerless. In the words of Lord Buddha, 'No one becomes an outcaste (*vasala*) by birth. No one becomes a high caste (*brahmana*) by birth. One becomes an outcaste by one's actions. One becomes a high caste by one's actions'.

As long as we retain caste labels the caste system will remain. As long as the caste system remains there will be discrimination, injustice and conflict situations. Today *Sarvodaya* is working in over 10,000 village communities and no one is interested in or talks of castes or caste differences. It simply is not in our thinking or day-to-day language. So any discriminatory deeds based on this ignorant conditioning are not heard of in our *Sarvodaya* villages.

II

Let me take your mind to a village scenario where the community is striving to build a better life for itself by harnessing self-reliance and community participation. They can conceive of their situation as hopeless if they look only at the dark side of the reality of their life such as lack of basic necessities like water, health care, shelter, education, a means to a livelihood and so on. They also see the political and economic injustices they are subjected to. They see corruption, waste and destruction of public and natural resources around them, which is truly a manifestation of structural violence at their level of society.

Some from outside the villages advocate violence and adopt violent revolutionary means in attempts to destroy the establishment. Violent clashes occur and the lives of the innocent as well as the not innocent are lost. Some are cast into prisons without trial. The establishment makes this an excuse to take away the fundamental freedoms of villagers by enforcing emergency powers. The village community falls from the frying pan into the fire.

The scenario in a *Sarvodaya* village is different. They see a small spiritual spark in their cultural memory. Here the villagers are seeking an alternative path to overcome the almost insurmountable obstacles they face in their everyday lives. They have inherited a cultural tradition which rejects hatred, violence and vengefulness as a means to resolve conflict. 'Hatred does not cease by hatred. Hatred ceases by non-hatred. This is the eternal Law'. They remember these words of the Buddha. How can they translate this noble precept into concrete action which will help them to bring about a change in their life both physically and spiritually? In other words, they are seeking a non-violent revolutionary path to justice and freedom.

Besides their cultural heritage, what people in our poor communities have is the power to think, to feel and to work physically. Can their cultural values motivate them to harness this power voluntarily to bring about the satisfaction of even some of their basic human needs? Can the success of such an experiment create a fundamental transformation in their collective consciousness? One of the instruments they use for this experiment is what is called *shramadana* (sharing of labour, skills, resources, etc., for the common good) camp. *Shramadana* camps are a regular feature in *Sarvodaya* villages. Besides six to eight hours a day of manual work, three to four hours of spirituo-cultural activities are also performed in these camps to build collective consciousness.

What are called family gatherings are held before starting work, after the midday community meal and after work in the evenings. This is psychological infrastructure building in the community. In addition to the village community, others from surrounding *Sarvodaya* villages also come to these camps to participate and gift their labour and skills. The physical work they do is decided upon by them depending on a felt need like an irrigation canal or a tank *bund*. What I am trying to describe here is not the physical aspect of this experiment. Let us listen to a young volunteer who steps forward and calls the attention of may be 300 to 500 volunteers, children, youth, women and men, before they go out in their work teams to the work sites.

Dear elders, brothers and sisters,

> In a few moments we will be going to the work sites to share our labour for the well-being of all. Our physical labour will certainly result in an accomplished physical task. No doubt this will help us to satisfy a need we have long felt. But more important is the human qualities we develop during the course of the day when we interact with one another. We will interact through thoughts that originate in our minds. We will interact through words that leave our tongues. We will interact through every deed that is performed by our bodily actions. In short, we have to be mindful of every thought, word and deed from now onwards. To the extent we can transform ourselves as human beings, we can transform our families, our villages, our country and our world.
>
> Let us close our eyes. Keep our heads straight. Have a slight smile on our faces. Let us now meditate for a few minutes. Bring our minds to our breathing in and breathing out. Let us breathe in and breathe out mindfully. Think. May my mind be free from greed, ill will and ignorance and be healthy. May all of us gathered here be well and healthy in body

> and mind. May all those who work with me today appear to me as members of my own family. May the entire humanity be well and happy. May the entire living world be happy and peaceful. . . . Thank you. Now the team leaders can take their groups to their respective work sites.

This kind of meditation is practised before, during and after every kind of physical or social activity. Special songs are composed and sung at these events. Dances, dramas and other cultural activities remind us over and over that we are one human family, compassion towards all life should be our guiding thought, we should share whatever we can with others, we should learn to get joy out of service. We should develop the capacity to accept name and blame, gain and loss, with equal detachment and equanimity.

When people are reminded of the four ancient principles of social conduct, namely sharing, pleasant language, constructive activity and equality in association, and are provided with a physical, social and psychological environment like a *shramadana* camp in which to practise them, it is our experience that the noblest qualities that human beings and human society possess can still be made manifest and flourish.

If I may summarise, a *shramadana* activity, properly organised, provides for the following:

- An opportunity for any participant from within the community or outside to practise respect for all life, compassionate service towards others, dispassionate joy arising out of such actions and equanimity.
- An opportunity for the community to practice sharing, pleasant discourse, constructive action and equality.
- An opportunity for the community to make decisions affecting their lives.
- Development of a sense of togetherness in the community. Helping one another and learning from one another irrespective of divisive considerations such as social position, wealth, political beliefs, family feuds, etc.
- An opportunity for non-traditional leadership to emerge, particularly from youth and women.
- An opportunity for people to show their talents in aesthetic, cultural and technical activities.
- A sense of pride, accomplishment and confidence at having met some common need largely through their own effort.

- An opportunity for learning and acquiring organizational skills.

On this psychological foundation the community can develop a social infrastructure where pre-school children, school-going children, youth, women and mothers, farmers and craftsmen, all can be organized into functional groups. After sometime they can form themselves into a legally constituted society which can plan and implement welfare and development projects which they think are feasible. Sarvodaya Divisional Centres, District Centres, Development Education Centres and the Headquarters provide leadership training, skills training and other needed services for them to help themselves.

III

From psycho-social infrastructure creation, through organization building and legalization, individuals and communities have to be guided to build their own instruments and methodologies for economic and political well-being. Mahatma Gandhi's vision of *gram svaraj* or Lord Buddha's teachings on a Right Livelihood (*samma ajiva*) society provide us with a lot of insights into this stage of the experiment. This experiment, including the economic and political aspects, is already going on in over 2,500 advanced villages out of the 10,000 villages where the movement is active. These villages are going through what we describe as social, economic and political empowerment.

The very fact that this people's movement working towards non-violent transformation of man and society has survived amidst many obstacles shows that change based on moral principles is still possible. The obstacles faced by *sarvodaya* from around mid-1986 to mid-1994 were of an unprecedented nature. During this period *sarvodaya* was persecuted by the State with all its might.

This kind of non-violent social transformation, I believe from my experience, is the only way to counteract and reverse destructive forces globally operative today. Both leaders and the led have to realize the collective suicidal danger we all are facing and overpower the culture of self-aggrandizement that has blinded our sanity. Our leaders should abandon petty-mindedness and become large-hearted. We all should turn to the spring of spirituality which is still within our reach, depollute and clean the stream of morality that flows from it, and on either side of the stream build a culture of peace, sustainability and joy of living.

May you all be well and happy.

22

Working Together for Peace
The Asian Perspective

M. Aram

INDIA, fortunately, is the home of all religions and birthplace of four: Hinduism, Buddhism, Jainism and Sikhism. Christianity, Islam, Judaism, Zoroastrianism and Bahaism have found a hospitable home in India.

The way Zoroastrianism came into India is a fascinating story. When the Parsis came as refugees seeking asylum and landed on the coast of Gujarat, their head met the king of the region and asked for land and permission to live in peace. They would put aside their weapons. The king granted permission. The Parsi leader said that they would be like sugar added to the milk. To this day, the small Parsi community is like sugar in milk, a precious part of Indian society.

Moral Basis: Satya and Ahimsa

The moral basis for peace comes from religions. Religion has been the source of values. Mahatma Gandhi identified truth and non-violence as the twin principles of morality. The genius of Gandhi was that he extended *satya* and *ahimsa* to the social realm. This was his historic contribution. Let me quote Gandhiji himself.

> We have to make truth and non-violence, not matters for mere individual practice but for practice by groups and communities and nations. That at any rate is my dream, I shall live and die in trying to realise it.

Indeed he lived and died for non-violence and truth.

Nagaland Peace Mission

The Nagaland peace effort was an example of the practice of non-violence and truth. First there was cease-fire — the eschewal of violence as a method of settling a political dispute. Then there was 'continuous dialogue'. It took many years of dialogue before we arrived at the Shillong Peace Accord.

There was also the policy of transparency — truth was not hidden. The Peace Observers' Team helped in finding out the truth and letting it be known to all concerned and to the public.

When there was a stalemate in political talks, two principles were identified and accepted:

1. The solution should be *honourable* to all concerned.
2. The solution should be *acceptable* to both parties.

We moved towards a final solution where there is no vanquished or victor. It would be a win-win situation — the path Lord Buddha had shown. A sincere approach was of the essence. It took time before confidence was built. I recall the underground leader saying:

> Many people say, 'Peace, Peace'.
> It is not heart Peace, it is mouth Peace.

The Asian Scenario

Last month the ACRP (Asian Conference on Religion and Peace) met in Thailand, at Ayutthaya, the ancient capital. Dr A.T. Ariyaratne was there. Let me quote excerpts from the statement we adopted.

The emerging scenario in Asia presents positive trends which favour peace, security and good neighbourhood.

> Economic power is gaining precedence over military power.
> New global values find increasing acceptance.
> Democratic processes and citizens' actions are on the rise.
> Growing economic independence is another positive development.

On the other hand, there were areas of concern:

> The people of Asia are profoundly concerned about the ongoing arms build-up and proliferation of nuclear weapons.

The ACRP statement suggested specific steps to promote peace and good neighbourly relations in Asia.

- to relax visa regulations to enable free movement of people — to reduce military spending
- to make more budgetary allocation for education and health
- to send inter-religious goodwill missions to areas of conflict like Sri Lanka
- to create a common Asian security system

And further:

> Asia is rich in diversity of race, culture and religion. Let us appreciate and celebrate our differences and live together in a spirit of mutual accommodation and acceptance.

Building a Sharing Community

Sharing is much better than gifting. Sharing means a sense of community. Building a sharing community is eminently practicable. Our cultural background nourished by our respective religious teachings provide a suitable environment to launch such endeavours. Let us launch them.

Building a Culture of Peace

> The culture of peace
> Has to be built
> brick by brick,
> Act by act,
> Community by community.

The vision was given by Gandhiji in his inimitable words, with which I close:

> In this structure composed of innumerable villages, there will be ever-widening, never-ascending circles. Life will not be a pyramid with the apex sustained by the bottom. But it will be an oceanic circle whose centre will be the individual, always ready to perish for the village, the village ready to perish for the circle of villages, till at last the whole becomes one life composed of individuals never aggressive in their arrogance but ever humble, sharing the majesty of the oceanic circle of which they are integral parts.

23

Public Opinion and the Movement for Peace

Ali Aksad

THE present situation of the world *vis-a-vis* the issue of peace seems to me to be one of great danger. The climate of the world is wholly hostile. A grave danger, particularly nuclear, even though considerably lessened in an improved international political atmosphere, still faces us all. A destabilized world is now at the mercy of many regimes with access to the most destructive weapons, chemical, biological and nuclear. The culture of peace is systematically being undermined by greed, selfish consumerism, terrorism, and the dehumanization of society. Thus war has become one of the common features of human activities worldwide. Alongside, the very serious problems of poverty, inequality, deprivation and unemployment, the rise of extremism, racism, religious communalism and fundamentalism, the violation of human rights and the threat of ecological disaster are besetting mankind's aspirations for peace. Efforts for disarmament, development and genuine security are faced with an escalated arms race, new projects of militarization, a growing arms trade and policies of domination and strategic hegemony.

We find a great contrast between the dismal reality of today and mankind's hopes, built after the defeat of Hitler's fascism and the end of the Second World War, for building a new world that would have no war, exploitation, national oppression, hunger, hardship, colonialism, racism and communalism. Fifty years later, poverty still stalks our globe despite the huge wealth of small privileged elites. The UN Human Development Report published this year reveals that a mere 358 of the wealthiest people in the world have acquired assets equal to the combined annual income of 230 crore people. With the backdrop of such appalling inequality and injustice, which nullify all sustainable peace, humanity is threatened with an upsurge of violence, extremism, abuse of drugs, cultural degradation and obscurantism.

The arms manufacturers and the weapons trading countries, rightly dubbed the 'merchants of death', who have been hit by a fall in demand for their products as a result of the end of the Cold War, are now assiduously seeking markets. Certain optimistic features such as partial arms reduction, easing of East-West tension and conflict resolution can be noticed; but unfortunately they have not been able to overshadow the stark facts of the continued wars in different parts of the world, increasing acts of military intervention, an ever-expanding arms trade, the expanded NATO military bloc and the covert attempts of certain countries to build new strategic alliances in various parts of the world.

Being an important theatre of the military activities of major powers, the Asia-Pacific region today faces complex security problems. Notwithstanding the improvement of East-West relations, the growing preoccupation with economic issues and commercial and financial linkages, the military deployment of the United States — under cover of the US Defence Department's 'East Asia strategic initiative' project (April 1990) for the forward projection of American military power remains intact. The US military presence in the Pacific stretches to the Indian Ocean and the Gulf. This comprises nearly half of the US Navy's strength, two-thirds of the US Marine Corps and an elaborate network of US military bases and facilities on foreign soil, which are an important element in the militarization of the whole region.

There are also other countries contributing to militarization. SIPRI estimates that arms imports by East Asia rose from $2.6 billion in 1983 to $4.1 billion in 1988. The corresponding figures for the South Asian subcontinent were $2.4 billion and $6.9 billion.

This dangerous spiral of military expense and rampant proliferation of sophisticated military hardware continues unabated, which inevitably heightens regional tensions, unleashes arms races and poses a growing threat to peace. This trend seriously jeopardizes the prospects of security, stability and development in these areas. Also, certain national and international circles, taking advantage of the situation, particularly in South Asia, seek to push the countries of the region into mutual distrust, suspicion and confrontation, fanning fundamentalist and communal violence and cross-border terrorism. All this is being done in covert collusion with the same elements and under the strategic framework that existed during the Cold War, aiming at thwarting people's aspirations for peace, stability and social progress through cooperation and good-neighbourly relations.

Peace is the first basic need for overcoming the problems facing mankind. An international order that guarantees peaceful coexistence and harmonious relations among nations is therefore to be considered an essential component and initial premise for tackling the problems of poverty, deprivation and underdevelopment which cruelly afflict much of Asia, Africa and Latin America. I prefer to consider the issue of peace in relation to culture in this context. Agreeing with the conference preamble describing the United Nations as the main political forum for world peace, we may here recall few lines from Chapter IX of the Charter: 'With a view to the creation of conditions of stability and well-being which are necessary for peaceful and friendly relations among nations based on respect for principles of equal rights and self-determination of peoples, the United Nations shall promote solution of international, economic, social, health and related problems and international cultural and education cooperation.' The linking of peace with cultural cooperation and development is very clearly emphasized here and Unesco was established on the basis of this principle.

A vital part of the programme of Unesco for this period is that of working towards a culture of peace. This culture inherently contains two main thrusts in its action: development for peace and peace for development, which is to be materialized through international cooperation. A large number of non-governmental organizations, the World Peace Council being among them, encouraged by the programmes of Unesco, joined in fulfilling the noble aim for world peace with justice and the building of a culture of peace. National, regional and international peace organizations and democratic public bodies have taken upon themselves the task of establishing a network of activities, uniting movements and popular efforts for the promotion of a culture of peace in the face of violence and war, cultivating and developing ideas of tolerance, of respect for and solidarity with all fellow beings. Following the Unesco programme, people in different countries, including Bangladesh, took active part in the prevention and solution of conflicts, in campaigns of peace education, mobilization of public opinion and the building of a mass movement promoting peace.

The prevention of war and the resolution of conflicts should be the primary responsibility of the UN and related agencies and organizations. Regrettably, the actual performance of the UN so far has in numerous cases been disappointing. In the recent period, with the UN being in the grasp of one major power, the Charter has been often flouted and UN bodies misused in the narrow interest of that power. Although nations nominally proclaim adherence to the UN Charter and describe peace as a prerequisite for social justice and progress, the precious resources of the world are being constantly wasted on the production of weapons of destruction, to the detriment of economic prosperity, national sovereignty and the growth of creative culture.

Keeping the true role of culture in view, Unesco declared in its constitution, 'Since war begins in the minds of men, it is in the minds of men that the defence of peace must be constructed'. In its own domain Unesco clearly realized the need for rallying the forces of the human mind to this cause — the cause of a culture of peace and the emancipation of human creativity. The defence of peace that is expected to be constructed in the minds of men through international cooperation and a joint struggle for peace, disarmament, development and social justice, therefore remain its top priority. It is here that various social movements expressing the popular and democratic will of the people and of organizations, for example anti-war organizations, trade unions, professional associations, development agencies and environmental groups have a vital role to play. They can set political agendas, mobilize public opinion and popular energies and create more lasting cross-national and cross-cultural links and an international network for the actors and builders of peace. Such a network, regionally and internationally composed of non-governmental organizations, popular campaigns and movements for a culture of peace and a world without nuclear and other weapons of mass destruction, seems likely to be effective, for it would reflect the fears, concerns and aspirations of a large number of people.

To fully understand the problem and to define solutions from a practical point of view, we need to examine and evaluate concrete issues in specific situations and particular geographical areas. Taking into consideration the situation prevailing in South Asia, I may propose an action programme towards the culture of peace as an agenda for action until the year 2000 by way of acting together for peace. This programme presupposes the togetherness and united action of all forces of peace in our region. The agenda for uniting different organizations and movements along with eminent public figures corresponds with the aims and objectives of Unesco. This would address the urgent problems of our subcontinent as well as of the world.

24

An Odyssey of Peace

Angelo Fernandes

THE Second Vatican Council, 1962-65, was one of the major turning points in the modern history of religion. The Church's openness to the world, to people of all living faiths and to all men of goodwill was one of its most striking features. Its message to humanity at the very outset emphasized the desperate imperative of peace and social justice as the key to God's rule on Earth and the improvement of the quality of life, economically and socially, of the poor and the lowly in the needy regions of the world. Peace and justice have thereafter been for me an abiding concern. Along with others from India, Asia and elsewhere, I was privileged to explore in numberless consultations and seminars all over the world the meaning and parameters of peace, peace-making and peace-keeping. Peace is an enterprise of justice and the outcome of love. That has been the burden of many discourses. I have occasionally envisaged the quest for peace as a personal and corporate journey towards a better human life for as many people as possible.

In the Bible, peace and justice are synonymous and connote a paradisiacal fulness and wholeness which is both a gift of God and a human enterprise to be carved out of the circumstances of life.

Towards Peace with Justice, published in 1981, is a collection of some of my essays on human dignity and human rights, on food for the hungry millions, on true and integral human development, on the goal of total disarmament and the futility of using force for conflict resolution. In more recent times I have been acutely seized of the danger to the planet from the fallout of industrialization and the ravishing of nature by unscrupulous individuals and corporations.

Experience of Dialogue, published in 1994, details at length twenty-five years of working for the cause of peace with persons of all living faiths. This was not so much for theological debate between belief systems as for the living dialogue of religiously committed persons applying the insights and experience of religion to the pressing problems of our age, which constitute obstacles to harmony and concord within and between nations.

One major obstacle not yet seriously addressed is that of national chauvinism. With the demise of communism and the gathering of the biggest ever meeting of heads of state and government at the Rio Earth Summit in 1992, hopes were raised that all the resources of the world — material, cultural, moral and spiritual — would be harnessed for a massive campaign for putting an end to destitution in the world by the year 2000 and beating the poverty problem within a decade or two thereafter. But that turned out to be a lost opportunity. The building of a human society based on freedom, solidarity, justice and love was given a fresh impetus by the UN Social Summit at Copenhagen in March 1995.

WCRP was closely associated with these seminal strategies and continues to function as one of the principal multi-religious awareness building and conscience raising institutions for lasting peace with justice in our troubled world.

This seminar, however, is of a different nature. Its focus is on the experience of peace of participants hailing from all parts of Asia and their experience in peace-making efforts. This innovative venture is a fresh contribution to the culture of peace starting from within the depths of our being, where all are bonded together in the spirit, and reaching out together for fulness of life for each and all with the wisdom that comes from on high. Faith in God and faith in man combine to make a specific contribution to the culture of peace from the standpoint of religion.

Pathways to Peace

If there is right in the soul,
There will be beauty in the person;
If there is beauty in the person,
There will be harmony in the home;
If there is harmony in the home,
There will be order in the nation;
If there is order in the nation,
There will be peace in the world.

Personal, Familial and Societal Peace

In the 1930s in the days of my priestly training, personal peace was first experienced as stemming from and inherent to union with God, and living in harmony with all my 200 confreres who, with one mind and one heart, were preparing for the common goal of becoming labourers in the vineyard of the Lord. 'How wonderful it is, how pleasant, for God's people to live together in harmony' (Ps 133/1). The growth of one's personality was thus seen as a matter of ever better relationships with God and neighbour and world.

This interior peace, which surpasses all understanding, has grown and developed over the years through daily prayer and meditation, first discursive and later more contemplative when the prayer encounter became a heart-to-heart affair — the giving and receiving of love.

Introducing people to the prayer experience through priestly ministry has added to the enjoyment of peace. This became even more pronounced when I published *As You Pray So You Live*, recently reprinted.

From 1993 the experience has been shared through a series of booklets, and they bring peace and joy to many everywhere. *Being In Love and Living to the Full* and the sequels — 'more', 'still more' and 'yet more' about 'Being in Love' — go to hundreds of friends who keep in touch. It is summed up in the logo 'Hand in hand with the Lord and with each other'. God's gift of peace comes through beautifully in the Church's New Year greetings to one and all: 'The Lord bless you and watch over you; the Lord make His face shine upon you and be gracious to you; the Lord look kindly on you and give you peace'(Numbers 6/24-26).

In the 1940s, through close association with hundreds of children, growing boys and girls, I learnt to see and experience life through the eyes of these unspoilt images of the Creator. I understood better why Christ said: 'Unless you change and become like children, you will never enter the Kingdom of Heaven' (Mt. 18/3).

It was a case of learning the beauty of peace from life, from God's showpieces, the darlings of the universe. Listening more to these harbingers of a better tomorrow, we might catch their sense of wonder, joy, inner serenity and relatedness to all, regardless of all man-made barriers and prejudices — a much desired boon.

My musical experience with a children's choir and school orchestra taught me the beauty of 'harmony', also in the ordering of human relations. I later discovered that this concept of harmony was a very Asian one from the days of Confucius onwards.

At this time, I also got a taste of experiencing unpeace. Thanks to being in touch with hundreds of military chaplains of the Allied forces of World War II passing through Bombay, from the north-eastern borders of India and the countries of South-east Asia. I experienced, vicariously, the scourge of war and the devastation it inflicts on innocent families and especially on women and children. The folly of trying to resolve conflicts through the use of force thus came home to me already then, long before I became actively involved in peace-making efforts with adherents of all religions. Group Captain Leonard Cheshire's return to the Church after his witnessing the horror of Hiroshima also had its effect on me. Cheshire Homes in Dehradun, Delhi and around the world proclaim loudly that works of mercy for the handicapped and unwanted are also works of peace. Mother Teresa's entire life and activities have been an exemplification of this.

Peace in the Family

A very significant memory of the 1950s was my experience with the Christian Family Movement. The many splendid couples and their families collaborating in the movement 'For Happier Families' communicated to me the beauty and splendour of familial peace. The family is the bedrock on which a better world has to be constructed.

Rampant individualism, seen also in schools and colleges, is spawning selfish and greedy persons with scant concern for others. The sooner peace-making efforts are focused on the basic cell, the family — the primary unit and nucleus of society — the better will it be for the world at large. The future of humanity passes through the family. This conviction of the 1950s has deepened over the years, and working with and for the renewal and enrichment of the family has become one of my ongoing endeavours. A few years ago I gladly introduced 'Family Fest' of the Focolare Movement to Doordarshan, our television network in India. I recently had an enjoyable Family Encounter for 170 persons in Mumbai on 'The Family, the School and the Media — Partners in Education'.

Christ Is Our Peace

Through the spiritual and educational ministry in which I was engaged at this time, I came to realize better that Jesus Christ is the decisive factor in history as planned by God. He is the supreme and everlasting gift which God offers to humankind. By breaking down all barriers by his death on the cross, Christ opened a path of freedom to all through his faithfulness to the Father. All can become sons and daughters of God through faith. We all can now have access in one spirit to the Father of all.

God's love is a love of friendship, and growing in intimacy and union with Christ, even the cosmic Christ, became for me the most powerful motive, the mainspring and springboard for further efforts to share God's Peace Plan with the world and work in the power of His Spirit, to bring it to fruition: Christ Is Our Peace. The conviction grew in me that the closer we all get to God in whatever ways are open to us, the easier becomes the challenge of healthy and wholesome human relations and the task of peace-building at all levels of society. Peace is both a gift of God and a personal and corporate thirst for justice.

In the early 1960s there burst upon the world the Second Vatican Council. I was closely associated with this momentous event in a variety of ways.

The opening message of the Council was to humanity, and it was one of well-being, love and peace. The two issues singled out as being of special urgency were peace between peoples and social justice. This was my first major involvement in peace-making at the societal level.

One prominent feature of the Council's great document on the Church in the modern world was the opening of the Church to the world, to all Christians and to persons of all living faiths on our common pilgrimage through life towards our common destiny. This was a whole new vision which led to many vital decisions and significant actions. One was the overture of the document, which proclaims:

> The joy and hope, the grief and anguish of the men of our time, especially of those who are poor or afflicted in any way, are the joy and hope, the grief and anguish of the followers of Christ as well.

Even more specific and germane to our purpose is the famous paragraph 90 of the same document:

> Taking into account the immensity of the hardships which still afflict a large section of humanity and with a view to fostering everywhere the justice and love of Christ for the poor, the Council suggests that it would be most opportune to create some organization of the universal Church whose task it would be to arouse the Catholic community to promote the progress of areas which are in want and foster social justice between nations.

Bringing this about has been one of my cherished memories.

The Council for Justice and Peace

Some years later, Paul VI published his epoch-making Letter on 'The Development of Peoples', wherein he declared that development is the new name for peace. He then established at the Vatican the Council for Justice and Peace. For ten years I was one of the thirty members from the five continents who met regularly to debate and relay to churches all over the world the dimensions of the crucial work for peace with justice. It was a great education in understanding the dynamics of societal peace-making, at international and world levels.

For two four-year terms, the Commission for Justice and Peace, of which I was Chairman, pursued this matter in India. We took the message to all areas of the country and today in practically all the 131 ecclesiastical units there are social service societies which deal with emergencies and rehabilitation, with welfare programmes, with self-help projects, and with issues of justice and peace for all, irrespective of caste or creed.

Caritas India, which functioned as our secretariat, has done and continues to do admirable work in such development, both by way of animation, awareness building and grassroots involvement in the villages of India and other needy areas. During my tenure as Archbishop of Delhi, this has also been done through what is known today as 'Chetanalaya', our diocesan social action organization in Ashok Place. It has a large network of field workers reaching out to the slums and rural areas of the capital and its environs in neighbouring Haryana.

Some Ecumenical and Multi-Religious Experiences of Peace-Making

The world's most practical Christian ecumenical venture was launched in 1967 when the Vatican and the World Council of Churches mutually agreed to establish a Joint Committee on Society, Development and Peace (Sodepax) with headquarters in Geneva. Its first venture was the historic international conference at Beirut, to consider the problem of world development. In concrete terms it spoke of the responsibility of all churches to awaken their constituents to their duty of swaying public opinion to the realization that in today's world every man is indeed his brother's keeper.

The splendid report helped the landmark conference to become a launching pad for the vital task of arousing the conscience of humankind to the problems of and the need for world development. It was a great blessing to have participated actively in this high-calibre encounter. It was peace education and experience of a higher order.

Peace Experience in the 1970s

The decade after that had a rich harvest of peace initiatives. Along with Christian leaders of all denominations in India, I helped organize a consultation in Delhi to examine the current Christian understanding of development in the Indian context and promote awareness, concern and involvement on the part of the churches. That was in February 1970. *Hunger for Justice* carries the full proceedings.

Also in 1970, in July at Tokyo, I was associated with a similar Asian Conference described in its report as 'Liberation, Justice, Development'. It drew together 180 participants from 19 Asian countries and included representatives of the major religions of Asia as well as consultants from the United Nations, the World Council of Churches and the Vatican, and fraternal delegates from Africa, the Pacific islands, Europe and North America.

Particularly significant was the consultation on 'Christian Concern for Peace' held at Baden, Austria, in 1970. The report — *Peace, the Desperate Imperative* — contains chapters on political conflict and the dynamics of peace, Christian responsibility for world peace, education for peace, human rights and world peace, etc.

Here is an interesting sidelight. At this major conference of Christians of the world, we grouped those from Africa and Latin America in one room, those from Europe, the US and Canada in another, and Asians in a third with the question: 'What does peace mean for you? Discuss and report back'. The first group summed up its findings as 'liberation', the second as 'peace-keeping' and the third as 'the integral development of each person, man on his way to God and all persons everywhere'. Presenting our findings to the assembly, we pleaded that all three approaches be taken together if we really wanted peace on Earth.

In Russia and Australia

At the request of the Vatican, I led a small delegation of Catholic scholars for a dialogue with the Russian Orthodox Church at Zazorsk on 'The Role of Religion for a World in Transformation'. All agreed when I suggested that we extend the dialogue to persons of all living faiths.

Working together from a religious standpoint on human issues is a form of inter-religious dialogue which is proving very effective. In early 1970 I gave the keynote address to the first ecumenical conference in Australia at Sydney on 'Action for World Development'. The burden of my message was the role of the churches in developed countries. The lecture was reproduced in the *Ecumenical Review*, Geneva, and summarized in *Theology Digest* in the USA.

In Canada and New Zealand

Yet another aspect of the peace-making spectrum came to the fore at the launching of WCRP Canada in November 1975, when I gave the keynote address on 'A New International Economic Order and the Role of Religion'. I wound up with the ten points of the 1975 Hammarskjold Report, which map out succinctly the field of the possible. Significantly, the first is 'Place the satisfaction of needs — beginning with the eradication of poverty — at the focal point of the development process'. And at the end: 'Adapt the United Nations system to new requirements'. Both are very relevant today.

In the same decade, in 1979, I addressed the Medical Guilds of Auckland and Wellington, New Zealand, on 'Social Justice Priorities in Health Care'. The burden of the message was that health is wholeness of body, mind and spirit. It calls for a community-based approach in health care that goes beyond the psychosomatic to include 'the great sickness of our age, namely, aimlessness, boredom, lack of meaning and purpose' (Viktor Frankl).

World Religions for World Peace

Already in the 1960s those who were working together ecumenically in this field felt the need to expand their vision and enlist all believers in the common struggle for peace with justice. This came about in a marked way at the beginning of the Gandhi Centenary Year in January 1968, when an International Inter-Religious Symposium on Peace took place in Delhi. It was of an exploratory nature and brought together 46 participants from 9 nations representing 9 world religions. In his preface to *World Religions and World Peace* — the book that published the proceedings — Dr Zakir Hussain stated, 'If religious leaders will stand for peace and justice unequivocally, then we take a big step towards world peace'. He went on to add, 'If the spirit of the Sermon on the Mount, Buddha's philosophy of compassion, the Hindu concept of *ahimsa* and the passion of Islam for obedience to the will of God can combine, then we shall see generated the most potent influence for world peace'.

At the symposium, an interim advisory committee of 16 persons of major religions was set up to explore the possibility of organizing a multi-religious world meeting with persons from around the globe to consider the world's most urgent problem — Peace. I was asked to act as Chairman and did so for the three exploratory meetings we had: the first with Patriarch Athenagoras at Istanbul, the second at the Boston Institute of Technology, Massachusetts, and the third at Kyoto, Japan. Only then did the historic Kyoto Conference take place in October 1970 in the International Conference Centre of that beautiful city. In a major address on 'Religion and Peace', apart from dealing with salient points of the components of peace-making and the main items of the agenda, namely human rights, development and disarmament, I made a strong plea for non-violence, not only as a citizen of the country that gave Gandhi to the world, not only as a follower of the Prince of Peace, but as a man, any man, a voice of the nameless millions of every creed and condition, of men 'who are weary of violence and persuaded that the time for peace is right now and the place to begin right here'.

The conference was a major event which was attended by more than a thousand persons including 219 full delegates. It was the fulfilment of a centuries-old dream often formulated as a question: 'When will the religions of the world make peace, not war?' Some initial steps were taken to fulfil the dream.

The Kyoto Declaration highlights the things on which all religions are united as being more important than the things which divide us. It has become part of the syllabus for education for peace, and also the basis of the 'global ethic' that emanated from a parliament of religions at Chicago in August 1993.

Given the success of the Kyoto Conference, it was felt by all that we should not disband but should continue to work together for the paramount goal of peace. And so was born the World Conference on Religion and Peace, which has its headquarters at 777 UN Plaza, New York, U.S.A. Elected Executive President, I guided the destinies of the nascent organization for 14 years with a splendid team of collaborators and a brilliant, dynamic Secretary General in the person of Dr Homer Jack, now with the Lord. His autobiography has just been published.

The findings of the Kyoto Conference were presented to the Secretary General of the United Nations, U Thant, in early 1971. I happened to be in New York and gladly joined the group.

Peace Experience at WCRP Assemblies

In addressing the subject of 'Religion and the Quality of Life', WCRP II brought in an additional issue: concern for the environment. It also called for 'food for the hungry millions' in view of an FAO consultation a few months later in Rome. Peace-makers cannot afford to bypass the basic rights of all to food, shelter, education and health, and expect peace to come about. Social justice is the key to a more peaceful world. All violence is traceable in the last analysis to injustice, real, alleged or imaginary, the last often created and projected by fundamentalist groups into their followers.

After the meeting, Europe got down to working at establishing WCRP Europe. Dr Maria Lucker at Bonn was identified as the chief organizer, and she provided very effective leadership. It was a pleasure to work closely with such an enlightened and committed leader. My first book in this field of endeavour was published at this time: *Religion, Development and Peace*. It reports on some of the principal events I have so far described.

The whole movement for peace got a great boost when the World Synod of Catholic Bishops meeting in Rome in 1971 declared in its report on 'Justice in the World' that action for the transformation of society is a constitutive dimension of the preaching of the message of Jesus Christ. That pronouncement has made the rounds and generated a greater social awareness all over the globe. Speaking for the bishops of India, I quoted Dr Raul Prebisch, then Secretary General of UNCTAD, to the effect that there was no political will to deliver the goods. That, he said, was an ethical and spiritual problem. It is still very much with us. At world assemblies of WCRP it fell to me to give the lead to the handling of the theme chosen for prayer, discussion and action. I did so at Kyoto in 1970 on 'Religion and Peace', at Louvain in 1974 on 'Religion and the Quality of Life', at Princeton, New Jersey, in 1979 on 'Religion in the Struggle for World Community', at Nairobi in 1984 on 'Religion Is for Life'.

At Nairobi we elected ten presidents representing the major religious traditions. As a founder of WCRP I was elected and have continued as president emeritus at the behest of our worldwide constituency.

Some Significant Highlights

The Princeton assembly of 1979 was a breakthrough. For the first time in recent years there were religious leaders from the People's Republic of China, and Mr Zhao Puchu became one of our vice-presidents and later on a president.

The Spiritual Dimension of Peace-making

WCRP assemblies are a marketplace for sharing ideas from various religious perspectives. At Princeton a distinctive contribution was the 'Strengthening of the Spiritual Dimension'. When in that same year, 1979, we met Mr Kurt Waldheim and others at UN headquarters, we were told: 'All the problems of the world are coming to us and they are clamouring for a spiritual input', which only an NGO like WCRP can give.

The definition of spirituality which emerged from WCRP III bears comparison with any other. It is proving very effective. 'Spirituality is the consciousness of responsibility (including responsibility for restructuring political and economic institutions) rooted in one's experience of the Divine'. The revitalization of our spiritual life through meditation, prayer, silent reflection and spiritual exercises was considered a fundamental matter in our struggle for world peace and justice. It empowers us for our work in the world.

Already a step had been taken in this direction at the First Asian Conference on Religion and Peace at Singapore in 1976, when 'Meditation and Integral Humanism as a

Spirituality for Today's World' was hailed as an Asian breakthrough. At Beijing in 1986 'Meditation and Religious Experience' was described as religion's specific contribution to peace-making.

At Nairobi we had the presence of the Nobel laureate Archbishop Desmond Tutu. In my address, 'Religion Is for Life', I quoted 80 Nobel laureates as saying that the current human behaviour at the world level was the 'silent genocide' of the poor and hungry of the world. An Irish philosopher has called it 'not injustice but blasphemy, the defacing of the image of God in His people'. Archbishop Tutu, after wittily dethroning the doctrine of apartheid, said the same: 'To treat a man, woman or child as if they were less than a child of the Divine destined for a life of unimpeded unity with the Deity is to commit not just a crime against humanity, but veritably to be guilty of blasphemy, for it is nothing short of dishonouring God Himself'.

Mostly Issue-Oriented Experiences of the Peace Spectrum

World Peace Day has been celebrated every year since 1968 on a facet of the peace spectrum, presented to the world first by Pope Paul VI and then by his successors. The world has a celebration on 1 January but India has it on or around 30 January, the death anniversary of Mahatma Gandhi. This was a decision of the Justice and Peace Commission of the bishops of India. The celebration has always been of all religious traditions together.

It was unexpected but very significant to join Christian business entrepreneurs at Zurich in 1976 as they sought to gear business, the motor of society, towards assisting the peace efforts of the nations. Economic justice is part of the peace-making process. Moving in the direction of profit for human development is the creative role of enterprise. WCRP Europe has recently held an important consultation on 'Economic Justice for Peace'.

Journalists and the Press in Cracow, Poland, got acquainted with WCRP and its thrust for peace when I was a guest of Cardinal Karol Wyotjila in 1975. It was a delight to share a peace experience in a country still under the heel of communism. Years later, in 1994, John Paul II hosted at the Vatican WCRP's Sixth World Assembly and delivered the opening address. The roughly 1,000 participants then adjourned to Riva del Garda, in the neighbourhood of Verona, Italy, for their six-day meeting. The next experience was at the Ramakrishna Mission, New Delhi, where I made my contribution to a series of addresses on 'Enlightened Citizenship'. The published work is reverentially dedicated to 'all those who love all, those who have no aliens at all, those who make the whole world their own as if they were their own kith and kin'.

A very satisfying experience was WCRP's role in bringing off the United Nations declaration on the elimination of all forms of intolerance and discrimination based on religion or belief. The November 1981 document is a triumph for religious freedom. This issue was previously highlighted in the Second Vatican Council, and was one of the Peace Day messages of Pope Paul VI.

It was an honour, a privilege and service to the country to have delivered the 8th Gandhi Memorial Lecture at New Delhi on 30 January 1982. 'God's Rule and Man's Role' highlights Gandhiji's total commitment to social justice and social change as a 'religious response'. 'I could not live for a single second without religion. . ; every activity of a man of religion must be derived from his religion, for religion means being bound to God, that is to say that God rules your every breath'. I went on to add: 'The earthly task and the heavenly vocation are different but this does not destroy their unity; they form a unity without being identical'. I also emphasized Gandhi's clear vision of the goals we have to achieve, the purity of means for the same, and the goodwill, commitment and option for the purpose we have to cultivate and bestow.

The National Disarmament Meeting in Delhi in 1983 was a unique experience for a religious personality in the midst of a host of scientists, military strategists, politicians, statesmen and leading journalists. Afraid that disarmament might be equated with peace, I presented — unasked — two papers, one on the morality of nuclear war the other on the quest for peace. The final report, which carries the technical papers and these two contributions, was presented to the 60 heads of state who assembled in Delhi a few months later.

'Summons to Dialogue' is a reprint of the Federation of Asian Bishops' Conference. It was delivered to the bishops and other major religious priests and sisters of Sri Lanka in 1983. It covers the entire field — the meaning and urgency of dialogue, its many forms and its requirements. I made a strong plea for working towards peace with justice through a fellowship of silence and a fellowship of service with persons of all living faiths in Asia and in the world.

Inter-religious dialogue has come to stay. The clock cannot be put back, especially after what happened at Assisi in October 1986, when fifty religious leaders of all Christians, and fifty representing all other religious traditions met, at the behest of Pope John Paul II, to pray, fast, and walk on a short symbolic pilgrimage to the tomb of Saint Francis, the poor man of Assisi. It was a dramatic expression of the universal longing for unity and worldwide peace. I was privileged to be a special invitee, and WCRP assisted with the organization of the event. To be present to the Lord in prayer with persons of all religious traditions of the world was an inspiring and elevating experience. The memory is a lasting gift to the making of a better future for humankind.

Living and Working Together with Persons of Other Faiths in Asia

This was a Christian ecumenical experience of the leaders of most of the denominations in the continent. Rising above their differences, Protestants and Catholics united in God's 'covenantal love' to embrace each and all in Asia and the world. Such motivation is a great incentive for further action.

Later meetings led to the opening up of fresh horizons for communion and cooperation. This peace-making process is from a theologico-spiritual standpoint. It is based on the action of the Spirit at work in the hearts of human beings in all cultures and all religions.

The movement of the bishops of Asia concerning the theology underlying inter-religious dialogue, led to a study on the theology of harmony. The Bible itself begins on a note of cosmic harmony and ends with 'the new Heaven' and the new Earth and the gathering of all of creation into that perfect harmony where God is all in all, the first and the last, the beginning and the end.

In 1990 I was elected President of OIEC, the International Catholic Education Office based in Brussels, with a far-flung constituency of 240,000 Catholic schools in the five continents. Asked to give the organization a new orientation, I focused on 'Basic Education for All By the Year 2000', a challenge to the existing school system. My address was based on the Jomtien (Thailand) Assembly of March 1990 and the Convention on the Rights of the Child of September 1990, at the first ever summit of heads of state and of governments of the world.

The special features of the movement are that children of the formal school system, acting as agents or levers of change, carry to family units of the slums in the neighbourhood a basic education package programme that includes, besides literacy, developmental components, basic skills, values and attitudes.

Distance learning centres attached to the school strengthen the concern for the underprivileged. I made a video cassette for the purpose which goes by the name of 'Outreach'. The message is put across in 35 minutes.

'The World's Religions for the World's Children' was a multi-religious effort that helped to provide ethical and spiritual insights to Unicef and the children's summit of September 1990.

The following year, the Institute for Objective Studies, Okhla, organized a symposium in Delhi on 'Pressing Issues Facing the Nation'. Given the state of the country — poverty and deprivation and its resulting prejudices; communalism and religious intolerance — I chose to speak on 'Poverty, Communalism and Violence'.

In particular, I analysed the causes of unrest and summed up by stating that 'the root causes of the unrest in the country are to be found in social and economic terms of poverty, unemployment, social injustice, widening disparities, corruption and unplanned urban growth'.

The remedy is respect for the basic humanity of man. The human person is more sacred than all the churches, shrines, mosques, temples or gurudwaras in the land. The human person alone is made to the image of God. All other signs of God are of relative value. Human dignity is in fact the very basis of true peace-making. I made a plea for non-violence and issued a call for common concern through inter-religious dialogue.

As preparation for making a multi-religious commentary on the agenda of the Rio Earth Summit, as requested by UNCED, leaders of WCRP and of Sao Paulo, Brazil, met in Campos de Jordao at the Jewish Centre there in April 1992. The year before, I had prepared and shared a paper on 'The Ecological Crisis and the Quest for Peace'.

Along with Hindu, Muslim, Buddhist and Christian theologians, I prepared a new study on 'Religion's Manifold Contribution to Ecological Consciousness'. It helped nuance the much talked of sustainable development, to 'equitable and sustainable development' and opened up a new vision of a 'Global Spirituality for the new Exodus'.

The movement of basic education for all was taken to Cairo by OIEC in 1992. For the benefit of our own constituency and the Arab world, I situated the basic education thrust as a first step in education for peace, which I spelt out in detail. The publication of *Building Bridges — the Missing Dimension in Education* (1993) helps to keep alive the need for nurturing the spirit and giving students a keen social consciousness of the reality outside the classroom.

Unesco took the initiative in April 1993 to invite about 60 religious leaders to share their views and discuss 'The Contribution of Religion to the Culture of Peace'. The papers have been published.

Then in December 1994 we met again in Barcelona, this time with a specific purpose. We hammered out a one-sheet 'Barcelona Declaration of Peace' which was signed in the Parliament Hall of Catalunya. A signature campaign to the declaration was launched. I collected and sent to Paris 12,000 signatures from across the world. Unesco intends to keep in touch with religious leaders in the interests of education, culture and peace.

The publication of *Experience of Dialogue* (363 pages) came in 1994. It contains most of the addresses referred to and some others too. It is seen and used by some as an introduction to inter-religious dialogue, the miracle of the twentieth century.

A Global Spirituality of Social Responsibility

After the failure of a World Parliament of Religions at Chicago in August 1993 to go beyond a 'global ethic', the same debate took place in November 1994 at the sixth World Assembly of WCRP at Riva del Garda. After conferring with many of the leading personalities in the field, I worked at developing a Global Spirituality based on the dignity, uniqueness and sacredness of every human being. Tentatively presented at the second Barcelona gathering in 1994, I later delivered it as the keynote address to the First International Ecumenical Assembly of Associations of Christian Colleges and Universities of the World at New Delhi on 16-20 January 1995. Expanded and improved, it was published in *Vidya-jyoti*, a journal of theological reflection, in December 1995 and January 1996. It seeks to apply human and divine wisdom to the handling of our life-size challenges and make it a norm for the conduct of human affairs in a troubled world.

At the Social Summit at Copenhagen in March 1995, the NGO world, and others with them, affirmed that a spiritual renewal is called for to reverse present trends and move together as one human family to make life more human and humane for all God's children everywhere.

Inter-religious dialogue and peace-making efforts of the future must take up the challenge of social justice at all levels and become a non-violent revolution of collective love that will hopefully carry all before it.

Vatican Two Revisited (400 pages), to be published shortly, gives today's generation the findings of the greatest religious event of the century, with a small update. It touches on many of the concerns of this paper on peace and peace-making.

I have also shared in Delhi, Nainital and in the second edition of *As You Pray So You Live*, a new piece on a collective spirituality, better fitted to deal with collective wrong-doing in India and in the world at large. It is accompanied by another essay, 'The Agony and Ecstasy of Contemplative Prayer'. Contemplative prayer, says Aldous Huxley, is the only place where God can change our thought patterns, attitudes, feelings and behaviour.

Prayer must come into its own, and contemplative living with it as a by-product;

individual spirituality must grow into a collective or communitarian one. A global spirituality of social responsibility must come to be accepted and practised by all peace-makers and lovers of humankind. Then may be generated the political will to deliver the goods and use the resources of the world, material, cultural, moral and spiritual, for a full human life for the peoples of the world.

Peace is both a gift of God and a personal and collective human quest. Religion has a prophetic role to play in denouncing the sinful, unjust structures of the culture of affluence which bring about the counter-culture of poverty and deprivation. It is the duty of every religion to teach its followers to look at this issue as a problem of conscience and to raise an accusing finger in the appropriate quarters. 'Poverty anywhere constitutes a danger to peace and prosperity everywhere' (ILO declaration in 1944). Social justice is the key to a better world.

Like the Asian search for harmony, this presentation proceeds from a world-view that is organic, interactive and cosmic. All Asian religious traditions, including the Judaeo-Christian, envisage wholeness of life for all humans everywhere, and a spirit of friendliness with nature and the cosmos. Such a harmony is not static but dynamic. It does not mean the absence of conflict and the threat of violence, but a continuously adjusting consensus in a process of give and take.

I hope that this Asian cosmic world-view founded on order, the well-being of the human person and the family and on truth, justice and love, will receive adequate recognition in the decades ahead. It acknowledges legitimate pluralism and respect for all people. But the quest for world justice and world equalization, in the wake of the Social Summit at Copenhagen, seems to demand that it replace the mechanistic mindset nourished by the Greco-Roman philosophies, the imposition of abstract principles and law, the use of force for conflict resolution which have led to a global war economy in which the world community continues to be trapped.

Highlighting the Asian cosmic world-view, this conference's findings, if shared with the United Nations and its agencies, could well become a positive and significant contribution towards implementing an agenda for peace and its supplement, currently being pursued by the comity of nations, as we all approach with fresh hope the dawn of the third millennium.

25

Bahá'í Principles of Education and World Peace

Dwight W. Allen

'Motion is life. . . . Nothing is stationary in the material world of outer phenomena or in the inner world of intellect and consciousness.'[1] The starting point for the application of Bahá'í principles to educational reform is the understanding that continuing reform and evolution of education is essential to the life of the mind and spirit. A Bahá'í perspective creates the expectation that education can and must change.

The expectation that change is desirable and to be expected has a profound impact on the reform of education. Current patterns presume stability, and change is an intruder. Because change is not built into the process, when reform takes place it is viewed as a temporary disruption which will be followed by a new stability. This quest for stability distorts the process of change. Seeking instant results leads to 'reforms of the day' — an endless procession of trendy, piecemeal innovations which are tried, quickly found wanting, and discarded. One important task is to design a strategy or strategies for the change process itself. Bahá'í principles can inform these strategies in important ways.

Shoghi Effendi, first Guardian of the Bahá'í Faith, defines an appropriate expectation when he states: 'All we can reasonably venture to attempt is to strive to obtain a glimpse of the first streaks of the promised Dawn that must, in the fullness of time, chase away the gloom that has encircled humanity. All we can do is to point out, in their broadest outlines, what appear to us to be the guiding principles underlying the World Order of Bahá'u'llah.'[2]

With such modest expectations we must forge ahead. Our strategies must be well considered, timely, and patient. It is important to realize that there is an awkwardness about change and reform, that new patterns will not immediately be smoothly implemented.

This patience is a part of the Bahá'í concept of moderation: don't be too quick to change, nor too quick to abandon change.

Bahá'í principles can influence material education and enhance its effectiveness. They can also focus the effort of material education to enhance the growth of spiritual education. But the animating force of Bahá'í principles is to enlighten the spirit so that the world of nature can become complete and allow human society to achieve the unity which is an essential component of world peace. The first task is to gain acknowledgement that these principles are important to the success of education. The process is not linear. Bahá'í principles of education can enhance the most flawed educational practice and improve its effect. They can be successfully applied without acknowledging their source. An ever-increasing awareness of the potential of these principles will create insights and precedents which only in the fullness of time will produce true Bahá'í education and enhance the process of achieving world unity and world peace.

Two of the specific Bahá'í principles of education that will influence the emergence of world peace are that education must become a virtuous process and that we must learn to celebrate error as a part of the essential processes and products of effective education. These fundamental principles will then foster the type of environment necessary to promote the independent investigation of truth to facilitate the interdependency of the process, content, and objectives of education.

A Virtuous Process

Much of current decision-making in education, as in all aspects of life today, is not genuinely motivated. The jockeying for such ends as power, credit and recognition, material gain, or favouritism confuses the agendas of reform. Motivations are almost always likely to be mixed, but there can be no substitute for striving to achieve a virtuous process. From the trust that such a process generates comes great strength, and a willingness to accept the inevitable difficulties and ambiguities that change will produce.

The Principle of Trial and Error

The traditions of education have seldom recognized the legitimacy of error. Ambiguity and error are to be avoided whenever possible. There has been a righteous insistence that excellence in education is an unerring path towards achievement. There are fundamental problems with this assumption. First of all, it is assumed that the objectives of education are clear and precise. They are not. They are ever-changing, and the rapidity of the changes is also increasing, creating ambiguity and confusion. The assumption that all objectives are clear and precise is an illusion. Second, it is assumed that the best — even the only — desirable model of learning is 'one trial learning'. The ideal student learns everything the first time. One trial learning is often not even desirable, let alone possible. These assumptions create false expectations and stereotyped responses prejudiced against exploration and change, and prejudiced against the newer objectives of education as they struggle even to gain recognition, let alone parity.

Bahá'í principles clearly identify trial and error as fundamental to human nature. Perfection in imperfection is one of the profound mysteries of God. One of the major tasks of educational reform is to find how to build the principle of trial and error into the process of change and into the practices of education.

It is impossible to learn to ride a bicycle without falling off. But there are better and worse ways to go about instruction. There are good mistakes and bad mistakes. But the expectation of error as a part of the learning process is indispensable to its full success. The educational process must find ways to reward the right kind of mistakes and to encourage them. The full learning potential of any individual is compromised without the knowledge of how to benefit from mistakes. The exploration of the implications of this great principle in planning both the process and objectives of education is one of the priority tasks of educational reform.

Encouragement

'Abdu'l-Bahá often mentioned the importance of encouragement. Current educational patterns rely dominantly on criticism. Encouragement is multi-dimensional. A proper educational environment is one where teachers encourage students, students encourage one another, and parents and community encourage schools and teachers — as well as their own children in their learning. And students must be trained to encourage their teachers as well.

Encouragement must be sincere and tied to real educational progress. However, progress may be incremental and reflect the legitimate errors which are part of eventual learning success. We need to reward the reduction of errors with encouragement. Just understanding the right approach or appropriate direction may unlock the potential for complete success and warrants encouragement. Encouragement spurs the learner to seek the next level of achievement.

Both teachers and students must become conditioned to use encouragement without thinking. It must become a normal, expected part of all interaction. The principle of using encouragement is not limited to formal education, but will gradually emerge as a major characteristic of Bahá'í society. Encouragement within the family, at the workplace, as well as at school and in all aspects of life, is important. For this reason mastering the art of encouragement must be an educational objective as well as an element of successful educational practice.

Feedback

Trial and error and encouragement together provide the means of consistent, focused, and successful feedback. 'Abdu'l-Bahá's concept of encouragement focuses on feedback, giving us a sense of incremental success, meeting expectations and gaining the will to continue. Current educational systems are basically flawed in their feedback processes.

Examination patterns are a good example. One of the prime purposes of examinations should be to provide feedback. For examination results to be really useful the student must have an opportunity to try again, to see if the lessons of feedback have been successfully learnt. Both the structure and timing of the current examination systems go against, and usually even preclude, this opportunity. Examinations come at the end of a course when there is no opportunity for further instruction. A second example is that writing after feedback will generally produce more learning than the original writing exercise. Only infrequently are students asked to rewrite. Even when feedback is given, often it is so general as to be useless for learning. 'Good job' does not tell a student what has been done well or why. 'Weak' does not tell a student how to make the point stronger.

Learning how to give and receive feedback effectively, in a timely fashion, with encouragement and with provision to try again is both a process and objective of effective education.

Too often there is little emphasis placed on the quality of feedback. Telling a student what she or he has done wrong is, in itself, not necessarily effective feedback. To be effective the feedback must include both how and why it is wrong, and what alternatives are available to give success or create the potential for future success.

Understanding and mastering feedback is vital to all aspects of life. In addition to being one of the foremost tools of the professional teacher, mastering feedback will give parents one of the strongest tools for the education of their children in the family setting. It is one of the prime mechanisms for creating a 'learning society', a society capable of systematic and ongoing improvement.

Interdependent Process, Content and Objectives of Education

The process of education itself is spiritual and must be examined for its effect. Learning how to learn is both process and objective, both method and content. Bahá'ís define the process of education to be the independent investigation of Truth. The purpose of education is to seek the transformation of each individual spirit through conscious knowledge.

One of the most promising fields of enquiry is to discover how the educational process can be made more 'conscious'. Fundamental to independent investigation is responsibility. At every stage of the educational process each individual must be made to feel responsible for the process and its results. Developing active learners is a starting point for successful Bahá'í education. Active student involvement becomes a focal point for defining both the process and the content of education.

Because Bahá'í education is seen to be a life-long process, it becomes obvious that teachers are never finished with their learning. Teacher learning must be integrated into the instructional process. As the sources of learning become more diversified — many of them outside the formal learning process — teachers will routinely have opportunities to learn from their students. At present they are not equipped to do so. We must learn how best to help teachers learn from students and for students to learn to be confident teachers. Properly conceived, this will not compromise the teacher's responsibility for instructional leadership. Teachers remain responsible for managing the educational environment, but a part of that environment should be the contributions of students to the teaching-learning process.

When the soul is conceived it enters the world pure and unblemished. The experiences of this world contribute blemishes and impurities. Paradoxically, it is the purpose of life to recognize and deal with these imperfections and to try to regain purity of motive and action. The purity of the infant is a bestowal of God. The imperfect purity we strive to regain becomes the conscious fruit of our lives.[3] Our nobility comes from successful choice. Successful choice has only one criterion, alignment with the spiritual premises of the active Divine attributes. Bahá'ís call the process of aligning our choices with Divine Will, personal transformation. Recognizing and making conscious choices which conform to spiritual virtue is the essence of education.

The process of spiritual growth and transformation has many settings. Obviously school is only one of them. But in modern secular education, school is often not considered a place for moral and spiritual transformation. It is not simply a matter of curriculum. The process of education, the premises of human relationships, the consequences of actions and how they are understood, all this is a part of spiritual growth. Put another way, if spiritual growth is not taken into consideration when designing the content and process of education, the result will almost certainly be at odds with spiritual processes, and effective education in the most fundamental sense will become impossible.

In the few examples we have of Bahá'í sponsored comprehensive schools, which include secular curricula, they are prone to copy, by default, both the content and the processes of secular schools. This is not their intent. They are simply applying a familiar academic template to create schools with recognizable academic excellence. The template is likely to be flawed in three ways: inadequate and inappropriately selected content and objectives which do not consciously integrate material and spiritual knowledge, obsolete processes which ignore both material and spiritual principles, and most important, a lack of understanding that one of the most important objectives of both spiritual and secular education is for students to master the processes of independent learning.

As the world around us becomes impossibly 'information rich' the simple acquisition of knowledge is no longer the prime objective of education. Knowing how to learn, how to evaluate information and knowledge, how to establish the credibility of sources, where to find appropriate information and principles, how to organize information for its effective use and to share it with others — all these are even more important. In Bahá'í terms, these skills are the foundation of the independent investigation of truth.

Cooperation and Competition

If world peace is to be achieved we must find a balance between competition and cooperation, between justice and mercy, and learn to appreciate tests, hardships and effort. Differences in human capacity will have to be acknowledged and respected as we consolidate our commitments to unity in diversity in a new world order. Vying for excellence is competition in its finest sense, strongly endorsed in Bahá'í principles. It is competition which encourages cooperation, which seeks the elevation of all performance as an integral consequence of its practice. Traditional models of education are based on a more destructive competition, and excellence has been defined in terms of competitive achievement with winners and losers. Cooperation has been seen as mutually exclusive with competition, a fundamental misconception.

There is value in saluting achievement so long as we also salute the achievement of the loser which has made the higher level of achievement of the winner possible. At an award banquet a few years ago honouring the winning women's swimming team, with times much slower than the men's, it was noted that if the women were to swim against the fastest men of two decades earlier, they would handily beat them all.

The ugly side of competition, winning at all costs, has fostered an equally extreme reaction in trying to create models of education where competition is completely eliminated. Competition, properly managed, can lead to overall improvement. It is interesting to note that in sporting competition today there is an expectation that records will continue to be broken, an expectation of continued improvement. In many individual sports there are increasing repertoires of strategies and moves (often named after the first competitor to develop them) which all competitors freely imitate and incorporate into their own repertoires. This mutual cooperation builds additional competitive advantage and higher levels of achievement. Many aspects of the current sporting model of competition are extreme and inappropriate. This does not detract from our ability to selectively learn from them.

In recent years competition for university places has been intense. One outcome of this competition has been the creation of more university places. Another outcome has been the creation of a variety of institutions to broaden the scope of competition. We have created more winners. But there is a residue of competition in the unhealthy sense, that true status remains limited to the narrow student body of 'prestige' institutions.

Justice and Mercy

A 'sense of justice' is perhaps the most powerful objective of all education. Bahá'u'llah states, 'Set your reliance on the army of justice, put on the armour of wisdom, let your adorning be forgiveness and mercy and that which cheereth the hearts of the well-favoured of God.'[4] It is a part of the mystery of God that justice should be embedded in paradox.

Children must be taught that this is not a world where absolute justice is possible or even desirable. This is a world of mercy. From a Bahá'í point of view it is vital for children to understand that injustice is an essential part of the world in which we live, for the opportunity for injustice gives us choice. And it is choice that makes education meaningful. If education were in any way an automatic process, we would be deprived of merit, and ultimately of our nobility. Nobility is derived from making the right choices in a world where wrong choices are possible and historically have dominated. This in turn goes back to the legitimacy and desirability of trial and error as a part of the educational process, and as a part of life.

Absolute justice would deprive us all of the opportunity to choose. So we must learn to celebrate our own and each other's errors — so long as they become a part of the larger process of achieving ever higher levels of perfection in an imperfect world. Justice is the grand, inescapable, yet unachievable objective, both for individuals and society. It is the foundation of world order.

Mercy is linked to the concept of forgiveness. If God can forgive the most grievous sins of man, then we are well advised to forgive one another. This means that we must each give others the opportunity to rise above past mistakes, however grievous, and to celebrate our progress in doing so. That is vital to the conduct of the teacher in the classroom. A learning environment is by definition a setting where mistakes are expected to be made frequently and dealt with mercifully. The consequences of mistakes in a controlled learning environment are dampened with effective teacher leadership. With feedback and encouragement the potential to enhance just action is enormous. Classrooms must be the laboratories of life. Teachers must be models, striving constantly to improve their own understanding and practice of justice. When we do not exploit the potential of formal education to use years of interaction to embed a sense of justice in students, we waste the greatest potential of formal education. We must be accountable for our actions but leave our mistakes behind by learning from them. Therefore teachers, more than other members of the society, must be trained to deal with the delicate balance between justice and mercy. Not only must teachers learn to deal with their own mistakes as well as the mistakes of their students, they are responsible to help students learn to deal with the mistakes of one another.

But we can become preoccupied with truth and justice. 'Abdu'l-Bahá said that not everything which is true is timely; not everything which is timely can be heard; and not everything which can be heard can be acted upon. This suggests that in educational settings in particular, a preeminent consideration must be to determine the timeliness of educational concerns — from the content and process of instruction to the correction and discipline of the child. Even truth and justice must be set forth in moderation. Understanding justice and mercy and their interrelationship both as processes and as prime objectives of education will grow gradually within the consciousness of individuals and society. It is time to transform the consciousness of society to achieve a completely new awareness of the importance of this agenda. It is this perspective which will guide true educational reform.

Tests, Hardship and Effort

Abdu'l-Bahá says that we must accustom children to hardship. The Bab tells us that he would not wish for his worst enemy a life without tests. Clearly tests and difficulties are an appropriate part of education. Again, it is a matter of balance. When we can see purpose in our tests and understand them, they become more meaningful and easier to accept. Not all tests, however, can be understood, and we must be prepared to accept tests and difficulties which we do not understand. It is the task of educators to make the process of education as focused and understandable as possible. It is the task of the learners to trust their teachers even when they do not understand. This places a moral responsibility on teachers to make the educational process as purposeful as possible, to make effort meaningful and productive.

The task of education is enormous. We must do everything possible to make the educational process as easy and as effective as possible, adding further levels of difficulty as students gain in capacity and understanding. There is so much to be learnt that hardship and effort are natural concomitants of any effective educational process, but they should become the source of high achievement and not the result of harassment, which has too often been the case in the past. There are many ironies in the process. Spiritual equilibrium comes from a series of challenges successfully met.

This is true on the institutional as well as the personal level. Each invention, each discovery, each achievement simply exposes multiple new challenges. As we learn to apply more spiritual principles to the processes of education we will be rewarded with the opportunity to further reform the system to achieve even more. The challenge we face now is to understand the dimensions which are required to begin the process in a confident direction so that our effort will be productive.

Dealing with Differences in Capacity

It is obvious that children thrive in different degrees in the same educational environment. Why? Partly because their innate potentials are different. Partly because of the influences and experiences they bring to the educational setting. Partly because of their own attitudes and dispositions. The teacher must make education as easy and effective as possible; the student must learn how to learn most effectively regardless of the quality of the teaching.

We must not confuse difference in intellectual potential with difference in spiritual worth. Current educational practice does not uplift the spirits of all children. Academic success is often confused with personal worth or spiritual capacity. To whatever extent possible we must learn from one another. Current practices of 'streaming' or 'homogeneous grouping' are overemphasized. Bahá'í teachings clearly endorse the different innate capacities of children. This would imply different educational levels and processes. There are also Bahá'í principles which suggest that some combination of multi-ability and multi-age groups as well as grouping by interest and ability will be appropriate. This is an area which will need the perspective of time, experience, and trial and error learning before effective practice can emerge.

Perspective

A basic Bahá'í principle is unity in diversity. Perhaps one of the most profound consequences of this principle is to provide perspective. Only when there is diversity is perspective possible. When only one viewpoint or one alternative is known, it is almost impossible to progress more than incrementally. We don't know what we don't know. Once a second alternative is introduced — diversity — it suggests a range of possibilities which can completely transform and redefine our approaches, our understanding: our perspective. One of the most vital lessons in education is for us to learn that our way is *a* way and not *the* way. Education must value a diversity of viewpoints, of processes and procedures, of content and method. But unity in diversity means that there must be coordination, a sense of direction and purpose, and a commitment to unity even as we actively seek to promote and appreciate diversity.

Unity in diversity implies a balance between top-down and bottom-up decision-making. Individuals must be encouraged to mount new initiatives and have the freedom to explore — and to fail. But they must accept the legitimacy of coordination and direction from institutions. Conversely, it becomes the responsibility of institutions not only to coordinate and direct, but to do so in a way which empowers and encourages individual diversity. Applied to education, this would suggest a whole new set of principles to guide educational development. The result will be a constant evolution of perspectives on which new educational initiatives can be based. The educational system alone will not solve problems of interdependency, but it can make a major contribution by providing the next generation of students with substantial new perspectives.

As the world becomes unified, we must have a greater understanding of one another — awareness of cultural diversity. But not all cultural practices are compatible with a unified world. The educational process must help students become aware of how cultural beliefs, their own as well as others', influence attitudes and behaviour. It is important to understand their history and context. Further, everyone must be taught to recognize how beliefs and practices must be modified to be effectively integrated into a world community. Students can gain the benefit of being able to incorporate other beliefs and practices to enrich their lives, from the food they eat or the entertainment they enjoy to an appreciation of alternative family structure and a willingness to change.

As global interaction increases, the tension between standardization and local choice will gain in consequence. Different voltages and alternating current frequencies are inconvenient, expensive and limiting when one travels or when goods and services are exchanged. The United States costs the world economy billions of dollars by refusing to join the world in adopting the metric system. Which side of the road one drives on is not very important unless you have to switch back and forth or build cars for both. We are rapidly moving towards a world currency and a world language (English). But because we are reluctant to support world standards in principle and have no mechanism to debate or decide the boundaries, we lurch along with expediency, our decisions constantly overtaken and preempted by events.

The basic school curriculum is edging towards worldwide standardization. In fact, there is very little difference among basic school syllabi. The best evidence of this is that students can attend the universities of almost any country in the world based upon the skills they have acquired in their local secondary schools. But nations, even local communities, cling to the right to determine their school curricula. It is more often an illusion than a reality. Mathematics, science, language, history and culture are considered 'basic' throughout the world. And the schools of all nations are concerned about increasing their emphasis on the arts. The same new subjects wait in the wings: the environment, health and nutrition, global awareness, thinking, interpersonal and analytical skills, and most crucial from a Bahá'í perspective, moral and spiritual education.

We desperately need to find a balance, to define the mechanisms to decide on common world curriculum elements, which will in turn encourage even more diversity in local curricula. Local curriculum diversity will prosper even more when there is confidence that the basic needs of education required to succeed in an integrated global community are met. The lack of a sure mechanism to establish common curriculum elements is one of the greatest barriers to successful educational reform and the achievement of the ultimate goal of the universal education of humanity.

Moral and spiritual education are, of course, not new, but they need to be newly reintroduced into almost all modern systems of secular education. As local populations have become more diverse in their beliefs, moral and spiritual education has retreated to the family. Societies have become confused in their spiritual values and have removed moral and spiritual education from their curricula. The continuing cascades of new knowledge and perspectives in secular education have disguised this gaping omission.

'Abdu'l-Bahá identifies two purposes for education, to make children good and to make them smart. He points out that a member of society who is 'good' but not 'smart' can be useful; whereas a person who is smart but not good is a menace. When a person is both good and smart, there is 'light upon light'. We have become preoccupied with making humanity 'smart'. The result has been to unleash well-educated and 'smart' members of society to wreak havoc with great ingenuity. Restoring the balance is an urgent need.

Bahá'í teaching affirms in the strongest theological terms the reality that education affects both outward and inner virtues — the material virtues and the ideal virtues. Civilization is the sign of the progress of the material virtues, but the inner and ideal virtues have been delayed. Now is the time for their development. The development of these inner virtues constitutes the rebirth of man, the second birth referred to by Christ.[5]

Consultation and Decision-Making

Bahá'í education focuses our attention on new modes of decision-making, defined by Bahá'u'llah as the spiritual processes of consultation. As humanity gains an appreciation of multi-cultural experiences, coalescing into agreed upon limits of diversity and a commitment to spiritual principles, and learns to speak out, to listen, and to respect diverse opinions, a new commitment will be forged towards the unified action and integrity of decisions and decision-makers.

There is a host of Bahá'í principles guiding the decision-making process. And there are many ways in which the decision-making process is applied to education. What to teach, how to teach it, who should teach, whom to teach it to, and when. Each of these decisions will enhance or constrain the process, appropriately and inappropriately. The process of educational reform should hold none of the current elements of education sacrosanct. All should be examined and alternatives considered. The principles of Bahá'í consultation can greatly facilitate and guide the process. As is the case with all of the principles we have been discussing, consultation is a process, and the mastery of consultation an important objective of education. The skills of decision-making are essential to success, in the family, in the workplace, in social institutions, and even in casual human interaction.

One straight point is to understand the definition of an effective decision: a decision based upon analysis of facts and circumstances and of the principles which apply; a decision which has been informed by the opinion and perspective of all those concerned; and a decision which is conscientiously implemented by all.

Part of the decision-making process, whether by an individual or a group, is to explain the decision and assist with its implementation. Conscious understanding is essential in both making and implementing decisions. Roles must be clearly defined and understood. There is a time to offer advice and input to a decision. After a decision is made it is essential for everyone to be united in implementing it; otherwise it is impossible to make a good judgement about its effectiveness. Its failure may simply be a function of strife rather than of its own weakness.

All opinions are sought, whether informed or uninformed. The only condition is purity of motive. To remain silent is to bias the decision inappropriately. At the same time, when an opinion is offered it becomes a part of the group decision-making process and should not be clung to by the person offering it. Every effort must be made to listen to what is being said, not to who says it.

In the classroom teachers have a leadership responsibility. They are in charge. But they have an obligation to listen to the viewpoints of their students and to take their opinions into account. They must help students understand why decisions are taken and the principles on which they are based. They must demonstrate how each decision relates to the welfare of all concerned and attempts to reflect justice and wisdom. Conversely, it is the responsibility of the student to conform joyfully to the expectations of the teachers, to constantly analyse the educational setting, and to offer opinions so they can be heard and appreciated.

Joyful students can have a visible impact on the entire class. Joy and enthusiasm are within our ability to achieve, independent of the circumstances in which we find ourselves. The environment around us makes it easier or harder to attain this state, but to the extent that we understand our own role and responsibility we gain a sense of power and direction. How great is the responsibility of the teacher to model joy. Bahá'í principles have a profound impact on the teacher-pupil relationship. Mutual respect and understanding, creating an atmosphere of joy, validating and celebrating trial-and-error learning, these must become the focus for decision-making and be prime evaluative criteria for the success or failure of decisions.

Defining a Comprehensive Agenda for Educational Reform

Educational reform continues to be muddled by conflicting, uncoordinated initiatives. There is constant tension between conflicting viewpoints. Principles themselves often appear contradictory. Bahá'í principles offer insights into the definitions of both the process and the objectives of reform.

In some respects Bahá'í teachings are harsh in their admonitions. 'It is evident that no vital results are now forthcoming from the customs, institutions and standpoints of the past.'[6] At the same time, they offer perspective and even specific guidance as to how we should build on the scientific body of knowledge which is being rapidly expanded, and incorporate both old and new knowledge into new institutions and practices.

There are three kinds of education: training and development of the physical body, intellectual and mental training, and the education of the spirit. The body of the world will receive its vivification through the animating virtue of the sanctified spirit of man.[7]

Some objectives of Bahá'í education stand alone, sometimes contradicting current educational theories such as the priority of spiritual education, achieving spiritual discipline, the memorization of the Holy Word, the preference for the education of girls, and the requirement of a profession without regard to economic necessity.

Bahá'í teachings identify the obstacles to human happiness as 'racial and religious prejudice, the competitive struggle for existence and inhumanity toward each other'.[8] Perhaps the most important way to define the purpose of education is to see true education as the ultimate source of human happiness. With unified action we will begin our journey to the achievement of true human prosperity and world peace.

References

1. 'Abdu'l-Bahá, *The Promulgation of Universal Peace*, Bahá'í Publishing Trust, Wilmette, 1982, p.140.
2. Shoghi Effendi, *The World Order of Bahá'u'llah*, Bahá'í Publishing Trust, Wilmette, 1974, p. 35.
3. 'Abdu'l-Bahá, *op.cit.*, p. 53.
4. *Tablets of Bahá'u'llah*, Bahá'í World Centre, Haifa, p.139.
5. 'Abdu'l-Bahá, *op.cit.*, pp. 330-3.
6. *Ibid.*, p.140.
7. *Ibid.*, pp. 330-31.
8. *Ibid.*, p. 468.

26

The United Nations and Permanent Peace in the 21st Century

A.K. Merchant

THE United Nations' 50th anniversary in 1995 coincides with a turning point in the life of our planet. The ongoing debate about its future role calls for serious rethinking of the ways the international organization deals with the issues of development, peace and security. The 50th anniversary is therefore a time not only for reflection on the achievements and difficult lessons of the past, but also for charting a course for the next century. 'The resolution of these problems — crushing poverty amidst vast sections of the developing world, oppression of women and minority groups, intractable political, religious, and ethnic conflicts; and disruption of the global ecosystem, among others — will require unprecedented levels of cooperation and coordination that surpass anything in humanity's collective experience',[1] and which must go beyond the present adversarial system of conflict resolution. Our present-day system is too costly, too painful, too destructive and too inefficient for a truly civilized people.

'From the remotest times men have told tales of golden societies — a submerged Atlantis somewhere off the African coast, a lost Lemuria in the depths of the Pacific, an immortal Shangri-la in the heights of the Himalayas, a vanished Eden in the region of four great rivers. . . . This is conjecture, to be sure, conjecture is not useless, for it leads to search. Search leads to knowledge and knowledge in turn breaks down false barriers which the ignorance of former generations has erected.'[2] Indeed, 'an onrushing wind is blowing through the archaic structures of the old Order, felling mighty pillars and clearing the ground for new conceptions of social organization. The call for unity, for a new World Order, is audible from many directions. The change in world society is characterized by a phenomenal speed. A feature of this change is a suddenness, or precipitateness, which appears to be the consequence of some mysterious rampant force. The positive aspects of this change reveal an unaccustomed openness to global concepts, movements towards international and regional collaboration, an inclination of warring parties to opt for peaceful solutions, a search for spiritual values.'[3]

Baha'is understand many of the complex problems of society to be inevitable features of a historical process that Baha'u'llah, Founder-Prophet of the Baha'i faith, foresaw would come to dominate the twentieth century. His vision of the eventual integration of humankind and the emergence of a global society in which unity in diversity would be the principal characteristic has been confirmed by the events of this century — accelerating as we near its close. Many of our most acute problems can be resolved if we become conscious of this historical process and respond in ways that take proper account of the oneness of humanity — the principle of social organization for the age now dawning in human history. Failure to understand and make the necessary adjustments in how human affairs are administered on this planet only intensifies the degree of suffering that is penetrating communities in virtually every country and region on earth.

Baha'is view the current phase of rapidly changing world conditions in a hopeful way, aware of the anguish created by current chaotic social dislocations but seeing them as part of a long-term process of adjustment, the pain of which can best be alleviated if we become conscious of its nature and direction. The current period of human history is one of these axial periods understood best perhaps in the phrase 'the coming of age of humanity'.[4] The period of relative isolation of various peoples of the world has ended. We have now collectively entered a new world where boundaries, if they exist at all any more, are no longer impenetrable. The interdependence of humanity with all its diversity of cultures, nations, and peoples will continue to increase. Exclusive sovereignties are no longer possible.

From our study of world trends and the forecast of the future of humanity as presented in Baha'i writings over a century[5] ago we can discern the following requirements on the part of present-day society for the establishment of a new World Order and permanent peace on earth.

1. Unity of nations resulting in the outlawing of war before the turn of the century. This will be a crucial achievement, marking a new phase in the sphere of international relations in the twenty-first century. The term used in the Baha'i Writings to describe this process is the 'Lesser Peace'.

2. Unity in the political realm with respect to the system of governance based upon the foundations of true justice.

3. Unity of thought in world undertakings such as exploration of outer space, sharing of scientific knowledge, combating global problems such as terrorism, rampant drug abuse, international crime, etc.

4. Unity of freedom, i.e. concentration of forces for social reform, especially a judicial system guaranteeing equal political, economic and social opportunity to every man and woman, to every nation and to every race.

5. Unity of religion and adoption by the majority of humankind of a world religion, thus fulfilling the prophecies enshrined in the utterances of the founders of extant religions.

6. Unity of races, i.e. all humankind will be regarded as one race. Truly, racism is one of the worst parts of the social malaise afflicting present-day humanity.

7. Unity of language, i.e., the selection of an auxiliary world language and script — one of the signs of the maturity of the human race.

Today several million people from virtually every race, culture, class and nation on earth are unitedly working for the speedy realization of the above objectives, the most important of which is the establishment of the oneness and wholeness of the human race. 'A new life,' Baha'u'llah proclaims, 'is in this age, stirring within all the peoples of the earth; and yet none hath discovered its cause, or perceived its motive. . . . The well-being of mankind,' He declares, 'its peace and security are unattainable unless and until its unity is firmly established.' 'So powerful is the light of unity,' is His further testimony, 'that it can illuminate the whole earth. . . . This goal excelleth every other goal, and this aspiration is the monarch of all aspirations.'[6]

In recent years much progress has been made in conflict resolution and management. I would like to cite the following examples given by Judge Dorothy W. Nelson of the United States Court of Appeals for the Ninth Circuit. She writes:

> In [1965] in 'Acca, Israel, I attended a hearing conducted by three Greek Orthodox priests in long black robes and long white beards. Court was conducted in a quonset hut with paint peeling from the walls, furnished only with a plain wooden table and chairs. A wife was suing her husband for divorce. As her lawyer rose to his feet holding a handful of papers from which to plead her case, he was waved gently aside by the presiding priest, who turned to the wife and asked her to tell her own story. She explained that for five years of marriage she had shared a house with her mother-in-law. The older woman, too old to climb stairs, occupied the ground

> floor, and the wife lived upstairs. Since there was only one entrance to the house she had to enter through her mother-in-law's living quarters to get to her own, and her mother-in-law continually questioned her about her activities and offered unsolicited advice. She loved her husband, she said, but the situation was intolerable.
>
> The wife sat down and the presiding priest, waving aside the husband's lawyer as he had the wife's, asked to hear the husband's side of the case. The husband said that he loved his wife but also his mother. As a Christian he felt responsibility for both, but he was a poor man and could not afford two households.
>
> The three priests retired by stepping into the dusty street outside and returned five minutes later with their judgment. The husband was to build a ladder. When the wife wanted to avoid her mother-in-law, she could climb the ladder directly to her second floor window.
>
> The practice of conflict resolution is as old as human civilization. From the Biblical story of Cain and Abel, to Homer's account of the Trojan War in the *Iliad*, to Thucydides' historical analysis of the war between Athens and Sparta, accounts of conflict across time have captured the interest of poets and scholars. We have moved from a primitive system of a clash of strength, brute force against brute force, to a clash of wills in an adversary system where vested interest is pitted against vested interest. Like the primitive system, the conflict continues until there is a winner and a loser.

A second example given by Judge Nelson is that of 'the Egyptian-Israeli peace treaty blocked out at Camp David in 1978. Israel had occupied the Egyptian Sinai Peninsula since the Six-Day War of 1967. When Egypt and Israel began to negotiate a peace, they had incompatible positions: Israel wanted some part of the Sinai for security reasons, and Egypt, on the other hand, insisted that every inch of the Sinai be returned to Egypt which had enjoyed sovereignty over it since the time of the Pharaohs. Looking to their interests instead of their positions, it was possible to develop a solution. The plan agreed upon was to return the Sinai to complete Egyptian sovereignty but to demilitarize large areas of the Sinai, thus assuring Israeli security. By looking behind opposed positions for the motivating interests, an alternative position was found which met the interests of both Egypt and Israel.'[7]

Going one step further, the late Professor Edward Azar, former Director of the Centre for International Development and Conflict Management, made an important contribution to conflict studies by suggesting that it is "needs" not "interests" which are at the heart of protracted social conflict.[8]

Professor Jerold S. Auerbach explains other drawbacks of the adversary system now prevalent almost everywhere in the world in his book, *Justice Without Law*, when he describes it as

> a chilling, Hobbesian version of human nature. It accentuates hostility, not trust. Selfishness supplants generosity. Truth is shaded by dissembling. Once an adversarial framework is in place, it supports competitive aggression to the exclusion of reciprocity and empathy.[9]

A report from the Department of Justice, Government of the United States, adds:

> The search for new ways of managing our differences can be seen as signalling a shift in public values. With increasing awareness that "we are all in this world together," traditional win-lose, adversarial processes may be personally and socially less satisfactory than more participative, collaborative problem solving that reconciles the interests of all involved parties.[10]

> There is a height of human experience where the instinct for combat sinks back into the inner spirit and finds rest. That height is our human future, if we take the mysterious step of conscious faith. The test is that of sincerity. The Baha'i Faith provides a comprehensive synthesis for bringing about a new cycle of human progress and endurance. What Baha'u'llah, its founder, has sought to accomplish is [to provide] the means for bringing about the promised Golden Age of humanity. Without the motivation of purpose to give meaning and usefulness to our experiences of life, we are bereft of hope and happiness.

> *ayam nijaparoveti gananam laghuchetasam*
> *udaracaritanam tu vasudhaivakutumbakam*
>
> (The Upanishads)[11]

> It is the small-minded who trivialize this world by their preoccupation with many kinds of divisions and demarcations which separate the peoples of the world. Those who are generous of spirit and have a larger vision regard the whole world as one family.' (Trans. by Dr L.M. Singhvi)

'The earth is but one country and mankind its citizens,' Baha'u'llah declared over a century ago.

Conclusion

A statement of the Baha'i International Community entitled *Turning Point for All Nations*, released on the occasion of the 50th anniversary of the United Nations, states: 'As the twin processes of collapse and renewal carry the world toward some sort of culmination, the 50th anniversary of the United Nations offers a timely opportunity to pause and reflect on how humanity may collectively face its future'.[12] The statement continues to outline three basic guidelines:

> First, discussions about the future of the United Nations need to take place within the broad context of the evolution of the international order and its direction. The United Nations has co-evolved with other great institutions of the late twentieth century. It is in the aggregate that these institutions will define — and themselves be shaped by — the evolution of the international order. Therefore, the mission, role, operating principles and even activities of the United Nations should be examined only in the light of how they fit within the broader objective of the international order.
>
> Second, since the body of humankind is one and indivisible, each member of the human race is born into the world as a trust of the whole. This relationship between the individual and the collective constitutes the moral foundation of the human rights which the instruments of the United Nations are attempting to define. It also serves to define an overriding purpose for the international order in establishing and preserving the rights of the individual.
>
> Third, the discussions about the future of the international order must involve and excite the generality of humankind. This discussion is so important that it cannot be confined to leaders — be they in government, business, the academic community, religion, or organizations of civil society. On the contrary, this conversation must engage women and men at the grassroots level. Broad participation will make the process self-reinforcing by raising awareness of world citizenship and increase support for an expanded international order.

As part of its contribution to the ongoing discussion on the restructuring of the United Nations, the statement among other things proposes the appointment of a commission to study borders and frontiers; to limit the use of the veto power in the UN Security Council to a limited number of issues; to investigate the possibility of adopting a single international currency; to explore the possibility of introducing a universal auxiliary language and a common script; and to create an International Force. There is also a call for a convocation of world leaders before the end of the twentieth century 'to consider how the international order might be redefined and restructured to meet the challenges facing the world'.

References

1. *Unity and Consultation: Foundations of Sustainable Development*, a statement of the Baha'i International Community, New York, 1994, p.1.
2. Marsella, Elena Maria, *The Quest for Eden*, Philosophical Library, New York, N.Y. 10016, 1966, p.1 and p.12.
3. 'Ridvan Message 1992', a statement of the Universal House of Justice, *The Baha'i World 1992-93*, Baha'i World Centre, Haifa, 1993, p. 26.
4. Baha'u'llah, *The Kitab-i-Aqdas — The Most Holy Book*, Baha'i Publishing Trust, New Delhi, 1993, para 189, p. 88.
5. Khursheed, Anjam, *The Seven Candles of Unity*, Baha'i Publishing Trust, London, U.K., 1991, pp.164-65.
6. Baha'u'llah, quoted in *Call to the Nations*, a selection from the writings of Shoghi Effendi, Baha'i World Centre, Haifa, 1977, p. 53.
7. Nelson, W. Dorothy, *Alternative Forms of Conflict Resolution — A Pathway to Peace*. The Second Annual Baha'i Lecture, the Baha'i Chair for World Peace, University of Maryland, 1996, pp.10-11 and pp.15-16.
8. Azar, Edward E., 'Peace Amidst Development', *International Interactions*, 6, No. 2, 1974.
9. Auerbach, Jerold S., *Justice Without Law?*, Oxford University Press, Oxford, 1983, p.1.
10. U.S.Department of Justice, *Paths to Justice: Major Public Policy Issues of Dispute Resolution*, Report of the Ad Hoc Panel on Dispute Resolution and Public Policy, January 1984, pp.7-8.
11. I have been unable to locate the exact reference to context of this ancient Indian tradition. My source is *Sambhuti — My Quest in the Fulfilment of Hinduism*, by S.P. Raman, Baha'i Publishing Trust, New Delhi, 1986, p.1.
12. *Turning Point for All Nations*, a statement of the Baha'i International Community issued on the occasion of the 50th Anniversary of the United Nations, New York, 1995.

27

An International Network of Peace

M. Ishaq Jamkhanawala

THE first thing about peace is that it is indivisible. It permeates the world in some form or it does not exist at all. Paradoxically, the physically enormous world of ours is still too small to contain peace and war together. Just as a house with many rooms may yet be too small to contain a family, if all its inmates are not harmonious and cooperative, in the same way the world may be a difficult and miserable place if all its inhabitants are psychologically and mentally at loggerheads with one another. Developments in Afghanistan, for example, are cause for concern not only in that country but also in the region.

The cardinal principle to remember about peace is that it is a positive quality and is not the mere absence of war. Things may be fine on the surface and yet hatred and bitterness may lie concealed in people's hearts. There, they fester and feed each day on imaginary iniquities and assume gargantuan proportions until they become unbearable. Mountains thus are made out of molehills and become unmanageable and get totally out of control. The result is a blazing inferno, and it is too late to put it out. The original participants are joined by newcomers who have various conflicting interests. The more, it seems, the merrier, it seems. Distance lends enchantment to the view, which beckons the mischievous, the curious, the avaricious as well as ideologists everywhere. The theatre of war spreads like wildfire and it is not long before it assumes the dimensions of a world war. At least its repercussions are felt and its reverberations are heard in many distant parts of the world, whose state of peace is rudely and suddenly broken. The world is in conflagration, and devastation is all around.

A universal problem of this nature demands a universal approach, and it is most fitting that an institution such as the United Nations should be engaged in dealing with its various ramifications. If it is to achieve its purpose, however, the approach must be universal, not merely institutionally, but with the backing of all. In other words, all citizens, communities and groups must participate actively, honestly and dutifully in a concerted effort to do away with war in all its forms. It is imperative not only to outlaw war but to banish it, not only from our conscious personalities but from our thoughts, our minds, our very psyche. Like the word 'impossible' from Napoleon's dictionary, the word 'war' must vanish from our dictionaries and be forgotten. It is a stupendous task but not beyond the capacity of man.

Which are the communities or groups who must be involved in this noble and sacred mission? Surely the younger generation, the youth, the students, and their teachers and instructors who are in charge of moulding their personalities. They in turn need to be hand-picked with care as to their suitability for the vital mission. Teachers' Day, observed in India on 5 September every year, reminds us of our duty to the community. Unfortunately it lacks the fire and passion that should mark such an event. If properly observed, it could perhaps serve as an important contribution to the creation of the necessary climate. The world could adopt it and shame the people and authorities concerned into playing their part in taking the world away from the scourge of war.

We have identified the critically important youth-student-teacher community as the potential movers and shakers of the world's nations. Add to them the sensitive community of the mothers of the young men and women. We have a sizeable section of the earth up in arms against the use of arms to achieve peace. They could be the all-important nucleus of the peace force which could unite to impose the rule of peace on a war-fearing world. There are, of course, others such as businessmen who wish to be left alone to do their work unhindered by the turmoil of war. These and many of their ilk would gladly enrol themselves in the movement for peace in all lands and for all times. 'Peace in all lands and for all time': what a sweet motto and how splendid and inspiring.

These sectors must form groups or associations in every important city in the world and get together as frequently as possible and express their desire to live in peace and to be left in peace by war-mongers. They are the powerful nucleus of the international network of peace and goodwill that alone can ultimately capture the world, if it is not to destroy itself.

Those people are happy who produce amidst themselves a fair number of such brahmanas as maulvis, priests and rabbis, who impart true education by precept and by example. We don't want professional religion-mongers, who are the source of hatred and destruction. The best people will be sure to possess a justly socialized civilization whose golden mean will give the greatest happiness to the greatest number of people. Realizing that no man liveth unto himself, we are all part of one another, that God has made human and of one blood. All creatures on this universe are members of one family. They will build stronger and surer nations on a foundation of world peace on earth by spreading goodwill among men. They will create such goodwill among men by establishing peace between the creeds, through the expression of unity as well as philosophical and scientific rationality and by explaining to them the principles of the purity of soul which will fulfil the just, reasonable and natural requirement of each and all, which will provide every person with suitable work and wages, so that human starvation is not increased and there is a real and widespread of general welfare.

The heaviest responsibility rests on our scientists. They can discover and spread knowledge which ought to be used for good. Therefore our scientists all over the world have to illuminate material science with spiritual science. They have to transfigure it into holy business and add to it determined philosophical theory. They must unite, confer together and show mankind the right way of organization.

The international effort for peace must find support and appropriate expression in a free and fearless press and an unattached body of writers. They do not have to go by big names. They must be independent of government and of all vested interests.

The householder who gives correct guidance to his household, the ordinary teacher who takes an interest in his students, the latter who take instructions from him and follow them, the mothers and the ordinary citizens who have learned to love their country and do not have to hate one another, who believe that all men are brothers and have equal rights and obligations, such are the stars on the earth, who guide the wayward. They are the players, the movers and shakers, the actors and heroes in the gentle exercise of keeping the peace in the world. Peace hath its victories more renowned than war. May such peace ever reign in this world of ours.

28

Self-Organizing Centres and Networks of Peace

Baidyanath Saraswati

I

It is all very well to talk about the 'global village'. It is exciting to think of 'global citizenship', a 'global civic society', a 'global ethic', and a 'global peace'. But what if this excitement were to rhyme with the darker side of the dawn — the globalization of war and violence?

Undoubtedly there is a growing global concern for peace. There is equally no doubt that the United Nations, Unesco and secular NGOs are working whole-heartedly towards the creation of a peaceful, equitable and sustainable future. Thousands of workshops and symposia are conducted around the world to find new concepts and actions for research. In spite of all these, acts of aggression have increased manifold. Doubts are now raised on the effectiveness of the worldwide network of development organizations. The question is not of abandoning them: rather, it is one of determining *how* much global organizations can really contribute to the culture of peace.

There is a difference between global awareness and cosmic consciousness. Modern man's global awareness is best explained by unenlightened anthropology, whose primary concern is to usurp 'time' and space and to prove the claim that man is the measure of all. Traditional cultures are gifted. Ever conscious of divine origins and cosmic diversities, they live in the utmost harmony with time and space. Tradition allows all creatures and cultures to self-organize in the spirit of the Whole. It presents a markedly cosmic life-view. The Indian tradition is one such example.

II

There cannot be a world without war. The cosmogonic myth of creation reveals the mystery of existence: In the beginning there was the Self alone, in the form of a Man. He performed an act of self-immolation so that the universe might come into being. From this sacrifice were born gods, demons, the four human castes, the five elements, and all that exists. Churning the milk of the ocean, gods or *deva* (lit. shining ones) and demons or *asura* (lit. self-indulgent ones) fought each other to win immortality. Ultimately the gods succeeded in seizing the jar of nectar; but since then the strife continues eternally. Many a time the gods are defeated and the demons win. Humans, even animals, come to aid the gods. The war between gods, who are few in number, and demons, who are more numerous, is the war between good and evil, truth and untruth. To maintain the cosmic order, the gods must win and the humans must abide by truth and goodness.

The righteous war (*dharmayuddha*) is an ontological necessity. Call it real or imaginary, the Mahabharat war goes on without cease within one's own body. The five Pandavas are the five sense-organs and the hundred Kauravas are the endless desires of all kinds. This is the war that man must fight.

III

There cannot be a world without peace. The ultimate goal of the righteous war is peace. But can this goal ever be achieved? Since the war continues without cease, one cannot admit the possibility of an all-time global peace. What the myth states is the *reality* of war and peace. The encompassing context of the myth is the war between gods and demons. Either we acquire the knowledge of the cosmic design as a theoretical construct, or we become deeply aware of the human responsibility of serving the gods, or we decide in favour of the demons, or else we adopt an attitude of holy indifference. There are different types of men, and different ways of war and peace.

All forms of religion use the power of prayer for human prosperity and peace. The ancient sages were concerned with peace for all, and in all the three worlds:

> To the Heavens be peace, to the Sky and the Earth,
> To the water be peace, to plants and all trees,
> To the gods be peace, to Brahman be peace,
> To all men be peace, again and again,
> Peace also to me!
>
> (*Yajurveda*, 36.17)

Peace cannot be achieved without freedom from fear. Hence there is a prayer for fearlessness.

May the atmosphere we breathe
Breathe fearlessness into us,
Fearlessness on earth
And fearlessness in heaven!
May fearlessness guard us
Behind and before!
(*Atharvaveda*, 19.15)

Peace and fearlessness bring happiness. In this prayer each element of the cosmos, the wind, the sun, and so on, is requested to be a conveyor of happiness.

The Vedic prayer reflects a dynamic world-view. What it shows is that there cannot be peace in the human heart if there is no peace in all the three worlds. The converse is also true. At the subtler plane, as already stated, both war and peace, evil and good, are within man's own inner being. This is wholly consistent with the conception that man is the microcosm and his real roots are nourished by the cosmic order.

IV

The seers have seen the universe as an organic whole. If man is the microcosm, culture is what makes human existence cosmic and divine.

The imagery of the shining cosmic egg (*hiranyagarbha*) is applied to man's cosmic constitution. Man is produced and processed within the womb of the ultimate. He has a fivefold constitution, each called a sheath (*kosa*) or envelope: namely, the beatific envelope (*anandamayakosa*), the poetic or intellectual envelope (*vijnanmaya kosa*), the mental envelope (*manomaya kosa*), the vital envelope (*pranamayakosa*), and the vegetative envelope (*annamayakosa*). These are hierarchical orders: the first and the highest is the beatific envelope.

The constitution of man is stated in yet another way. Man is made up of the five primordial elements (ether, air, fire, water and earth), the ego, the intellect, the mind, the ten organs and the five senses (sound, touch, colour, taste and smell). The human body is spoken of as the field (*kshetra*) and the one who lives in the field is called the knower of the field (*kshetrajna*), the Supreme Being.

Man moves upwards in the cosmic plane through the ritual process of transformation. From the moment of conception to the last rite of cremation, a number of body-cleansing rituals are required to be performed. Only then can he become a full-fledged member of society.

To make the material man capable of transforming himself into a cultural person, there are ways of establishing a correlation between the transcendent order of nature and the natural order of culture. Cultural activities are determined by body, mind and spirit. The satisfaction of bodily needs is a critical factor in survival. The mind responds to physical needs and creates an urge for satisfaction. The spirit, which transcends both body and mind, mediates and allows the satisfaction of needs to an extent to which the living physical world can be maintained. This has been the contexture of all traditional cultures, in and outside India.

V

The natural theory of culture creates an image of a self-organizing human world. In the tradition of India, human life is organized along a fourfold path of progressive complexity. Four is a conceptual number signifying totality: 'All beings are one-fourth of Him (the infinite Brahman); three-fourths, the immortal in the sky' (*Chandogya Upanishad*, 3.12.6).

There are four successive stages in life: *brahmacharya*, learning and practising; *grahastha*, performing household duties; *vanaprastha*, holy indifference; and, finally, *samnyasa*, complete withdrawal from the social life. Man moves from one stage to the next. Each stage is directed towards a specific goal. The first two are concerned with social life and the second two are aimed at a final cosmic goal.

There are four human castes, each having a hereditary, non-competitive occupation. Thus, minimum economic security is provided to each and every individual in society. The divine legislation lends powerful support to an equitable distribution of power and wealth. The all-powerful intellect, the highest brahman caste, has to live in holy poverty; the all-sovereign authority, the kshatriya caste, has to remain subordinate to those who live in poverty; and the producers of material wealth, the vaisya and the sudra castes of commerce and industry, have to serve with humility the first two.

Human desires are fourfold: *dharma*, the desire to uphold the divine ordinance; *artha*, the desire connected with wealth and power; *kama*, the desire pertaining to pleasure and procreation; and *moksha*, the desire to transcend all desires.

Human life carries with it a fourfold obligation on the part of every individual. The obligations that accompany one throughout life are the debts to the gods, the sages, to ancestors and to humanity. Accordingly, man moves from one station of life to another, sustains the human world, and establishes the link between the human and the divine.

All the four fundamental forces of human organization are predetermined by tradition.

Both individually and collectively, each is drawn towards a predetermined goal. In the Indian scheme of life, man moves *centrifugally*. The individual self splits into two: male and female. The husband receives his wife from the gods. Their relationship is indissoluble: in so far as the two make a unit, each is only half the body of the other. The more perfect unit is formed of husband, wife and offspring — the trio (*trivarga*). The continuity of a trio depends, first, on maintaining the order of legitimacy, and secondly, on its extension in time through several generations of similar trios forming larger units. The family extends to lineage, to clan, to subcaste, to caste, to village, to subregion, to region and eventually to the organization of life called the 'universe as family' (*vasudhaiva kutumbakam*). The essential character of each of these units (centres) is to remain self-organized and yet functionally interdependent. No single individual is in the privileged position of claiming freedom without duties.

VI

The organizational complexity of the ancient Indian model creates the right conditions for a culture of peace.

Like *Purusha*, the Cosmic Person, who sacrificed Himself in the beginning, the man of matter performs sacrifice. It is by self-sacrifice that the individual lives. By sacrifice he links himself with the whole of existence. It is by sacrifice that he performs his duties of a householder (husband-wife, parent-child). By the elimination of his little self, the individual lives in peace and harmony. The four stages of life minimize the generational conflict within the family. Kinship is regulated by joking and avoidance relationships, as also by obligatory life-affirming rituals and festivals. The conflict between the four castes is reduced to a bare minimum, because each is culturally autonomous while they are functionally interdependent. Together they share an ordered spiritual value.

The ancient law-givers adopted a *laissez-faire* attitude towards all the members of society on purely family matters originating from regional customs and traditions.

VII

The creation of peace in the concretion of man's living relationship with his world demands Faith. There is, in all traditional societies, an in-built complex of metaphoric actions of faith. The core of man is faith. Faith is the 'inner source' from which real human growth proceeds. There are three types of faith, each rooted in the human heart: acting faith, thinking faith and loving faith. The path of peace is the path of faith. It is paved by the virtue of unconditionally giving up all ego.

Prayer is the veneration of the highest value in the hierarchy of existence, not the adoration of a creature. Prayer is an expression of the deep desire for peace, personal and universal.

Pilgrimage is a path of devotion. It is an act of truth-seeing and truth-saying. It is imperative to use the hands and feet to move into the shrines of the gods and to let the wings of the soul fly. The human body is compared with the place of pilgrimage. Both are called *kshetra,* in which the gods reside. The presiding deity (the Self) is a point in the circle. All holy places and all gods and goddesses are believed to be present in the *kshetra.* Pilgrims are enjoined to circumambulate the *kshetra* clockwise. There are various types of pilgrimages in space and time. Pilgrimage offers peace and happiness.

Purity is a state of perfection. Purity of food produces purity of body and mind. With mind and heart purified, the body attains peace. Man attains perfection.

Patience is a virtue which combines with compassion and non-violence. With patience one achieves peace, and thereafter there is nothing left to be achieved.

Poverty is shining purity and the practice of loving faith. Holy poverty is a necessary good because, as Kabir says, 'In pain everybody remembers Him whilst in enjoyment and pleasure He is forgotten.' After the Mahabharat war Kunti, the mother of the victorious Pandavas, prayed to God Krishna:

> O Teacher of the world, let calamities
> Always overtake us, because we would then
> Have Thy sight which prevents reincarnation.
> The man whose pride is swelled by
> Birth, power, learning and fortune
> Is not worthy of taking Thy name,
> Which is within the reach of only those
> Who own nothing.
>
> (*Srimad Bhagavatam*)

VIII

Peace is an unassailable, unagitated state of mind and body. It creates a spirit of dispassion, which is a requisite for the knowledge of Reality. The Sanskrit word for it is *shanti.* The dormant state of the body as in sleep or in death is called 'lying in peace' or 'becoming peace'. Those who accept this life-view will say: Peace is inseparable from Reality. Truth is also inseparable from Reality. Hence, peace is none other than Truth. War, the opposite of peace, is untruth (unreal). Both are designed by the Gods and are independent of human cognizance.

Man is the actor (*liladhar*). He acts in war and in peace. What matters is his role in the cosmic play (*lila*). He plays a specific role in the course of living. His destiny lies in the role that he chooses for himself. Depending on the self-reflexivity with which he is gifted, he relates himself either to Truth (gods, light), or to untruth (demons, darkness). He is, thus, the maker of his destiny. He has an innate tendency to self-organize. Moving from one body to another he is re-made, renewed and re-organized again and again. In truth, he is without a centre. His roots are upward.

Peace is rendered visible in and through the tradition of faith and fidelity. The universe of a traditional society is criss-crossed by the human network of organizations that weave a culture of peace. It is designed as a collection of individuals, each independent in his self-making and yet functioning together with others as cogs in the wheel of life. The fundamental forces of the human organization operate *centrifugally*. Each centre is closely linked to the others by the cognizance of the divine ordinance of rights and duties. A pattern of peace emerges with prayer, pilgrimage, purity, patience and holy poverty. A geometrical structure (of fivefold man) is built around the triangle (of husband, wife and offspring) and the quadrangle (of the four human castes, the four stages and four orders of life, and the four obligations) in a circle (of birth-and-death), with multiple centres (of the individual self). This pattern of peace repeats itself in space-time.

The traditional model of human organization is diametrically opposed to the *centripetal* pattern of the modern 'global village', organizing itself in fear and tension.

References

Agrawal, Vasudeva S., *Matsya Purana: A Study*, Varanasi, All-India Kashiraj Trust, 1963.

Behari, Bankey, *Sufis, Mystics and Yogis of India*, Bombay, Bharatiya Vidya Bhavan, 1991.

Hume, Robert Ernest, *The Thirteen Principal Upanishads*, Delhi, Oxford University Press, 1984.

Panikkar, Raimundo, *The Vedic Experience; Mantramanjari*, London, Darton, Longman & Todd, 1977.

———, *Myth, Faith and Hermeneutics: Cross-Cultural Studies*, Bangalore, Asian Trading Corporation, 1983.

Pavitrananda, Swami, *Hymns and Prayers to Gods and Goddesses*, Calcutta: Advaita Ashrama, 1992.

Saraswati, Baidyanath, *Brahmic Ritual Traditions in the Crucible of Time*, Simla, Indian Institute of Advanced Study, 1977.

———, 'The Kashivasi Widows', *Man in India*, 65, 2, 1985.

———, 'Ksetra', in Bettina Baumer, ed., *Kalatattvakosa*, vol. II, New Delhi, Indira Gandhi National Centre for the Arts and Motilal Banarsidass Publishers, 1992.

———, 'Culture as Inverted Tree', in *The Contribution by Religions to the Culture of Peace*, Barcelona, Unesco, 1993.

———, 'Elements of Nature and the Order of Culture', in Baidyanath Saraswati, ed., *Prakriti: The Integral Vision*, Vol. 5, New Delhi, Indira Gandhi National Centre for the Arts and D.K. Printworld, 1995.

———, 'Lifestyles in Traditional Cultures: A Conceptual Framework', in Baidyanath Saraswati, ed., *Computerizing Cultures*, New Delhi, Indira Gandhi National Centre for the Arts and New Age International, 1995.

List of Contributors

M.M. Agrawal	Department of Philosophy North-Eastern Hill University Mayurbhanj Complex Shillong - 793 014
Ali Aksad	Bangladesh Peace Council 6/4 Humayun Road Dhaka 1207 (Bangladesh)
Dwight William Allen	College of Education Old Dominion University Norfolk, Virginia 23529 (USA)
Félix Martí Ambel	Director Centre UNESCO de Cataluyna Mallorca, 285 08037 Barcelona (España)
M. Aram	Shanti 11, Janpath New Delhi - 110 001
Ahangamage Tudor Ariyaratne	President Lanka Jathika Sarvodaya Shramadana Sangamaya Inc. 98 Rawathawatte Road Moratuwa (Sri Lanka)

Tan Chung	Indira Gandhi National Centre for the Arts Central Vista, Janpath New Delhi - 110 001
Angelo Fernandes	Archbishop's House Ashok Place New Delhi - 110 001
Satya Narayan Goenka	Vipassana Research Institute Dhammagiri Igatpuri - 422 403 Distt. Nasik (Maharashtra)
Sirima Kalanawathie Goonesinghe	No. 36-B, Sir Marcus Fernando Mawatha Colombo 07 (Sri Lanka)
Bharat Gupt	PB No. 8518 Ashok Vihar Delhi - 110 052
Som Raj Gupta	4, Staff Quarters Kirori Mal College Delhi - 110 007
M. Ishaq Jamkhanawala	Anjuman-I-Islam Anjuman Secretariat Badruddin Tayabji Marg 92, D.N. Road Mumbai - 400 001 (Maha.)
Minoru Kasai	International Christian University 3-10-3 Osawa, Mitaka Tokyo 181 (Japan)
Natalia Kravtchenko	Central Post Office Crimea Simferopol - 333000 (Russia)

Keshav Malik
5/90, Connaught Circus
New Delhi - 110 001

S.C. Malik
5/90, Connaught Circus
New Delhi - 110 001

A.K. Merchant
Baha'i House
6 Canning Road
New Delhi - 110 001

Khaliq Ahmad Nizami
Nizami Villa,
Sir Syed Road
Aligarh - 202 002 (UP)

Mira Aster Patel
Auromodele
Auroville - 605 101 (T.N.)

Cao Xuan Pho
Research Institute of South East Asia
National Centre of Social Science and Humanities
27 Tran Xuan Soan
Hanoi (Vietnam)

Devi Prasad
52, Godavari Apartments
Alaknanda
New Delhi - 110 019

N. Radhakrishnan
'Sabarmati'
Mitrapuram
Paranthal (Post)
Kerala - 689 518

Mohamad Reza Rikhtehgaran
Department of Philosophy
Tehran University
Tehran - 14174
(Iran)

Baidyanath Saraswati	Unesco Professor Janapada Sampada Indira Gandhi National Centre for the Arts Janpath New Delhi - 110 001
Biswanarayan Shastri	"Ritayana" Red Cross Road Chandmari Guwahati - 781 003
Ramjee Singh	Gandhian Institute of Studies Post Box No. 1116 Rajghat Varanasi - 221 001
Pataraporn Sirikanchana	Headquarters of The World Fellowship of Buddhists 33 Sukhumvit Road (Between Soi 1 and Soi 3) Bangkok 10110 (Thailand)
Kapila Vatsyayan	Academic Director Indira Gandhi National Centre for the Arts Janpath New Delhi - 110 001
Jin Weinuo	68 Xiaoweihutong Pong Cheng Dist. Beijing - 100 005 (People's Republic of China)
Vladimir Zaitsev	Central Post Office Crimea Simferopol - 333 000 (Russia)

ॐ द्यौः शान्तिरन्तरिक्षँ शान्तिः पृथिवी शान्तिरापः शान्तिरोषधयः शान्तिः । वनस्पतयः शान्तिर्विश्वेदेवाः शान्तिर्ब्रह्म शान्तिः सर्वँ शान्तिः शान्तिरेव शान्तिः सा मा शान्तिरेधि ॥ ॐ शान्तिः शान्तिः शान्तिः ॥